Second Edition

CULTURES *in* CONTACT

DOROTHY L. DAVIS

Kendall Hunt
publishing company

Kendall Hunt
publishing company

www.kendallhunt.com
Send all inquiries to:
4050 Westmark Drive
Dubuque, IA 52004-1840

Copyright © 2008, 2017 by Dorothy I. Davis

ISBN 978-1-5249-1333-5

Published in the United States of America

Contents

Unit IV
Tasmania, Australia, Japan and Conclusions   99

Conclusion

Introduction

This anthology has been assembled as a text for an anthropology course titled Contemporary Non-Western Cultures. The mission of this course is to help students achieve a better understanding of cultural diversity in the modern world. Most students sign up for this class because it meets university and college requirements, but the long term goals of the course are to help students become better citizens in an increasingly global environment. Many students come to college with limited knowledge and understanding about the lives of people in other parts of the world. Globalization is nothing new, but the challenges of living in the twenty-first century make an understanding of this process increasingly important.

Anthropology is a discipline that is ideally suited for this type of study. The origins of the discipline coincide with the Age of Discovery and the expansion of European cultures, which brought them into contact with many different societies throughout the world. Early anthropologists attempted to explain these differences, but from a very biased perspective. They shared the values of the times that they lived in. They often saw their own societies as superior to all others and believed that the best future for these other cultures was to become just like the West. Anthropology today is a science and has come a long way from its beginnings. Today many anthropologists use their knowledge to help people around the world improve their lives. This includes believing that native peoples should have a role in determining their own future and finding ways to help them achieve these goals.

The focus of this course is culture contact. We are studying what happens when Western and Non-Western cultures come into contact with each other. Most students educated in this country have only a one-sided view, the Euro-centric view, of these events and their consequences. This course tries to put the study of culture contact into a more holistic perspective, to put it in context. That means looking at both sides of a contact situation. The readings in this text are chosen because they illustrate this theme. The articles come from different sources and the authors may have many different backgrounds, but they all attempt to help us understand the perspective of Non-Western peoples. Of course, we have to recognize that no one from one culture can totally understand what it is to be a member of another culture. Never-the-less, we are going to attempt to begin to see ourselves as others see us. In some cases this may be easy to do; in others it will be difficult or even impossible. Even if we don't agree with them, at least we have made an attempt to appreciate their perspectives and this leads to greater understanding and empathy. In doing this, and as in any anthropology course, we will not only get a better understanding of others but a greater understanding of ourselves.

The term Non-Western is problematical. It is never good to define a group of people by "what they are not." However, there is no widely accepted alternate term. We may refer to groups as indigenous cultures or native cultures, but sometimes this would not be an accurate description. There is also the ever present issue of political correctness. Native peoples often have a preference for certain names for themselves, while other names may be considered insulting. In this text we will use the term Non-Western, acknowledging its limitations. The term does function well in a course that examines the contact between Europeans and others.

It is also necessary to explain the anthropological use of the term, contemporary. Anthropologists study events that may have occurred millions of years ago. Our discipline has a very deep time frame, so contemporary does not mean right now. In this course we are definitely taking a historical perspective. The starting date for the information in this course is 1492. This is the year that Columbus "discovers" the New World. Of course he wasn't the first person on this continent, there were many millions of people already here, but 1492 is an important impact date. Columbus returned to Spain and the New World and the Old would never be the same.

The text is divided into four units. The first unit is an introduction to the discipline of anthropology. In this section, students are introduced to the basic concepts of anthropology. They learn what anthropology is, what anthropologists do, and how they do it. They also learn about the practical application of anthropological knowledge and expertise in the real world. The focus of the course is on culture change. There are several themes that will be seen running through the various units. These themes are modernization, commercialization, and globalization.

The five areas that are covered in the text are: North America, South America, Africa (including parts of the Middle East), Oceania, and Japan. Obviously this does not include the whole world, but there is a limit to how much material can be covered in a semester. In each of the area sections there will be a discussion of the natural and social environments of native cultures before and after contact, the nature of subsequent changes, and how these cultures are presently adjusting to the impact of modern sources of change.

The articles in the text have been selected to offer reflections on these different topics from varying points of view. The articles have been selected because they are easy to read and they correspond well with topics discussed in class. I realize that most of you are not anthropology majors, so I have tried to include articles that relate to other disciplines. Hopefully, you will find them both enjoyable and enlightening.

Introduction to Anthropology and the Study of Culture Change

Topics Covered in Class

Definition of Anthropology
Brief History of the Discipline
Four (Five) Branches of Anthropology
Anthropological Method
Concept of Culture
Fundamental Characteristics of Culture
Culture Change
Globalization and localization

About the Readings

There are six articles in this unit. The first one is by Brian Fagan, an archaeologist and a popular writer in his field. Over 30 years ago, he wrote the first edition of a book about the contact of Western and Non-Western cultures. He titled this book *Clash of Cultures*. If you like history and archaeology, you may enjoy reading the whole text. The book covers the same geographical areas that is covered in this course. Although this is primarily a course in cultural anthropology, it often borrows from the work of archaeologists to learn about both the prehistoric and the historic past. Fagan explains that whenever two cultures come into contact there will be a "clash." You may assume that the term *clash* implies violence. This is not necessarily the case. First contact can be peaceful and can benefit both sides, but it would still be classified as a "clash." No matter what the nature of the initial contact, peaceful or otherwise, both cultures are going to begin to change. Further-more, because cultures are integrated a change in one part of culture can lead to subsequent changes in other parts creating what Fagan calls a "ripple effect." These changes not only affect the cultures in direct contact, they have an impact on their neighbors and the environment as well.

Fieldwork is often referred as the "cornerstone" of anthropology. It is traditionally the method that anthro-pologists use to gather their data and test their hypotheses. Anthropologists actually go out and live with the people that they are studying. An accurate description of this method is "participant observation." Doing field-work is challenging and often unpredictable. The article by Andrew Cornish presents a good example of "-fieldwork by accident." This tongue-in-cheek, self-deprecating account gives us a new insight into what "par-ticipant observer" actually means.

Immediately after the accident, Cornish expected that it would be handled just like a similar accident in the United States, but it was not. The anthropologist had the opportunity to experience how the Thai justice system works and to become aware of his own ethnocentrism.

The articles by Mark Plotkin and Horace Minor are both about medical practices. Taken together they make a number of interesting points. The two articles help us to become more aware of our own biases in regards to modern and tribal medicine. Most of us would assume that traditional medicine is just based on magic and superstition. The author is not an anthropologist. He is an ethnobiologist who recognizes the value of traditional medicine. Plotkin is especially interested in studying the use of plant and animal products in treatments by local medicine persons or Shamans in the rain-forests of South America. When their "recipes" are tested in modern medical labs, we often discover that they actually successfully treat illnesses. Of course there is always the hope that people like Plotkin will discover the cure for the common cold or cancer. That has not happened yet and may never happen, but the value of shamanistic knowledge is recognized and valued by the modern multi-national pharmaceutical companies who are researching ways to treat and cure diseases. Unfortunately, many of these shamans are dying out without passing on their medical knowledge. The article about the Nacirema gives us a different perspective on our own medical practices. While Plotkins study gives us a greater appreciation of the effectiveness of traditional medicine, Minor's article makes fun of Western medicine. It also shows how an outsider's point-of-view and vocabulary can distort our understanding of a culture.

Ted Bestor's article focuses on globalization. When we think of the spread of culture from one part of the world to another, we often think of the far-reaching impact of the spread of Western culture to other parts of the world. We overlook the fact that we are a relatively young society and have borrowed from many other cultures. The anthropologist Ralph Linton estimates that 90% of our culture has foreign origins. proceeds to point out the origins of our material culture and behaviors. He estimates that the impact rate of diffusion on American culture is 90%. One good example of diffusion is food. Ethnic restaurants and markets are very popular in this country.

Ted Bestor's article is about the globalization of business. His focus in not on medicine but on food. The world-wide popularity of Japanese cuisine is the topic of this article. He explores the globalization of Sushi from the fish who can travel 70MPH across the ocean to the table and even the ballpark. Even tough Sushi has become a global phenomenon. it has still kept it's Japanese Cachet and cultural identity. We will return to this theme of international or global and local again and again throughout the semester.

In the final article in this section, Wilma Mankiller writes about what it means to be an aboriginal person in this country and the world today. Mankiller was the Principal Chief of the Cherokee Nation (Oklahoma) from 1985 to 1995. Aboriginal Peoples are not disappearing. Their numbers are actually increasing and so is their influence. We have introduced the concepts of agency and voice in class. This article explores the future that Native Peoples are making for themselves. According to Mankiller, two important things that all aboriginal peoples have in common is their unique view of the natural world and the importance of reciprocal relationships. The value of communalism as opposed to individualism is a constant theme in native cultures.

Prologue

Brian M. Fagan

Land has grown, the sky has grown, and the ocean has grown; all these are filled with living creatures.
The room for gods is filled with gods, and now what shall be done for the room for people?

Tahitian origin legend recorded in 1822, quoted in Douglas Oliver, *Ancient Tahitian Society* (1974)

In the year 1772, a small band of French seamen led by an explorer named Marion du Fresne landed on a sandy beach in southern Tasmania. As du Fresne's boat grounded, a band of about thirty aborigines carrying pointed sticks and sharp stones emerged from the trees to greet the strangers, exotic-looking people "in color black, the hair woolly and all were naked." It was perhaps surprising that the Tasmanians recognized their visitors as fellow humans. Marion du Fresne was the first outsider to greet them in at least 8,000 years.

The Tasmanians had been isolated on their remote island home by the rising waters of the Bass Strait at the end of the Ice Age. At the time of du Fresne's visit some 3,000 to 5,000 aborigines occupied Tasmania, divided into at least eighty different bands of thirty to fifty people. Their descendants survived less than a century of Western civilization. Branded as the most primitive people on earth, savages who were "the connecting link between man and the monkey tribes," the aborigines were decimated by exotic European diseases and literally hunted into extinction by land-hungry colonists. From the very beginning a vast chasm of incomprehension had separated the Tasmanians from their unwelcome visitors.

Du Fresne and his men advanced cautiously up the beach, while the locals piled up a heap of driftwood. The aborigines greeted the white men in a language that seemed to draw words "from the bottom of the throat." An officer offered them beads and other trinkets of the type carried by every expedition to the South Seas at the time. The Tasmanians rejected the gifts with scorn. When the French proffered live chickens, the aborigines flung them away in disgust and ran into the woods. Eventually du Fresne himself managed to prevail on them to return. The bandleaders again gestured at the woodpile. Confused, the captain set fire to the dry branches. The Tasmanians fled precipitately to the top of a nearby hillock and bombarded the astonished seamen with volleys of accurately flung stones. The French fled for their boats. Once safely out of range, they rowed along the shore looking for another place to land. The Tasmanians pursued them with showers of rocks. Du Fresne lost his temper when they hit two of his officers, and ordered a volley of musket fire. The Tasmanians scurried for cover, leaving one of their band sprawled on the beach. The expedition lingered in the cove for another six days in the hope that the aborigines would return. In the meantime, the officers laid out the abandoned corpse and measured it in the cause of science, noting that its owner was five feet, three inches tall, with "reddish brown hair." Then they sailed away to New Zealand, where Marion du Fresne was "devoured by natives."

Du Fresne's experiences with the Tasmanians were by no means unusual in the adventurous centuries of the Age of Discovery when Western explorers were penetrating every corner of the globe. In most cases, the first encounter with a hitherto unknown society was but a fleeting kaleidoscope of curiosity, sometimes horrified fascination, and often romantic excitement. The "natives" could be respectful and hospitable, even amorous. However, all too often they could act in seemingly unpredictable ways. Even navigators with a vast experience of exotic peoples like the celebrated Captain James Cook had difficulty understanding people like the Tasmanians and Australians. "They wander about in small parties from place to place in search of food," Cook wrote. "They are all together an ignorant, wretched race of mortals, though at the same time the natives of a country capable of producing every necessity of life, with a climate the finest in the world" (Reed 1969,

163). What bothered Cook and other observers most of all was that such people had no interest in improving their individual lot and were absolutely content with just "being." Such values were completely alien to goal-oriented, individualistic Westerners exploring the world with specific objectives in mind, whether a search for China, pure exploration, missionary activity, trade, or colonization.

We live in such a well-explored, familiar world that it is difficult to imagine what it is like to encounter a society that has never had contact with Western civilization before. The famed BBC traveler David Attenborough is one of the few people who have had this experience in recent times. During the late 1960s he accompanied a party of government officials to the headwaters of the Sepik river in New Guinea, where a bush pilot had reported mountain dwellings where none were suspected to exist. After two weeks of marching through unknown country, Attenborough's small party came across two sets of footprints.

The group followed the footprints and laid out gifts in the forest. The strangers left telltale spoors that showed they were watching constantly. The Europeans cried out greetings in a known river dialect, but to no avail. Eventually they lost the trail and almost gave up hope. Then suddenly one morning seven small, almost naked men appeared in the bush near their camp. As the travelers tumbled out of their tents, the strangers stood their ground. Attenborough recounts how he and his companions made hasty gestures of friendship, for the tribesmen did not understand any known river dialect. Fortunately both sides had many gestures in common: smiles, and eyebrows that could frown, signify wonder, disapproval, or ask a question. The gestures were the only way to understand one another, to barter iron knives for fruit, to deepen the relationship between two absolutely incompatible societies. Such gestures are one of the few common communication inheritances of humanity; the early explorers used them to the full.

The traveler of two centuries ago was much better versed in the procedures for landing on unknown shores and apparently deserted beaches. Indeed, the British Admiralty had standard instructions for its captains to follow. A small party would land with the utmost caution, firearms within easy reach, the ship's cannons and an armed pinnace at their back. If anyone approached, an officer would offer gifts—perhaps iron tools, clothing, or glass trinkets—and make appropriate gestures of friendship. Everyone held his breath and waited for the local people to react. Sometimes they would accept the gifts or hang back until one bolder individual came forward to take the offering. Sometimes violence would erupt or the group would take to their heels. Captain Cook and his contemporaries learned the value of expressive sign language, the irresistible lure of iron tools, the power of their own firearms. "Some of the men Grunted and Cryd lyke a Hogg then pointed to the others—others crowed Lyke cocks to make them understand that we wanted fowls," wrote one of Francis Drake's officers in the early years of the Age of Discovery (Shipton 1973, 14). After centuries of experience, and despite the overwhelming advantages of gunpowder and large ships, Europeans always feared the unpredictable and the unexpected, the fatal miscalculations that could bring sudden danger and terrible slaughter.

Historical Background

The discovery of the extraordinary biological and cultural diversity of humankind between the so-called Age of Discovery between the late fifteenth and nineteenth centuries was one of the great intellectual watersheds of Western civilization. Long-term forces of history led to this discovery. After A.D. 1000, the rulers of western European states allowed merchants greater freedom and enhanced privileges, in marked contrast to those of the more centralized, tributary polities of the Near East and Asia. Western Europe was impoverished, on the periphery of a wealthy Asian and Mediterranean world. Merchants and their widespread networks were vital to ambitious European lords, for they provided the capital for warfare, conquest, and peaceful expansion. The same merchants had access to well-established river and sea routes, which provided cheaper, reliable transportation without all the tolls and other hazards of overland caravan travel. As the western Europeans expanded their sphere of mercantile operations, money turned over more rapidly and profits increased in the hands of people whom many historians regard as the ultimate founders of capitalism.

However, tributary surpluses continued to be the mainstay of rulers and their courts, of entire states. In New Spain (Spanish colonial Mexico), the conquistadors paid a fifth of their profits to the King. During the early centuries of the Age of Discovery, these tribute networks expanded dramatically, as producers in every part of the world—fur traders in northeastern North America, silver miners in Mexico and Peru, sugar plantations in the Caribbean—were drawn into vast webs of economic interdependency. In many areas, the merchants and visitors offered exotic commodities of little value such as glass beads, cotton cloth, or iron axes for raw materials. As the producers of these materials acquired a taste for exotic baubles, they became ever more dependent on those who bought their furs, slaves, or copper ingots. In many cases, merchants eventually supplied tools, even raw materials, receiving reimbursement in finished products in a system of unequal exchange that was a form of peonage. The African slave trade provided the labor to grow sugar, mine precious ores, and cultivate cotton.

From the fifteenth to eighteenth centuries, European voyagers traversed the sea-lanes of the world. They found sources of gold, silver, and precious stones. They found places where fur-bearing animals abounded and tropical savannas where large tusked elephants flourished. Wherever they sailed, they tapped into existing trading networks, linked them together, and manipulated them for maximum profit. Back in Europe, artisans working in villages and in sizable manufactories produced goods and commodities for overseas colonies and suppliers. Thus was born a global commercial network, a "World System," as many scholars call it, with roots in much earlier trading alliances in many areas of the world. Over many generations, societies large and small, Western and non-Western became linked in a vast web of interdependency and interconnectedness. With the notable exception of the Atlantic slave trade, these connections were mostly confined to merchants and missionaries, with a few settlers far from home, laboring in coastal communities close to well-established sea routes.

For four centuries, European commerce operated under the protection of its government sponsors, hedged around by a morass of constraints and monopolies. International trade flowed along predictable routes, most of the profits lying in commodities such as human beings, sugar, or elephant ivory rather than in manufactured goods. Throughout these centuries, the state was still a tribute-collecting organization, dominated by rulers who sought to enhance their wealth at the expense of their rivals. Then, in the late eighteenth century, the British textile industry turned mercantile wealth into capital with the dawn of the Industrial Revolution.

England had become a major wool producer in the fifteenth century, exporting its manufactures throughout Europe and further afield. As a result, landowners turned increasingly to sheep herding and more intensive agriculture. Communities of merchants and their financial backers dwelt in towns large and small, acting as middlemen in an increasingly more complex trade. By the eighteenth century, landowners and merchants were intermarrying, with major landlords and nobility controlling between 80 and 85 percent of the land. Increasingly, those who had once been medieval serfs, then tenants, were forced off the land. By the late seventeenth century, as much as 40 percent of the population had left the land, many of them going into manufacturing as salaried workers. The new, more commercial agriculture was capital-intensive, while at the same time merchants acquired more political power and held increasing control over rural craftspeople, who manufactured the goods they distributed elsewhere.

English society was changing rapidly, but the country's manufacturers faced stiff competition from the Dutch, who were expert wool finishers, and from Indian cottons and calicos, woven to suit European tastes. The English manufacturers responded to the Dutch by producing wool mixed with silk, linen, or cotton, and worsteds made with combed wool. They reduced their labor costs, first by moving their cloth production to the country, and then by increasing the mechanization of the production process. Indian competition was met politically by banning imports of calicos. At the same time, English manufacturers developed linen and cotton fabrics that were virtually identical to Indian cloth, using mechanization to undercut Asian labor costs with machine-made fabric. Provincial merchants and manufacturers began to exercise ever closer control over production techniques, using their wealth from other sources such as brewing and real estate to acquire the simple machines that were speeding up both weaving and finishing by 1750. Then, in 1779, Samuel Crompton developed the "mule," a machine that not only allowed a spinner to spin several threads of yarn simultaneously, but also wound the twisted fibers and drew them out. Eleven years later, this revolutionary device was powered by steam engines, resulting in a staggering increase in productivity. An Indian hand spinner would take about 50,000 hours to spin 100 pounds of cotton. Crompton's mule cut the time to 2,000 hours, while steam-powered machines reduced the time to 300 hours and could be operated by unskilled labor, mainly low-paid women and children. The figure fell even lower in the nineteenth century (Wolf 1982).

Inevitably, greater efficiency in the manufacturing process led to the abandonment of cottage industries and small workshops, which were replaced by well-organized factories. Factories gave the manufacturer much greater control over the entire process, as well as over the formerly kin-based, now wage-earning labor force.

At the same time, pilfering could be controlled, transportation costs reduced, and delivery times shortened, while expensive machinery paid for with valuable capital was kept operating as intensively as possible. The changeover did not come easily. Many cottage workers strongly resisted the discipline and unrelenting labor of the new factories, many of which resembled prisons. Prolonged social unrest, indeed near-civil war, permeated English society after 1815, until the mid-nineteenth century saw the factory system develop its own institutions and factory labor forces stabilized.

The appearance of factories coincided with the growth of enormous textile-manufacturing cities, among them Manchester, which rose from a mere 24,000 inhabitants in 1773 to more than 250,000 in 1851. The new cities became magnets for immigration from the surrounding countryside, as well as from countries like Ireland. Displaced from the land and unable to find employment in the country, thousands of families moved to the new cities, where they worked for wages. Cotton textiles were the catalyst that produced the Industrial Revolution and the capitalism that went along with it. The ripples of the Industrial Revolution were felt throughout the world after the Napoleonic Wars. By that time, half the total value of all British exports was cotton, and up to 20 percent of Britain's imports were raw cotton. By 1807, more than 60 percent of all this cotton came from the United States. The rise in production was staggering. In 1790, 3,000 American cotton bales reached England. By 1850, the figure had reached 4,500,000.

The Industrial Revolution, fueled by English textiles, brought a new social order based not on tribute, but on the deployment of capital, mechanized manufacturing, and the employment of laborers for hire. The reorganization of English agriculture created a huge reservoir of unemployed, free laborers, providing a unique work force, and a society not based on tribute or slavery, but on wages paid by deploying capital. The same capital financed railroads and steamships, improving communications, permitting the movements of raw materials, and of migrants, on an unprecedented scale. This same revolution created an insatiable demand for raw materials in many corners of the world, placing demands on native populations far from the factories of Lancashire and Yorkshire. At the same time, thousands of artisans and land-hungry farmers left their homeland and migrated to distant lands in search of wealth and new opportunity, and acreage of their own, "purchased" or seized from its long-term indigenous owners.

Non-Western societies in many parts of the world withered in the face of a flood of immigrant farmers, who believed they had the right to carve out a new life in an alien land without any reference to the indigenous population whatsoever.

The Age of Discovery connected all parts of the populated world to one another in lasting ways that still impact on our lives. These centuries of intermittent, then continual contact between Westerners and an enormous range of human societies dramatically changed European attitudes to the unusual and the exotic.

The Clash of Cultures

The changing attitudes of Westerners to non-Western societies form a fascinating backdrop to what we may loosely term the *clash of cultures*. the clash was a progressive confrontation between an expanding, sophisticated civilization with radically alien beliefs and dozens of societies that lived in careful balance with the natural resources of their environments. The long centuries of Western discovery are a story of confrontation and non-comprehension, of cautious encounters between strangers, of searches for gold and brutal military campaigns, of profitable trading, land grabbing, and missionary endeavor. They are also a weary chronicle of pathos and tragedy, of bitter disillusionment between societies living in totally incompatible worlds. The intellectual, moral, and spiritual effects of the clash are with us to this day.

The clash of cultures played out against a backdrop of ever-changing attitudes towards, and expectations of, the non-Western world. By the same token, the perspectives of non-Westerners changed just as radically over the centuries.

At first, voyaging Europeans searched for paradise on earth, the last domain of a once universal Golden Age. At first, paradise was a remote and ancient dream, then it was located on earth, a mythical golden kingdom sometimes associated with Ethiopia, later with the Indies and the lands to the west. Ironically, the first Portuguese explorations brought Westerners in touch with the actual realities of some of the least complex of fifteenth-century human societies. Our story begins with the discovery at the southern tip of Africa of the

Khoikhoi, simple herders whose way of life seemed so primitive that they soon became the epitome of savagery in European minds. The Khoikhoi seemed beyond Christian redemption.

Not so the American Indian, revealed to an astonished Europe by Christopher Columbus only a few years after the Portuguese reached the Cape of Good Hope. It was in the Indies and New Spain that images of the Noble Savage, of paradise and utopia, lingered to haunt peoples' minds for centuries. It was here also that the learned and greedy fought out their arguments over the morality of bringing Indians to the True Faith and to forced labor. Mexico was the land where the confrontation between Western civilization and the non-Western world was played out.

The Europeans who came to the New World, explored the Pacific, and coasted past Africa to India were members of a civilization that had only recently emerged from medieval feudalism. They were ruled by monarchs who governed rigidly stratified states. In this sense, the Spaniards or English were no different from the rulers of the Aztecs or Incas, who ran their empires on the premise that power and privilege were the right of only a few. Inequality and social stratification were for the common good, a tacit reality no one thought of questioning. But the Europeans were Christians, members of a faith that taught that individual freedoms and the equality of all people were fundamental doctrines for all humanity. To convert people to Christianity was to expose them to doctrines that in the long term undermined the established notion that inequality was a permanent condition. In due time these subversive teachings—for in a sense they were nothing less—were to overturn the colonial empires of every European nation.

Nearly five centuries have passed since the Conquest of Mexico, centuries during which the full diversity of humankind has been exposed to European eyes. While hundreds of societies underwent traumatic cultural change and the forces of reality played out on remote beaches and battlefields, philosophers and travelers developed a whole range of myths and stereotypes that plague our understanding of human diversity to this day. This strange dichotomy between myth and reality is ever present, ever-changing. Western perceptions of other societies have often fluctuated with the esteem in which Westerners held their own civilization. English and French philosophers sighed with nostalgia for a simple, uncomplicated life when Tahiti was discovered in 1769. Noble Savages and people living with nature became fashionable in the eighteenth century, bursting on Western civilization with an intensity that is startling even today. By no means did everyone believe in nobility, however. It was but one strand in white perceptions of the non-Western world at the time. The Noble Savage gave way to disillusionment at the time of the Napoleonic Wars, when the Industrial Revolution and fervent nationalism changed global politics forever, bringing in their wake a new intellectual confidence about industrial civilization and its astonishing technological achievements.

Nineteenth-century Europeans believed, as had their predecessors, that Western civilization was the pinnacle of human achievement, a signpost of inevitable progress for the future. But their belief was now couched in far less tolerant terms. The non-Westerner became an even more inferior being in European eyes, often considered as having the intelligence of a ten-year-old child. From there it was a short step to the ardently racist doctrines of late nineteenth-century imperial Europe. Colonist and settler took refuge in doctrines of racial superiority to justify the annexation of tribal territories, or prime framing land, usually on specious arguments that the acreage was not used properly by its indigenous owners. The specious argument was simple and to the point: How could mere intellectual children learn the latest farming methods or govern themselves in a "civilized" manner? Leave such problems to a superior race, went the litany of imperial powers, with devastating consequences for the non-Western world. Hundreds of little-known societies, many hunter-gatherer cultures like the Tasmanians and Yahgan Indians, others elaborate societies like those of the Maori and Northwest Indians, were radically changed by contact with nineteenth-century missionaries, traders, and colonists. Some peoples, like the Khoikhoi of the Cape of Good Hope and the Tasmanians, vanished rapidly. Others, like the Aztecs and Maori, fell apart, the survivors becoming an impoverished and often oppressed minority on the fringes of the new society. Only a few non-Western societies managed to adapt with some success to a new world.

No one knows why some groups adapted better to European domination than others. A great deal depended on their political structure, for many non-Western societies, with their loosely structured, sometimes coercive, forms of government, were riven with factionalism, which made it hard for them to unite in the face of outside threat. Many of the societies that adapted with some success to the new order did so as a result of charismatic and shrewd leadership at the right moment.

King Moshoeshoe (1786–1870) of the BaSotho people of southern Africa was such a man. He was born into an isolated society of farming villages organized in small chiefdoms, a world that knew nothing of horses, firearms, or of white people. During his thirties, African refugees fleeing from the great Zulu ruler Shaka invaded his homeland and disrupted the centuries-old order. It was then that Moshoeshoe emerged as a leader. Through moral influence as much as military acumen, he rallied the survivors and built a small kingdom bounded by the massive Drakensberg Mountains of what is now Natal in South Africa. This kingdom he named Lesotho, the homeland of the Sotho people. Lesotho was still in its infancy when Western civilization expanded out of the Cape. For the rest of his life, Moshoeshoe grappled with the problems created by marauding plunderers, missionaries, British officials with treaties in hand, and Afrikaner farmers encroaching on his lands. He was a humane, self-disciplined man who ruled by popular consent and only resorted to warfare in self-defense or under extreme provocation. Above all, he was a realist who saw the selective advantages of such European innovations as guns, horses, European crops, and writing. This realism gave him a sophisticated understanding of changing power relationships in the Africa of his day. To survive, he navigated his people along a fine line, keeping one foot firmly in traditional society while embracing at least some evangelical Christian doctrine. The political and social reasons for his pursuit of such a course were so compelling that he was never baptized, despite frantic last-minute efforts by both Catholic and Protestant missionaries. He died as he had lived, in two worlds.

Moshoeshoe kept Lesotho together during a period of intense competition between Afrikaner and British interests for his lands. He fought bitterly with Afrikaner commandos, complaining to their leaders that he would not give his country away. "It belongs not to me, as you know yourself very well that every country in the world does belong to the people which dwells in it. If I remove the Basutos, I have nowhere else where I can establish them" (Thompson 1975, 294). His final diplomatic coup was to have his people annexed by the British, who had little interest in exploiting the BaSotho. Had the Afrikaners of the Orange Free State done so, they would have seized almost all their arable land. In the event, Lesotho was a British colony for nearly a century. The British forbade whites to own land and left the structure of society more or less intact. They did little to encourage economic development or higher education, or to prepare the country for independence. Moshoeshoe's family occupied most positions of power and prestige in the newly independent Lesotho on 4 October 1966. But the problems were and still are daunting: land shortages, an ever-rising population, and a single major export, mine labor for South Africa. A period of political instability followed, partly because Lesotho's new political institutions did not reflect the fine line that still bridged the new and traditional elements in BaSotho society.

But Moshoeshoe left a vital legacy behind him, for the BaSotho possess much more cultural integrity and social cohesion than their black neighbors who suffered for so long under the repressive rule of white South Africa. By shrewd political maneuvering, this great African king secured the best options for his people that he could, in a world where the options were at best unsatisfactory. Few other non-Western rulers achieved such a long-term legacy.

While many African and Asian societies were battered and profoundly changed by their encounters with European civilization, they managed to adapt and survive—as did the Japanese or the Kikuyu of Kenya— emerging as the dominant society in a nation that has gained independence from colonial rule.

People Without History

Clash of Cultures is based on one fundamental, and perhaps obvious, assumption: that world history during the past six centuries has not been merely the history of Western expansion, but of thousands of diverse human societies interacting with one another in an increasingly interdependent and interconnected world. This important point lies behind historians and social scientists' notion of a "world economic system" that was the consequence of the spreading tentacles of the Age of Discovery. The notion of a "world system" has some conceptual value, provided it is confined to the post-Medieval world, and not carried back into the remote world of the Late Bronze Age, as some archaeologists have suggested.

World systems theory argues that events in distant Europe could affect peoples thousands of miles away, who had never heard of London or even seen a white person. By the same token, a shortage of furs along

North America's St. Lawrence River or reports of Maori cannibalism across the world in New Zealand could alter the course of European events in various ways. For instance, the international fur trade already had a long and highly profitable history that began when sixteenth-century European fishermen on the St. Lawrence River started trading for Canadian beaver pelts with the Indians along its banks. Beaver fur-wool was an immensely lucrative product, imported to Europe by the Dutch West Indies Company and later by the British and the French, and then redistributed throughout Europe. Canadian beavers revolutionized European fashion. The importers controlled redistribution so carefully that prices remained stable. Soon fur hats replaced the woolen headgear of earlier centuries. To own a beaver fur-wool hat was a sign of social status, even of political affiliation. Only in the early nineteenth century did the fur hat give way to silk and other materials.

From the very beginning, the North American fur trade involved not only competition between European powers, but between Indian groups as well. The frontiers of the trade moved rapidly, as one beaver population after another was hunted out, and the trappers had to move further into the interior. The new commerce had profound effects on both European and Indian society, as our essay on the Huron shows. At first the Huron profited from the trade. Their culture and ceremonial life were enriched. They and their confederacy partners controlled the fur trade over thousands of square miles, despite only minimal contacts with European colonists. However, as competition for furs intensified, both European powers and Indian groups competed for the rich harvest of pelts that flowed down the St. Lawrence. Eventually the Huron succumbed to the irresistible spiritual pressures of the Jesuits and fell prey to their fur-poor Iroquois neighbors, who took over their territory and the trade that went with it. Thus, men and women living hundreds, even thousands, of miles apart had their lives and their societies shaped by distant commercial and spiritual forces of which they were totally ignorant. It is both naive and simplistic to consider the history of either Western civilization or of the societies in these pages in isolation. Their destinies were shaped not only by their own actions, but by those of others as well.

World systems theory is conceptually useful for such broad issues, but does it have value on a smaller historical scale? It does, if it forces anthropologists, and archaeologists for that matter, to think in global and historical terms. As the distinguished anthropologist Eric Wolf pointed out in his magisterial study of capitalism and non-Western societies, *Europe and the People Without History* (1982), anthropologists have tended to ignore the forces of history in studying the non-Western world. He argues that events in Europe, as well as in remote lands, had a profound influence on the course of history, that the "people without history" were a major factor in global history. It is not enough, he argues, for anthropologists to study even the smallest of societies without considering their wider connections and their history, in whatever form it is recorded. In other words, anthropologists and historians should look at the world as a whole, not as a "sum of self-contained societies and cultures." Wolf speaks of unraveling "the chains of causes and effects at work in the lives of particular populations . . . [that] extend beyond any one population to embrace the trajectories of others—all others" (Wolf 1982, 385). Europe played an important role in this process, but what Wolf calls "chains of causation and consequence" within individual societies encompassed entire continents, and brought together the entire world.

Eric Wolf restored the "people without history" to the center stage of history at a general level, calling on a staggering array of scholarly sources to achieve his remarkable synthesis. The approach he calls for means researchers must venture far beyond documents and government archives into a realm of multidisciplinary scholarship unimaginable even a half century ago. Explorers' accounts, missionary journals, and Western sources tell but one side of a complex, multidimensional story. How can we correct this historical imbalance, examine the clash of cultures from both Western and non-Western perspectives, when many of the societies we study have completely different perceptions of history, and of the world around them? What weight can one place on oral histories, passed down from one generation to the text, on archaeological evidence, and on documents set down by native informants under the watchful eyes of Catholic friars? A new generation of multidisciplinary scholarship searches for fleeting clues. Australian historian Inga Clendinnen, herself the author of a memorable study of Aztec civilization, aptly calls us "Ahabs pursuing our great white whale." She adds: "We will never catch him . . . it is our limitations of thought, of understandings, of imagination we test as we quarter these strange waters. And then we think we see a darkening in the deeper water, a sudden surge, the roll of a fluke—and then the heart-lifting glimpse of the great white shape, its whiteness throwing back its own particular light, there on the glimmering horizon" (Clendinnen 1991, 275).

A Quartet of Sources

The new scholarship relies on unselfconscious multidisciplinary thinking, which evaluates a patchwork of traditional and scientific sources to create a historical synthesis with many dimensions. Such approaches mean grappling with incomplete, often tantalizing, sources such as oral histories or material clues left in abandoned archaeological sites from contact times. As Clendinnen says, there are many things we will never know, such as the Tasmanians' reaction to Marion du Fresne. However, the sheer diversity of sources allows us to obtain at least glimpses of complex events and reactions. The detective work involves a quartet of major sources—historical sources, ethnohistory, anthropology, and archaeology—as well as insights from many other academic disciplines.

Historical sources are the conventional tools of the historian and come in many forms. Explorers' accounts of their voyages and travels, their journalism annotated and published by modern scholars, government archives, missionary accounts, early settler diaries, even the texts of treaties, all are the raw material of the events of the past five centuries. Almost invariably, they give the Western perspective and take on events, people, and societies.

Ethnohistory, traditional history derived from non-Western sources, is a burgeoning field of historical inquiry, involving not only analysis and collecting of hitherto unrecorded oral histories, but also the critical examination of native sources written down after European contact. The most important American ethnohistories come from central America, where native accounts of Aztec and other societies were recorded by sixteenth-century friars, and sometimes by native speakers working under European supervision. Fray Bernardino de Sahagun used informants to set down a definitive account of Aztec civilization a generation after the Spanish Conquest. Sahagun's twelve-volume *General Things of the History of New Spain* covers the early history of Aztec civilization, its social, religious, and economic institutions, and ends with an account of the Conquest as seen through indigenous eyes. An entire academic specialty has developed around Sahagun's work alone, quite apart from other native documents such as the *Codex Mendoza,* an ethnographic account of Aztec society commissioned for the King of Spain in 1547.

Such sources bristle with scholarly challenges. Though Bernadino de Sahagun's *General Things* has an immediacy that comes from speaking to people who lived the traditional culture in their youth, he worked a full generation after the Conquest in a hostile political environment. While Sahagun considered his informants reliable, he edited their narratives for his book to meet his own Christian objectives. An intellectual chasm separated the informants and Sahagun's young Nahuatl interpreters, born since the Conquest into a quite different cultural environment. A similar gully divides modern scholars from the worthy friar. The modern Sahagun expert wrestles with the problems encountered by earlier scribes copying the prelate's original text and a hitherto unwritten language of highly inflected, compound words for the first time. Nahua discourse is full of allusions and unspoken implications, which escape us five centuries later. The Aztecs memorized their history through a combination of structured pictographs on codices and formal orations. This form of "alternative literacy" provided a reasonably standardized account of the Mexican past, which relied heavily on mnemonics and formal schooling, where pupils learned by rote, just as ancient Egyptian scribes did. The early friars wrestled with the complexities of a skeletal history transmitted by word of mouth. What follows is a summary of a once carefully managed past, for the Aztecs inherited a complex legacy of religious beliefs and philosophies from their predecessors, which their leaders refined for their own purposes.

Oral histories, whether recorded in textual form or captured by tape recorder, have serious limitations as historical documents. At their best, they echo with the resonance of confident memory, which lay easily in old mens' memories, and rolled easily from their tongues. The scientist has to reconstruct the context and content of their experiences from fragile oral clues and casual allusions. Most have an agenda—to legitimize a dynasty of chiefs, to make a political point, to lay claim to a piece of land. To dissect them requires extraordinary linguistic and critical skills, but a skilled expert can use oral traditions highly effectively to pinpoint memorable events such as solar eclipses or major population movements. Fortunately, the arrival of strangers from over the horizon in big ships was a major event by any standards, one quite out of the experience of human memory. The occasional oral traditions that have survived the centuries reflect a moment of shock, of gods perceived as arriving from outside the known world. A Maori chief in his old age remembered Captain Cook's men rowing backwards toward the shore like "goblins" with eyes in the back of their heads. Ethnohistories tell us that European contact came as a rude shock, like a divine thunderbolt let loose in well-ordered, predictable worlds. How does one reconcile these accounts of visiting gods with the observations of hardened explorers? We can never be entirely sure. A long drawn-out controversy has surrounded Captain Cook's arrival and death in Hawaii. Did the Hawaiians actually greet him as their returning god Lono, or is this portrayal a figment of Europeans' imaginations or of anthropology itself? The debate surrounds both the reliability of contemporary European sources and scholars' preconceptions of other societies of which they are not members. On the whole, the veracity of the contemporary observers prevails in the debate.

Anthropology is the study of humanity in the broadest possible sense, ancient and modern. However, the societies first contact by Westerners are long vanished, changed beyond recognition by exposure to industrial civilization. Our knowledge of pre-contact societies comes from contemporary sources such as Captain Cook's journals or pioneer missionary accounts, written long before prolonged interaction with Europeans. Such writings sometimes have an immediacy that reaches across the years, but their value varies infinitely from observer to observer, and inevitably reflect the biases of their authors. Cook was a sober chronicler of the Tahitians. His botanist colleague Joseph Banks was of romantic inclination, with a classical education and a penchant for the writings of the French philosopher Jean-Jacques Rousseau, who praised the natural state of humanity among savages.

Such accounts have value when combined with modern-day anthropological (ethnographic) studies undertaken by fieldworkers, who spent years living among their subjects. The scholar, however, must always remember there is no such thing as the "ethnographic present," a moment of first European contact when, say, Khoikhoi or Tahitian society was frozen in time in a "pristine" state. The so-called ethnographic present is a myth, for human cultures have changed constantly, ever since the first hominids fashioned stone choppers. European contact was simply another historical event that triggered cultural change, just as earlier innovations, such as, for instance, the Australian Aborigines' boomerang, sparked adjustments in hunting methods and society as a whole.

Ethnography provides a wealth of background information on the non-Western societies of the past five centuries, but we must never forget that each observation, each study, is but a snapshot of a brief moment in time. As Eric Wolf pointed out, relatively few anthropologists have a well-honed historical perspective, which contributed, and sometimes still contributes, to the impression that non-Western societies did not change dramatically over time.

Both ethnography and ethnohistory provide us with vital perspectives on the remarkably diverse worldviews of human societies. Many non-western societies share broadly similar cosmic views—a universe arranged in layers, a continuum between the living and spiritual worlds, and a central role for shamans and ancestors, intermediaries between the present generation and the intangible cosmos. These perspectives have deep roots in antiquity. Ancestor worship is well documented at early Jericho in western Asia at least 9,000 years ago. Bernardino de Sahagun's *General History* reveals an astounding complex Aztec pantheon and cosmos, many elements of which have survived the trauma of the Spanish Conquest to endure today in a subtle melding of Catholic and indigenous belief.

Westerners espouse a linear history, which unfolds over centuries and millennia, measured by major events, the reigns of kings and queens, the deeds of generals and statesmen. The relatively dispassionate historiography of modern Western scholarship that produces the recorded history learned by Westerners in school might serve political and ideological ends upon occasion, but is always a completely different conception of the past than that of the Tahitians, Huron, and other non-Western societies. The explorers of the Age of Discovery encountered cultures with a cyclical view of time and human existence, based on the eternal cycles of spring, summer, fall, and winter, of planting, germination, and harvest. This farming cycle replicates the verities of human life: procreation, birth, life, and death. Human existence unfolds in inexorable rhythm, through birth to death. One generation replaces another, in a world that the living inherit from the dead, and pass on to their successors, with the expectation that it will always remain the same. Everyone enjoys close material and spiritual ties to the land, which nurtures them and is the crux of cyclical human existence. Many non-Western societies have a linear sense of history, too, measured by glyphs or calendars as the Aztecs and Maya did, or remembered in oral tradition with reference to known ancestors, or major events such as solar eclipses or the arrival of outsiders. Such linear history serves to subdivide time, to justify imperial ambitions or the rule of lords, or is simply the stuff of generational memory, something quite different from the long time spans of

Western history compiled from centuries of documents and millennia of archaeology. Reconciling the cyclical and linear views of history is a major challenge for a historian of the Age of Discovery.

Archaeology is unique among all academic disciplines in its ability to describe and explain cultural change over long periods of time. For example, excavations in southwestern Tasmania chronicle human occupation in the southern extremities of Australasia by at least 32,000 years ago, during the late Ice Age. Recent research by archaeologist Herbert Maschner in southeast Alaska has shown that coastal native American societies in that region varied dramatically in their cultural complexity and forms of settlement over time. His research suggests that the elaborate contact-period societies of the country's northwest coast may not have been long established in all areas.

Archaeology provides a long view, and is also a powerful ally when used in conjunction with historical documents to reconstruct life at early European settlements, like, for instance, the fifteenth-century Portuguese fort at Elmira on West Africa's Ghanian coast. Evidence for interaction with outsiders is harder to find in indigenous sites, except in the form of exotic artifacts of unquestioned foreign manufacture such as the imported glass beads, sea shells, and other baubles used in long-distance trade from Africa's coasts into the far interior. Historic period Huron and Iroquois archaeological sites in the St. Lawrence Valley also provide evidence of trade between Europeans and native American groups that predate, and are contemporary with, the expansion of the fur trade.

By its very nature, archaeology is an anonymous discipline, concerned with the generalities of human culture rather than the deeds of individuals, providing relatively little information on European contact. However, excavations, field surveys, and meticulous analyses of historic and prehistoric artifacts can provide extremely valuable information on the earlier origins of societies such as the Khoikhoi or the Aztecs.

This formidable quartet of historical sources provides the tapestry for our story. However, remarkable, and sometimes startling insights come from unexpected sources: the florid prose of Victorian adventure novels, children's books, the artistic styles used by explorers' artists such as the Scottish colors used by Cook's first artist to evoke Tahitian landscapes, even handbooks for explorers and official directions to government expeditions. Biological anthropologists provide forensic and medical data; linguistic researches give clues to ancient migrations; and fragments of animal bones and long discarded seeds reveal dietary stress or evidence for human diets modified when fisheries are exhausted or crops fail in the face of cycles of drought. The list of potential, and sometimes imaginatively developed sources is unending. Five centuries of sometimes dramatic and always complex culture contact provide a unique opportunity for creative and unconventional research. These inquires are still in their infancy.

Even in today's global world, few people find it easy to accept those who are different from them, whether the difference be that of color, creed, or simply ways of thinking. This inability of humankind to comprehend others heightens the tensions in our industrial and nuclear world. *Clash of Cultures* uses contemporary scholarship and nine human societies to explore some of the ways our forebears reacted to human diversity. Our present attitudes to non-Western cultures are colored by powerful and little known forces of history that developed in medieval times and reached a crescendo in the imperial heyday of the late nineteenth century. We live with the legacy of racist doctrines and stereotypes that developed over a century ago, sharpened by the events of the twentieth century.

Participant Observation on a Motorcycle

ANDREW CORNISH

A short while after arriving in the field in southern Thailand, I managed to acquire a motorcycle. While I did not actually possess a licence to ride it, some kind words to those in high places by patrons who had taken me under their wing had cleared the way for me to be turned loose on the roads of Thailand without hindrance unless, it was sharply stressed, I was foolish enough to get involved in an accident. At an early stage I had wondered whether I should mention that my licence at home had been repossessed by a couple of incredulous policemen who took a very dim view of creative driving, but I felt that to try and explain this in Thai would probably lead to misunderstandings, and might well have caused my hosts unnecessary anxiety.

Come St. David's Day, the inevitable accident occurred. I had been on an afternoon jaunt on my freshly cleaned motorcycle, merrily weaving through the traffic, and thinking how interesting it was that Thai motorists actually lived out the theory of loose structure in their driving. During this course of musing I decided to make a right-hand turn, and still being rather set in my Western ways, slowed down to do so. This was an ethnocentric mistake. As I began to turn, another motorcyclist, complete with an ice chest full of fish and a large basket of oranges on the pillion seat, decided that this was the ideal moment to overtake. I was much too slow, he was far too fast, and our subjective constructions of existence spectacularly collided with the limits of the material world.

What followed was actually quite pleasurable for the brief but slow-motion moments it lasted. A massive surge of metal, flesh, fish, and disintegrating oranges swept me from behind, then passed overhead in a surrealistic collage as my body easily performed a series of gymnastic stunts that I had been totally unable to master at school. As always in life, the brief pleasure had to be repaid with an extended flood of unwelcome pain, relieved only by the happy realization that I, and the other motorist who had flown so gracefully above me, had narrowly but successfully avoided truncating our skulls on a Burmese ebony tree.

Anxious to reassure myself that nothing was broken, I got quickly to my feet, dusted myself off, and walked over to switch off my motorcycle engine, which by now was making a maniacal noise without its exhaust pipe. Then I walked back to the other rider, who was still lying rigidly on his back and wondering whether he should believe what was happening. I politely asked him if he was all right, but the hypothesis that in a crisis everyone reverts to speaking English clearly required some revision. Months of Thai lessons began to trickle back, but far too slowly, and in the meantime he had also stood up. It was only then that I realized the pair of us had been surrounded by a rather large crowd of onlookers.

Television in Thailand does not commence broadcasting until 4:30 p.m. so our little accident had a good audience, with local residents coming out of their houses and shops, and cars, motorcycles, and trucks stopping to take in the scene. The other rider began talking to some people near him, and a shopkeeper who knew me came and asked if I was all right. From that moment, I never had a chance to speak to the other rider again. We were slowly but surely separated, each of us in the centre of a group, the two groups gathering slightly apart from one another. I had a sudden and horrible realization that I was in the middle of one of those dispute settlement cases that I had intermittently dozed through as an undergraduate. With an abrupt and sickening shock, participant observation had become rather too much participation and too little cosy observation.

Some of the other rider's newly acquired entourage came over to ask the fringes of my group what exactly had happened. I pleaded my version to those standing close to me, and it was then relayed—and, I should add, suitably amended—back through the throng to be taken away and compared with the other rider's tale of woe. While this little contest was going on, a number of people from both groups were inspecting the rather forlorn wreckages of our motorcycles and debating over which one appeared to be more badly damaged. "Look at this!" someone cried, lifting a torn section of the seat and helpfully making the tear more ostentatious in the process. "But look at this!" came the reply, as someone else wrenched a limply hanging indicator light completely off its mounting. After a series of such exchanges, the two groups finally agreed that both motorcycles were in an equally derelict state, though I could not help feeling, peering from the little prison within my group of supporters, that those judging, the damage to the machines had played a more than passive role in ensuring a parity of demolition.

Physical injuries were the next to be subjected to this adjudication process. I found my shirt being lifted up, and a chorus of oohs and aahs issuing from the crowd, as someone with jolly animation prodded and pinched the large areas of my back which were now bravely attempting to stay in place without the aid of skin. My startled eyes began looking in opposite directions at the same time, while somewhat less than human groans gargled out of my mouth. From similar sounds in the distance I deduced that the other poor rider was being subjected to a similar treatment. He frankly looked rather the worse for wear than I did, but whenever his group claimed this, my supporters would proceed to show just what excruciating pain I was suffering by prodding me in the back and indicating my randomly circumambulating eyes as if to say "see, we told you so."

On issues of damage, both mechanical and physical, we were adjudged by the two groups to be fairly evenly scored. Fault in relation to road rules had never been an issue. Then came a bit of a lull, as if something serious was about to happen. A senior person from the other group came over and spoke to me directly, asking if I wanted to call the police. A hush fell over everyone. I, of course, was totally terrified at the prospect—no licence, visions of deportation, and so far only one meagre book of field notes to my name. I put on my best weak pathetic smile and mumbled that I thought it was not really necessary unless the other chap insisted. A culturally appropriate move: Everyone looked happily relieved, and the other rider's spokesman said generously that it would only be a waste of time and cause unnecessary bother to bring the police out on an errand like this. It was to be a few months before I realized that, like many other motorcyclists, the other rider was also probably roaming the roads without a licence, and that in this part of the country calling the police was generally regarded as a last, and unsporting, resort.

The final agreement was that we should settle our own repairs—to both body and vehicle—and let the matter rest. A visible sigh of relief passed through the two groups that had gathered, and they slowly began to disperse. For the first time since the collision, I saw the other rider face to face, so I walked towards him to offer my apologies. I never managed to reach him. The dispersing groups froze in horror, then quickly regathered around me. "What is wrong now?" I was interrogated on all sides. Was I not happy with the result? I had clearly made a serious blunder, and it took a while to settle things down once more. A perceptive shopkeeper from nearby grabbed my arm and dragged me off to his shop for coffee, explaining to me that the matter had been settled and that further contact for any reason with the other rider or his group would only prolong an unpleasant situation that could now be forgotten by all involved.

so it was that later that evening I was able to start my second book of field notes with an entry on dispute settlement, though painful twinges up my back and throbbing between the ears made me wish I had relied on some other informant to provide the ethnographic details. I made a silent vow to myself to discontinue this idiosyncratic method of participant observation, and managed to some extent to keep the vow for the rest of my stay. Thereafter I successfully steered clear of motorcycle accidents, and instead got shot at, electrocuted, and innocently involved in scandal and otherwise abused. But all that, as they say, is another story.

Shamans

MARK J. PLOTKIN

Contrary to popular belief, the medicine man, or shaman (usually an accomplished botanist), represents the most ancient profession in the evolution of human culture.

—Dr. Richard Evans Schultes, 1963

He didn't look like a medicine man to me when I first met him.

Having been raised on a steady diet of Tarzan films, I first entered the rain forest expecting to find the medicine man (or "witch doctor") outfitted in full forest regalia: grass skirts, carnivore tooth necklaces, feather headdress. And indeed I did eventually work with shamans wearing even more fantastic costumes (or almost nothing, in some instances) when I entered the jungles of the northeast Amazon in the late 1970s. But as ever-encroaching Western civilization began making its appearance throughout the most remote corners of Amazonia, the young indigenous people lost interest in the old ways. Living in a world where the cultural global icons were people like Bruce Lee, Madonna, and Michael Jordan, the young Indians showed little or no interest in their own traditional cultures. The world of the shamans, with their belief in magic spirit worlds and astral travel, seemed less useful and effective than antibiotics. And if the missionaries or government-sponsored nurses insisted that shamanism was a sham, why pay any attention to a great-grandfather who said otherwise? So I would enter villages to find ancient wizards and plant masters wearing traditional breechcloths and jaguar-tooth necklaces but their descendants dressed in National Basketball Association T-shirts and high-top tennis shoes. In fifteen years of field experience, I had met few shamans who were not at least twice as old (and, more often, thrice as old) as I was.

But this fellow was different.

It was the first day of August, 1995, and I was seated in a cotton hammock under a thatched roof in the western Amazon of Colombia. To get there, I had to fly south from the Andean city of Bogota to the burgeoning frontier town of Florencia, the capital city of the state of Caquetá; then an all-day bus ride past the military checkpoints and through the depressingly deforested landscape. In the 1960s, the national government, with the best of intentions, had encouraged landless peasants to settle on the "fertile" soils of the "uninhabited" Amazon region. The peasants' inability to manage the (admittedly challenging) tropical landscape resulted in forest destruction of staggering proportions. When my mentor Richard Schultes carried out ethnobotanical research here in the 1940s and 1950s, he marveled at "the seemingly limitless forest that stretched unbroken to the far horizon." Schultes returned to the area only a decade later, and writer William Burroughs was there to record the scientist's reaction: "My God, what have they done to the forest. . . . It's all gone!"

I had traveled to the area at the invitation of a Colombian colleague to participate in an ayahuasca ritual, the vision-vine ceremony conducted by Amazonian shamans for purposes of curing and divination. In South and North America, ayahuasca had attained an enormous and devoted following among certain New Age groups, though none of the practitioners whom I met were Native American shamans. The invitation to the Colombian Amazon seemed to represent the opportunity to participate in a truly traditional ceremony.

On that torrid afternoon, sweat poured off me and a few mosquitoes buzzed hungrily around my ears as I conversed with a fellow who stood leaning against the wooden post from which one end of my hammock was strung. He stood about five-foot-two, the typical height of a forest Indian, though the local campesinos (peasants) were not much taller. He had jet black hair and spoke excellent Spanish, again making it difficult for me to ascertain whether he was a Native American or not (knowing that such a question can be considered ex-

15

tremely rude by both cultures, I would not ask him outright). He took a last, long draught of his warm beer, and asked me if I'd ever been to the jungle before. I replied that I had worked in several South American countries searching for healing plants. A brief smile flickered across his face. "Have you ever participated in a *toma,* an ayahuasca session?" he asked.

"Once," I replied, "in Peru. But I know I have much to learn about the use of the vision vine for curing purposes." A fleeting, Mona Lisa smile played across his face as he stubbed out his cigarette on the dirt floor and said, "Then I'll see you at the ceremony tonight." And with that, he wandered off.

The session was held at a small tribal meetinghouse constructed at the edge of the village. I was crestfallen—the poured concrete floor, cinderblock walls, and corrugated aluminum roof seemed the very antithesis of rain forest culture. Where was the traditional *maloca,* the fantastic elongated conical roundhouse that was supposed to be the characteristic indigenous dwelling of the northwest Amazon? I asked a local Ingano fellow who wandered past. "The ayahuasca journey only begins here," he said, pointing with his chin at the structure. "But you will depart very quickly and travel very far away." He smiled and walked on.

The light of the moon on that clear evening was strong enough to illuminate enormous sandstone boulders that marked the edge of a small river running a few hundred meters to the west of the meetinghouse. On the other side of the water began the Andean foothills, home to the only pristine forest in the area. Surrounding the other sides of the meeting hall was nothing but depleted cattle pastures that had harbored magnificent rain forest until a few decades before.

There was an audible murmur from the other Indians as the shaman entered the hut. I marveled at the traditional *cushma,* the sky blue cotton tunic that covered him from shoulders to waist. Wrapped tightly around his thick biceps were dense strings of *shoroshoro* seeds that produced a hissing rattle as he walked. And around his neck was a magnificent necklace of jaguar teeth, the symbol of the shaman in many Amazonian tribes. It was only after admiring the medicine man's finery that I was startled to recognize him as the fellow with whom I had been chatting earlier that afternoon. In his ceremonial garb he looked every inch the great shaman, and I wondered how I could have ever thought otherwise.

The shaman took his seat on a low bench at one end of the hut while the rest of us sat in a circle on the dirt floor at his feet. A chilly breeze blew in from the Andean slopes and I shivered as much from anticipation as from the cold. The night was alive with jungle sounds: crickets buzzed and chirped, frogs croaked and trilled, night jars cooed and whooped. Howler monkeys hooted briefly, indicating that rain would fall the next day.

The shaman dipped a calabash into an earthen pot between his feet. Holding it high over his head with both hands, he mumbled a few incantations before drinking the ayahuasca in a single draught. Wiping his mouth clean with the back of his hand, he refilled the container from the pot, repeated the incantation, and passed it to me.

I looked down at the cup and saw it filled to the brim with a thick reddish brown liquid. I tried to knock it back in one swallow as I had seen the shaman do. The dreadful bitterness of the potion, however, caught me by surprise and I struggled to keep from retching. The Indian seated on the other side of the shaman noted my distress and passed me a cup of *aguardiente,* a fiery sugar cane brandy whose sweet anise aftertaste erased the disagreeable brackishness of the ayahuasca. I sat and watched the shaman slowly repeat the procedure with everyone in the circle.

All seemed quiet and peaceful until the shaman picked up a handful of *wai-rah sacha* leaves and began to shake them in a fanning motion. The leaves produced a whistling sound not unlike a high wind rushing through the rain forest canopy before a heavy thunderstorm: *shhhhhh-shhhhhh.* He shook it in a slow, rhythmic pattern that proved hypnotic, and felt as if my brain waves were being organized in a fixed laser like pattern under his control. My body began to relax, and I lay back onto a blanket I had brought to ward off the cold. Glancing around, I noticed that everyone else had also reclined, as if the shaman had willed us to do so. Only the medicine man remained seated upright, and he began a mesmerizing chant: *Hey-yah-hey! Hey-yah-hey!*

What seems simple in retrospect was emotionally enrapturing at the time. And the shaking of the leaves added a layer of complexity and fascination that reverberated through my brain from the right front lobe to the rear left lobe to the rear right lobe to the front left lobe, and back again. By now the shaman seemed master of time, space, and my entire being.

I drifted off into a gentle trance. I felt myself lying in a tucum palm fiber hammock as comfortable as a giant feather bed. I was floating as in a dream. Looking up, I could see a beautiful blue tropical sky with only a few wisps of clouds above me. The hammock was slung between two towering columnar *epena* trees with a dark Amazonian lake below me. At the far edge of the lake I could make out the tiny figure of the shaman in this blue tunic continuing his chant. By the peaceful look on his face that I could just make out at this distance, I could tell that he was deep into his own ayahuasca visions. As I floated there with my hands propped comfortably behind my head, I peacefully reviewed scenes from my life that reenacted themselves for my analysis. Aside from a few mild waves of nausea, all seemed peaceful and calm; I was at one with the cosmos.

Soon the shaman ceased his chant, and I opened my eyes to find myself seated at his feet once more. He refilled the calabash, prayed over it, and drank it down. Repeating the first two steps, he then passed the container to me. I drained it but it didn't sit right in my stomach. I tried to ignore the volcanic nausea welling up inside. I promised myself that I would lie back down as soon as everyone had had their turn and began to feel a bit better by focusing all my attention on the shaman. I knew that he was able to feel my gaze, and he turned to me. As he did so, the beaded bracelets on his biceps produced the sound of rushing water and turned into tiny glowing diamonds that all but obscured my field of vision. As the diamonds dissipated, I could see that the shaman was staring at me with a look that combined equal parts power, disdain, humor, and kindness. I stared at his black pupils growing larger and larger, finally combining into one giant black vortex into which I was sucked. I was underwater now in waters as pitch-black as the Rio Negro. Huge black caimans and anacondas swarmed in the river, menacing me with their size and demeanor, though not attacking me directly. Running out of air, and afraid of the creatures that surrounded me in this aquatic realm, I swam desperately.

I broke the surface and crawled on all fours onto a white sandy beach along with riverbank. Having been underwater too long, I became sick, vomiting and vomiting. I was unable to stop; the life began ebbing from my body. I could not regain my feet and sank face down into the sand, rising up enough only to retch over to the side. I began weeping and begging for help as I continued to fade. Pain racked my body and my head felt as if it had exploded. I tried fighting for my life but no longer had the strength. I had managed to crawl up the riverbank toward the jungle but only made it far enough to pass out in the grass at the edge of the forest. I lay face down. I died.

I don't know how long I lay in the grass, inert, comatose, inanimate. But I could hear something in the back of my head. The shaman continued to chant, deep in the forest in front of me. With a Herculean effort, I managed to raise myself on all fours. I began weeping again because I did not have the strength to go to him. As I sat mired in this predicament, I was frightened by a deep guttural grunt in the jungle in front of me. A jaguar! Now I was weak *and* terrified. But a most extraordinary thing happened: the great cat's roar caused a wave of nausea to well up inside me and I puked as I never had before. Horrible things poured out of me: purple frogs and bloodred snakes and phosphorescent orange scorpions. I thought I was dying a second death, yet when it stopped I felt a bit stronger. So close was the jaguar that I could smell him, yet I was no longer afraid. I stumbled a bit as I followed him into the jungle; I knew that he was leading me toward the shaman. Tripping over roots, I tried to keep pace with the great cat. I momentarily worried about snakes until I realized that nothing could be worse than what I was enduring.

Falling to my knees, I looked up to see the shaman standing over me. He began a peculiar chant that made my head hurt even more until he pressed his palms against my temples and started to squeeze. As he twisted my neck to the right I felt my vertebrae pop; the pain began to abate, ever so slightly. He seated me on a tree trunk and began to dance around me. Taking a swig of an herbal tea, he circled me, spitting the aromatic liquid at me in a cold spray at each of the four cardinal points of the compass. The pain and confusion that racked my body began to subside as he massaged my arms and neck. The sun had started to rise in the east. He sang and rubbed my upper body with leaves, pausing every now and again to cast off some invisible film he seemed to be scraping off me. I managed to croak out a question: "Why did you do this to me?"

He gave a cryptic, Cheshire cat smile and replied: "You have had a glimpse of our world. You have been purged, cleaned, healed. You will never again fear death as you have now died and been reborn."

In a classic treatise on ayahuasca (1979), R. E. Schultes wrote:

> There is a magic intoxicant in northwesternmost South America which the Indians believe can free the soul from corporeal confinement, allowing it to wander free and return to the body at will. The soul, thus untrammeled, liberates its owner from the everyday life and introduces him to wondrous

realms of what he considers reality and permits him to communicate with his ancestors. The Kechua term for this inebriating drink—ayahuasca ("vine of the soul")—refers to this freeing of the spirit. The plants involved are truly plants of the gods, for their powers are laid to supernatural forces residing in their tissues, and they were the divine gifts to the earliest Indians on earth. The drink employed for prophecy, divination, sorcery, and medical purposes, is so deeply rooted in native mythology and philosophy that there can be no doubt of its great age as part of aboriginal life.

In the northwest Amazon, ayahuasca represents an essential component of most—if not all—shamanic healing ceremonies. Yet there are aspects of these shamanic practices that are used by other cultures around the world, only some of which employ psychotropic plants in their healing rituals. According to Dr. Piers Vitebsky, an authority on Eurasian shamanism, the word "shaman" comes from the language of the Evenk peoples, reindeer herders in Siberia. To the Evenk, a shaman is a person who can "will his or her spirit to leave the body and journey to upper or lower world." Common elements unite the shamanic tradition found on every continent except Antarctica.

Curing disease, preventing famine, controlling the weather, entering trances, fighting evil spirits sent by malevolent shamans of other tribes, traveling up to the spirit world, or conveying souls to the underworld are common denominators among most practitioners of what we consider shamanism. In most groups, the shaman serves as the only tribal member who fully comprehends both the "real" world and the "spirit" world and is therefore responsible for maintaining the balance between the two.

Within the context of the source culture, shamanism is often considered a profoundly holy profession. Unlike in much of the industrialized world, in which healing is essentially divorced from spirituality, the shaman also functions as the priest-rabbi, which greatly augments his or her ability to heal. As Western science finally begins to study and appreciate the therapeutic benefits of spirituality, the practice and effectiveness of shamanism becomes not only more comprehensible but also more appreciated.

An integral component of shamanistic healing is what has been called "the placebo effect." Many leaders of the Western medical establishment came of age during the antibiotic revolution, the single greatest therapeutic advance of the mid-twentieth century. However, the development of these drugs also led several generations of physicians to equate (to a large degree) chemistry and healing. Spirituality (its nature and its role in healing) was part of few (if any) medical school curricula. The placebo effect, in which patients recovered because they believed they would, was not in and of itself shunned, but more often noted with bemusement rather than harnessed and put to work.

Shamans, on the other hand, are masters of the placebo effect. Much has been made of the shamanic practice of sucking the "evil darts" (or other foreign substances) out of the patient's body by the healer. References in the literature often refer to it as trickery or sleight of hand, usually in a condescending way. Two aspects, however, are overlooked. First, it often provides the patient some relief, convincing them that they are on the road to recovery and creating a mind-set that facilitates healing. Second, therapeutic compounds, usually in the form of plants, are also employed because the shaman is customarily a master botanist. The shaman's genius as a healer stems from his (or her) ability to combine the spiritual (sucking out evil darts, communing with the forces of nature, etc.) with the chemical (the plants, insects, etc.)

Chief Pierce of Flat Iron, an Oglala Sioux, explained the inextricable link between the holy and the botanical almost a century ago: "From Wakan-Tanka, the Great Mystery, comes all power. . . . Man knows that all healing plants are given by Wakan-Tanka: therefore they are holy. . . . The Great Mystery gave to men all things for their food, their clothing, their welfare. And to man he gave also the knowledge how to use these gifts . . . how to find the holy healing plants."

The sophisticated botanical knowledge of these "uneducated" shamans astonishes Western researchers. In the rain forest, these healers can sometimes identify almost every single species of tree merely by the smell, appearance, or feel of the bark, a feat no university-trained botanist can accomplish. And their knowledge of the ecology of these plants—when they fruit, when they flower, what pollinates them, what disperses the seeds, what preys on them, what type of soil they prefer—is no less impressive. As nature continues to provide us with a cornucopia of new medicines, these shamans (in the rain forest and elsewhere) will prove to be the ultimate sources of knowledge about which species offer therapeutic promise and how they might best be employed.

Almost every plant species that has been put to use by Western medicine was originally discovered and utilized by indigenous cultures. Despite the fact that a single shaman may know and employ over a hundred species for medicinal purposes, or that a single tribe (which may have several shamans) may know and utilize several hundred species for medical purposes, few of the world's remaining tribal peoples have been the subject of comprehensive ethnobotanical/ethnomedical studies. Yet the more we study, the more we learn how little we know about how much they know.

Ayahuasca, the vision vine, represents a classic example. The early accounts of ayahuasca focused on a single species of vine *(Banisteriopsis caapi)*. Subsequent research has revealed that other plants added to the mixture determine the actual type, intensity, and duration of the hallucinations—proving the sophistication of these shamans as both botanists and chemists. For example, leaves of a species of the *Psychotria* shrub of the coffee family are often added to the ayahuasca mixture. These leaves contain chemicals called tryptamines that induce hallucinations. The compounds, however, are inactive when taken orally unless activated by the presence of another type of chemical known as monoamine oxidase inhibitors. The psychotropic compounds in the ayahuasca vine not only induce hallucinations but also function as monoamine oxidase inhibitors. The result: a brew much more potent than one prepared from either species.

Furthermore, the shamans often have the remarkable ability to distinguish between, describe, and make use of distinct healing and/or chemical properties of different parts of the same plant. A shaman, for example, will note that bark from the upper stem of the ayahuasca vine may cause visions of jaguars, while the root bark results in scenes of anacondas. Schultes wrote:

> Among the Tukano of the Colombian Vaupes, for example, six "kinds" of Ayahuasca or Kahi are recognized. . . . *Kahi riama*, the strongest, produces auditory hallucinations and announces future events. It is said to cause death if improperly employed. The second strongest, *Mene-kahi-ma*, reputedly causes visions of green snakes. . . . These two "kinds" may not belong to Banisteriopsis or even to the family Malpighiaceae. The third in strength is called *Suana-kahi-ma* ("Kahi of the red jaguar"), producing visions in red. *Kahi-vai Bucura-rijoma* ("Kahi of the monkey head") causes monkeys to hallucinate and howl. . . . All of these "kinds" are referable probably to *Banisteriopsis caapi* [e.g., what to Western botanists is all the same species].

Hallucinogens, while an integral part of shamanic healing practices in the western Amazon, still represent only a very small portion of plants employed for therapeutic purposes. As we have seen before, natural products employed for a particular purpose in one culture may offer promise of a different use in our own culture. In the case of ayahuasca, for example, Western-trained physicians in both Brazil and Peru are using the vine as an experimental treatment for chronic alcoholism and crack addition, with promising results.

An example of using one therapeutic plant for different purposes in a different culture comes to us from the tropical forests of American Samoa in the South Pacific, where the herbal healers—the *taulasea*—are primarily women. These herbalists know 200 species of plants and recognize 180 types of diseases. Ethnobotanist Dr. Paul Cox of the National Tropical botanical Garden had been working with this culture for over a decade when, in 1984, a *taulasea* named Epenesa Mauigoa showed him an herbal treatment for acute hepatitis prepared from the inner bark of a local species of rubber tree. Cox was particularly intrigued when she insisted that only one "variety" of the tree could be employed when, in Western botanical terms, both varieties were the same species. Investigation of the plant in the laboratories of the National Cancer Institute outside Washington, D.C., yielded a new molecule that the scientists named prostratin. This compound belongs to a class of chemicals known as phorbols, many of which cause tumors in the human body. Intriguingly, however, prostratin not only inhibited the formation of tumors but, in the test tube, prevented cells from becoming infected by the HIV-1 virus and extended the life of infected cells! Of course, it is a long way from the jungle to the laboratory and, in some ways, an even longer trail from the test tube to the pharmacy. Nonetheless, research on prostratin continues. And it is precisely these finds that validate indigenous wisdom in Western eyes, leading to pharmaceutical companies' increased interest in shamanic wisdom.

Scientists continue to be astonished at the breadth and depth of indigenous wisdom. Ethnobotanists at the New York Botanical garden recently conducted a classic comparative study of indigenous ethnobotanical sagacity in the Amazon Basin. Working with the Chacobo tribe in Bolivia, Dr. Brian Boom found they used 95 percent of the local tree species. His colleague Dr. Bill Balee learned that the Tembe peoples of Brazil employed 61.3 percent of local tress while the Ka'apoor tribe used 76.8 percent.

The effectiveness of this wisdom is being validated in the laboratory. Dr. Bernard Ortiz de Montellano of Wayne State University sifted through accounts of the ethnomedicine of the Aztec peoples of ancient Mexico and was able to identify 118 plants that they employed as medicines. When he subjected them to laboratory examination, he found that almost 85 percent were at least somewhat efficacious, strikingly similar to data gathered by Paul Cox and his colleagues in Polynesia. The joint Swedish-American research team tested the Samoan medicinal plants in the laboratory. The results: 86 percent demonstrated significant pharmacological activity.

Of course, new mechanisms must be developed to protect the intellectual property rights of these local peoples and local governments: fortunately, the colonial/neocolonial model of "Let's take what we need of local plants and wisdom and cart if off to the marketplace" is completely unacceptable as we enter the twenty-first century. New economic models and legal frameworks are being devised and put in place to share benefits from these new discoveries and avoid the "rape and run" approach to commercializing natural resources that characterized much of human history.

Nonetheless, an enormous body of shamanic knowledge remains untested (or untestable) in the laboratory because we cannot (or have not yet been able to) understand it outside of the context of indigenous culture. The Tirio Indians of the northeast Amazon, for example, employ a series of plants to treat ailments that (they claim) are caused by the breaking of hunting taboos. One ancient medicine man showed me a plant that he explained was "boiled into a tea and given to an infant who was crying at night because he couldn't sleep because his father had killed a giant anteater." Another species was used for the same purpose, except that the child suffered insomnia because the father had killed a tapir. Most Westerners would regard these ailments as imaginary. A much more effective utilitarian approach, instead of dismissing this seemingly incomprehensible claim, would be to investigate whether the plant potion contained compounds that might serve as the basis for a safe, effective, nonaddictive sleeping pill—a potion that Western medicine has been unable to devise.

In our culture, we have been taught that our system of medicine (and other things!) is the most advanced, the most successful, the most sophisticated, and so on—a valid statement, in many regards. This "lesson," however, often results in a cultural arrogance that underestimates or even denigrates other systems, either because they seem "primitive" and/or because we don't understand what they are trying to tell or teach us. In his brilliant book *Witchdoctors and Psychiatrists,* Dr. E. Fuller Torrey wrote: "A psychiatrist who tells an illiterate African that his phobia is related to fear of failure and a witch doctor who tells an American tourist that his phobia is related to possession by an ancestral spirit will be met by equally blank stares."

Our culture teaches us to "cut to the chase," to get that one plant or (better yet) one molecule that is responsible for the shaman's cure—and you can spare us the magic rattle and the sacred smoke, thank you very much. Some of these cures only work within their cultural context, be it a treatment for possession by an ancestral spirit, a cure that involves ceremony, ritual, and healing plants, or a mundane remedy that simply requires rubbing a few crushed leaves on the afflicted area. Clearly, some of these treatments harness powerful chemicals that can be used effectively far from their site of origin and within a Western (or other) clinical context.

The Western tendency to adopt a reductionist approach is not just an interest in getting to the basic chemistry (preferably a single molecule that is responsible for the therapeutic effect) or merely a question of being in a hurry—it is also a question of safety and economics. It has proven difficult, if not impossible, to patent a complex plant extract that may contain a multitude of chemicals, even if proven safe and effective. Still, our cultural propensity to reduce everything to the simplest common denominator can cause us to underestimate or even deny the shaman's healing wisdom. A recent example: two ethnobotanists were intrigued by a West African medicine man who appeared to have an extremely potent potion for reducing blood-sugar levels in diabetic patients. They asked whether he might be willing to provide them with the plants he used so they could take them back to the United States for testing. The shaman readily agreed and gave the scientists three different plants. In the lab, they tested species A, which had no effect; they tried species B, which had no effect. They tested species C, still with no positive results. Finally, they boiled them all together and analyzed the resulting potion. Nothing! A year later, back in Africa, they returned to the medicine man. "Your potion doesn't seem to work," said one of the ethnobotanists to the witch doctor.

"What do you mean?" he replied. "You saw me give it to my patients, and measured their blood-sugar levels with your instruments. You yourself told me that the blood-sugar level went down. How could you now claim it doesn't work?"

The ethnobotanists then asked the medicine man if he would be willing to prepare a batch of the potion they could then take with them. He agreed. The shaman boiled water in a big aluminum opt over a wood fire. He added the first plant species, then the second, then the third. Just as he was preparing to take the pot off the fire, he reached into a wet muslin sack, extracted a crab, and dropped it in the pot.

"What is that?" asked one of the ethnobotanists.

"What does it look like?" replied the shaman. "It is a crab!"

"Yeah, I know," responded the scientist. "But why did you add it to the pot? You didn't tell us that was part of the recipe."

The shaman smiled. "Look," he said, "you asked me if I would give you the plants used to make the potion. I did!"

The scientists took the potion back to the United States, found it to be effective at lowering blood sugar, and it is currently being investigated in the lab.

Of course, a shaman's healing wizardry does not necessarily entail the use of nature's chemistry. Dr. Charles Limbach, and American physician with extensive experience in Latin America, recently related an intriguing encounter. A friend of his, also a physician, had returned from a sojourn in the Oriente, the Amazonian territory of eastern Ecuador:

> My friend was visiting a missionary acquaintance who was working with the Shuar people, also called the Jivaro, who were once renowned for their then common practice of removing and then shrinking the heads of their enemies. He was sitting on the porch of the missionary's house and chatting with his fellow American and an elderly Shuar who had a reputation as a powerful shaman. While they were conversing, another Shuar arrived and asked the missionary for help with a botfly larva (through a complicated process, botfly eggs enter the human body and hatch into larvae which feed on human flesh. The standard western treatment is to cut them out with a scalpel). The missionary, who had received some medical training, ducked into the house and came back out with alcohol, cotton swabs, a bandage, and a scalpel. The Shuar shaman asked what he planned to do with all that equipment. The American replied that he would cut out the larva. The shaman smiled, and said he would handle it. He sat the patient in a hammock, leaned over the arm with the botfly and began to sing. Within minutes, the botfly larva emerged from the man's arm, fell onto the floor of the porch, and the shaman crushed it beneath his bare foot.

Neither Limbach nor his colleague was able to explain the incident. Had the shaman sung a particular frequency maddening to the insect, as opera singers are able to hit a note that can shatter glass? Or did the shaman surreptitiously exhale tobacco smoke into the larva's breathing hole, causing it to crawl out in search of air? In some ways, this situation is analogous to the use of aspirin for most of the past century: even though we didn't fully understand how it functioned in the human body until relatively recently, we nonetheless used the drug because it was safe, effective, and painless.

The extraordinary antiquity of shamanistic practices is well documented. Southern France has long been famous for a series of caves, the walls of which are covered with the oldest known art of human origin. Several years ago, the most ancient of all was discovered not far from other subterranean caverns that had been known and studied for over a century. This cave, christened Chauvet, contained art that was noticeably similar to that found in the earlier discoveries, with portrayals of large mammals like the cave bear and woolly rhinoceros that flourished in Europe at that time. On a hanging rock near the entrance, however, is a striking portrait of a composite creature, the bottom half of which is a human, the upper half a bison. Here, in the earliest known example of human art ever discovered, we see the portrait of the shaman.

Chauvet Cave has been dated at well over thirty thousand years old, which means that this art was created twenty-five thousand years before the more familiar paintings and sculpture of "ancient" Egypt. Similar half-man half-beast motifs are found in many caverns painted and carved in the distant past. The best known and most thoroughly studied of the caves is at Lascaux; a man in a bird mask lies next to a staff with a bird on the end of it. The bird that—unlike most humans—can soar over the forest and through the heavens represents the symbol of the shaman in many cultures. Joseph Campbell suggested that this particular figure lies "rapt in a shamanistic trance" and that "in that remote period of our species the arts of the wizard, shaman, or magician were already well developed."

The Trois Frères sanctuary dates from fourteen thousand years ago and harbors what is probably the most famous prehistoric painting of a shaman: the Dancing Sorcerer. The magnificent portrait features a male creature composed of the parts of many different animals. It has antlers on its head, yet dances on its hind legs in a clearly human manner. Adding further credence that this is a human rather than an animal is the headdress of caribou antlers worn in sacred dances by shamans of Arctic and subarctic tribes, much as Indian medicine men on the Great Plains wore headdresses of buffalo horns.

The antiquity of healing-plant knowledge is assumed to be equally great. A Neanderthal grave at Shanidar in Iraq, near the Iran border, held seven species of plants carefully buried around the corpse. People living in the region today use five of these seven species for medicinal purposes. At Monte Verde in southern Chile, recently concluded to be the site of the earliest known habitation in South America, researchers found what had been gardens of medicinal plants. A ubiquitous species was an evergreen shrub known locally as *boldo,* and widely used as a diuretic, a laxative, and a treatment for liver problems. Laboratory research has proven that this plant is an effective diuretic; investigations in Germany have led to its official approval for the treatment of stomach and intestinal cramps as well as dyspepsia.

The question then arises as to the source of ethnomedical wisdom: simply stated, how did the shamans learn which plants had healing properties? Trial and error undoubtedly played a central role. But in it place like the Amazon, with eighty thousand species of flowering plants (not to mention tens of millions of other organisms), how would the healers know not only which plant to employ but which part of the plant to use? And at what dosage? How did the shaman learn at which phase of the moon these plants should be collected? Even more curious is how they devised such clever recipes that sometimes consist of over twenty components. In the instance of the diabetes case history presented in the introduction, the shaman made the potion from four plants. What would be the odds of recreating that potion using the correct dosage, species, and particular plant parts from a forest of eighty thousand species if we tried to do it based on random collections, which has been the major approach used by most pharmaceutical companies up to the present date?

One key as to how the shamans and others have found and utilized species with therapeutic compounds is the taste test. The concept of "bitter" exists in most cultures, and bitterness often indicates the presence of alkaloids, which represent the single most important chemical components of modern medicine. Quinine and ayahuasca are some of the bitterest substances known.

Yet another clue for the shamans also serves as a lead for Western scientists like David Newman or William Fenical, who look for new medicines from marine organisms: color equals chemistry. If a plant (particularly a tree sap) has a peculiar color, it may well contain interesting chemicals. The clear red sap of the *Virola* tree led shamans of the Yanomami people of Venezuela to develop it into a powerful hallucinogenic snuff, just as the brilliant orange sap of the *Vismia* bush of Suriname led the Tirio shamans to use it as an effective treatment for fungal infections of the skin. The milky red sap of the *Croton* tree led Shuar shamans to employ it as a safe and effective agent for healing wounds.

Another key is the so-called doctrine of signatures. Simply stated, if a plant (or plant part) looks like something, it is somehow good for that something. In other words, because a walnut looks like a brain, it must be good for diseases afflicting the brain (a common belief in medieval Europe). As ludicrous as it sounds, the doctrine has yielded at least one medicinal compound in wide use until recently. The Vedas of ancient India were written about four thousand years ago and included a remedy for snakebite from the snakeroot plant, so named because the twisted roots resembled squirming serpents. Tested in the laboratory in the 1950s, it was found ineffective for countering the toxic effects of the snake venom. One of the problems associated with snakebite, however, is that the trauma of being bitten causes the heart to beat faster, thus pumping the poison throughout the system. What the alkaloid in snakeroot does do is slow down the heartbeat and, because of this, was developed into one of the first effective tranquilizers used by Western medicine.

Once again, this demonstrates why we should not reject ideas, gleaned from other medical systems without first investigating them. The Aztecs valued a Mexican species of magnolia with a heart-shaped fruit as a treatment for cardiac problems. Recent investigations in the lab have found that this fruit contains compounds with a digitalis-like activity.

The most intriguing source of ideas for which plants can be utilized medicinally is perhaps the most difficult concept for Westerners to accept: a shaman's dreams. After a ten-year hiatus, in 1995 I returned to the village of Tepoe in Suriname while searching for diabetes treatments and sought out the great shaman Mahshewah. The old healer, though he appeared pleased at my return, said that he was unable to help me. "I'm sorry," he said, "but I don't recall ever seeing that disease so I can't tell you what plant might be useful for treating it."

Six days later, Mahshewah summoned me to his hut, where he related a most interesting occurrence: "This afternoon I was sleeping in my hammock and I had a dream. And in this dream I saw a tree, and the bark of this tree may help to treat this disease that you said is killing your people. If you canoe down the river for about an hour and a half, you will find a trail on the west bank. If you walk up this trail for about an hour, you will find an enormous tree with yellowish peeling bark. That is the species whose bark may help your people."

I followed his directions down the river and found the trail. I followed his directions up the trail and found the tree. Mahshewah's legs have been paralyzed since he was born. When I asked the other Indians if the old medicine man had ever been up that trail, they told me unequivocally that he had not. How does one explain this through the prism of Western science? I gathered a few scrapings of the bark because my guide said it was a rare and sacred tree that could not be collected in bulk. We still do not know if it might prove efficacious in treating the disease.

The question as to whether something useful can be "discovered" through dreams is one that many people in our society would be inclined to answer negatively. Yet how many remember the discovery of the structure of benzene? Friedrich August Kekulé von Stradowitz, one of the greatest chemists of nineteenth-century Europe, simply could not figure out the structure of the molecule of this enormously important industrial solvent. Quitting in frustration, he decided to turn in for the night and tackle the problem again in the morning. Soon he was dreaming and in his dream he saw several snakes. One of the reptiles began chasing another and then the others joined in, forming a circle. Kekule woke up with the solution to the problem: benzene is a ring! When British scientists dream the answer to perplexing problems, they may become famous, rich, well-respected, and sometimes offered a knighthood. But when Amazonian shamans do it, we dismiss it as "unscientific."

Mother Nature herself is a great teacher. In the words of the gifted natural history writer Sy Montgomery: "In other, older cultures than our own, in which people live closer to the earth, humans do not look down on animals from an imaginary pinnacle. Life is not divided between animals and people, nonhuman and human: life is a continuum, interactive, interdependent. Humans and animals are considered companions and cop layers in the drama of life. Animals' lives, their motives and thoughts and feelings, deserve human attention and respect; dismissing their importance is a grave error."

Characteristic among indigenous cultures of North America was the famous "vision quest," in which a young man (often an apprentice shaman) would go into the wilderness to pray and fast, fast and pray. After several days, he would be visited by visions, often in the form of an animal that would, in the words of the great Inuit shaman Igjugarjuk, "open the mind of a man to all that is hidden to others." As a result of this vision quest, the boy often ended up with a totemic spirit, an animal that served as his personal symbol or protector. The shaman may conclude the process with "animal familiars" or "power animals"—an animal or animals that help him learn and heal. So close is the identification with the animal that the shaman may be perceived as part animal, an essential component of sacred tribal dances around the world and the ancient cave paintings from Europe. In some cultures, the shamans believe that they actually become the animals, as do the Tirio shamans in the northeast Amazon, who claim the ability to turn into jaguars and roam the jungle at night. Among many tribes, the shaman becomes a bird, omniscient by virtue of his or her ability to look down from above and see things invisible to all others. In the case of the Navajo, as we saw in the last chapter, the bear is the medicinal plant master who taught the Indians about *Ligusticum* and all other healing plants.

The realization that much of shamanic knowledge is based on animals' use of plants is relatively new to Western scientific thought. Many healing plants employed by tribal people have probably been learned from local animals. The legends of these cultures often feature sagas explaining how people first learned of useful plants (agricultural and medicinal) from forest creatures. In these cases, animals are, perhaps both metaphorically and literally, the bringers of wisdom.

Joseph Campbell suggested that true shamanism is the religion of the original hunting societies; with the advent of agriculture, cultures became more communally oriented and their religious beliefs changed. While this argument is somewhat hypothetical, what is more certain is that the manifestations of shamanistic religion have been seen as a threat by other organized religions, particularly Christianity, which saw itself in direct competition with belief systems that offered extraordinary experiences to the adherents: "The white goes into his church and talks about Jesus; the Indian walks into his teepee and talks to Jesus," wrote one anthropologist, describing peyote rituals among Native American peoples. But consider this passage from the Book of Job: "But ask now the beasts, and they shall teach thee; and the fowls of the air, and they shall teach thee."

The supreme irony of our suppression of, or disregard for, shamanic religions or other medical practices that rely on natural products is not only the extraordinary therapeutic gifts they have already provided us, but our undeniable need for more of these healing potions to treat "incurable" diseases. The witches of medieval Europe, burned at the stake for their heretical beliefs, were the shamans and/or herbalists of their day. It was their ethnopharmacopeia that gave us aspirin and digitalis. And if we had paid closer attention to their custom of applying moldy bread to wounds, we might have "discovered" penicillin several centuries earlier than Alexander Fleming's research in the 1920s.

A similar situation transpired in our own country. We have all heard about how Squanto and his fellow Indians taught the Pilgrims how to farm the land, but what did the settlers use for medicine? Native American medicinal plants cured the Pilgrims' ailments just as Native American crops filled the European bellies. And prior to the arrival of these Europeans, some of the original Americans had learned that mold could hasten the healing of wounds and local foxglove could treat certain heart problems. Native American healers independently invented syringes and enemas, developed a local anesthetic, and conducted head surgery. Every medicinal plant valued by the settlers was taught to them by local tribespeople. Some of these species entered into commercial, over-the-counter drugs: the yellow color of Murine eyedrops was until recently due to alkaloids extracted from the goldenseal herb. Others, like cascara sagrada (a common ingredient in many laxatives), are sold in many pharmacies. And new medicines are still being developed from plants originally employed by Native Americans: extracts of American bloodroot now serve as an antiplaque agent in toothpastes.

Even some of the most troublesome medical problems are being treated by ancient Indian medicines. Benign prostate enlargement (BPH) afflicts tens of thousands of American men. The fruits of the saw palmetto, a scrubby palm from the southeastern United States, have proven extremely effective at reducing the symptoms: as effective, it has been claimed, as a medicine marketed by Merck. Neither nature nor the shaman has all the answers to the ills that plague us, but both have some—I would say many—of these answers. Urgently needed is an approach that is more humble, more spiritual, more environmental, and more open-minded. The great anthropologist Weston LaBarre, who collaborated with R. E. Schultes on his early peyote research, wrote of the South American Indian:

As scientists we cannot afford the luxury of an ethnocentric snobbery which assumes *a priori* that primitive cultures have nothing whatsoever to contribute to civilization. Our civilization is, in fact, a compendium of such borrowings, and it is a demonstrable error to believe that contacts of "higher" and "lower" cultures show benefits flowing exclusively in one direction. Indeed, a good case could probably be made that in the long run it is the "higher" culture which benefits the more through being enriched, while the "lower" culture not uncommonly disappears entirely as a result of the contact.

Twenty years ago, I stumbled across the most moving account of this ongoing tragedy that I have ever seen—and it was all because of an earache.

A common and painful ailment suffered by researchers working in the rain forest is fungal infection of the ear. The hot and wet environment of the tropics turns eardrums into Petri dishes ripe for the cultivation of fungal invaders. When I began working in the Amazon in the late 1970s, I developed these infections on such a regular basis that before departing I would schedule appointments to have my ears examined at the university clinic upon my return to the States. I quickly learned that if I mentioned my occupation to the physician on duty, she or he would often tell me at great length that ethnobotany was what they really wanted to do with their careers but that they had student loans, a mortgage, a family, and so on, which was why they had been unable to pursue this dream.

I vividly remember going into the clinic with a terrible earache after an expedition to the jungles of southern Venezuela. After examining my ear, attending physician Dr. Jonathan Strongin asked if I had any idea where I might have picked up such a peculiar fungus. "Sure," I replied, "I've just returned from South America."

He asked what I had been doing south of the border, and I gave a distinctly noncommittal reply. He said, "You know, I lived with Indians in the Peruvian Amazon for several years while I was doing my Ph.D. in anthropology, which is how I became interested in healing."

Intrigued, I made a mental note of his name, looked up his dissertation, and found one of the most poignant statements ever recorded on the inextricable interrelationship between people, plants, healing, and belief:

Since the time of their initial contact, the missionaries have openly discouraged the [shamans], viewing them as AntiChrists. . . . [Another anthropologist reported] that in the Shimaa region there was a powerful [shaman] who had to abandon his craft because he felt he no longer had the support of the Machiguenga people in his area. This shaman used ayahuasca to take the form of a bird to travel far and wide at a great height to discern the cause of illness. However, he felt that because the missionaries had so successfully eroded the traditional faith of his people, he could no longer continue to cure. For without the faith of the population, while in the avian form he would not be able to return to his body and [would] crash in the forest far from home . . .

Body Ritual among the Nacirema

HORACE MINER

The anthropologist has become so familiar with the diversity of ways in which different peoples behave in similar situations that he is not apt to be surprised by even the most exotic customs. In fact, if all of the logically possible combinations of behavior have not been found somewhere in the world, he is apt to suspect that they must be present in some yet undescribed tribe. This point has, in fact, been expressed with respect to clan organization by Murdock (1949: 71). In this light, the magical beliefs and practices of the Nacirema present such unusual aspects that it seems desirable to describe them as an example of the extremes to which human behavior can go.

Professor Linton first brought the ritual of the Nacirema to the attention of anthropologists twenty years ago (1936: 326), but the culture of this people is still very poorly understood. They are a North American group living in the territory between the Canadian Cree, the Yaqui and Tarahumare of Mexico, and the Carib and Arawak of the Antilles. Little is known of their origin, though tradition states that they came from the east. According to Nacirema mythology, their nation was originated by a culture hero, Notgnishaw, who is otherwise known for two great feats of strength—the throwing of a piece of wampum across the river Pa-To-Mac and the chopping down of a cherry tree in which the Spirit of Truth resided.

Nacirema culture is characterized by a highly developed market economy which has evolved in a rich natural habitat. While much of the people's time is devoted to economic pursuits, a large part of the fruits of these labors and a considerable portion of the day are spent in ritual activity. The focus of this activity is the human body, the appearance and health of which loom as a dominant concern in the ethos of the people. While such a concern is certainly not unusual, its ceremonial aspects and associated philosophy are unique.

The fundamental belief underlying the whole system appears to be that the human body is ugly and that its natural tendency is to debility and disease. Incarcerated in such a body, man's only hope is to avert these characteristics through the use of the powerful influences of ritual and ceremony. Every household has one or more shrines devoted to this purpose. The more powerful individuals in the society have several shrines in their houses and, in fact, the opulence of a house is often referred to in terms of the number of such ritual centers it possesses. Most houses are of wattle and daub construction, but the shrine rooms of the more wealthy are walled with stone. Poorer families imitate the rich by applying pottery plaques to their shrine walls.

While each family has at least one such shrine, the rituals associated with it are not family ceremonies but are private and secret. The rites are normally only discussed with children, and then only during the period when they are being initiated into these mysteries. I was able, however, to establish sufficient rapport with the natives to examine these shrines and to have the rituals described to me.

The focal point of the shrine is a box or chest which is built into the wall. In this chest are kept the many charms and magical potions without which no native believes he could live. These preparations are secured from a variety of specialized practitioners. The most powerful of these are the medicine men, whose assistance must be rewarded with substantial gifts. However, the medicine men do not provide the curative potions for their clients, but decide what the ingredients should be and then write them down in an ancient and secret language. This writing is understood only by the medicine men and by the herbalists who, for another gift, provide the required charm.

The charm is not disposed of after it has served its purpose, but is placed in the charm-box of the household shrine. As these magical materials are specific for certain ills, and the real or imagined maladies of the people are many, the charm-box is usually full to overflowing. The magical packets are so numerous that people forget what their purposes were and fear to use them again. While the natives are very vague on this

Miner, Horace. From *American Anthropologist,* by Horace Miner, June 1956, pp. 503–507.

point, we can only assume that the idea in retaining all the old magical materials is that their presence in the charm-box, before which the body rituals are conducted, will in some way protect the worshipper.

Beneath the charm-box is a small font. Each day every member of the family, in succession, enters the shrine room, bows his head before the charm-box, mingles different sorts of holy water in the font, and proceeds with a brief rite of ablution. The holy waters are secured from the Water Temple of the community, where the priests conduct elaborate ceremonies to make the liquid ritually pure.

In the hierarchy of magical practitioners, and below the medicine men in prestige, are specialists whose designation is best translated "holy-mouth-men." The Nacirema have an almost pathological horror and fascination with the mouth, the condition of which is believed to have a supernatural influence on all social relationships. Were it not for the rituals of the mouth, they believe that their teeth would fall out, their gums bleed, their jaws shrink, their friends desert them, and their lovers reject them. (They also believe that a strong relationship exists between oral and moral characteristics. For example, there is a ritual ablution of the mouth for children which is supposed to improve their moral fiber.)

The daily body ritual performed by everyone includes a mouth-rite. Despite the fact that these people are so punctilious about care of the mouth, this rite involves a practice which strikes the uninitiated stranger as revolting. It was reported to me that the ritual consists of inserting a small bundle of hog hairs into the mouth, along with certain magical powders, and then moving the bundle in a highly formalized series of gestures.

In addition to the private mouth-rite, the people seek out a holy-mouth-man once or twice a year. These practitioners have an impressive set of paraphernalia, consisting of a variety of augers, awls, probes, and prods. The use of these objects in the exorcism of the evils of the mouth involves almost unbelievable ritual torture of the client. The holy-mouth-man opens the client's mouth and, using the above mentioned tools, enlarges any holes which decay may have created in the teeth. Magical materials are put into these holes. If there are no naturally occurring holes in the teeth, large sections of one or more teeth are gouged out so that the supernatural substance can be applied. In the client's view, the purpose of these ministrations is to arrest decay and to draw friends. The extremely sacred and traditional character of the rite is evident in the fact that the natives return to the holy-mouth-men year after year, despite the fact that their teeth continue to decay.

It is to be hoped that, when a thorough study of the Nacirema is made, there will be a careful inquiry into the personality structure of these people. One has but to watch the gleam in the eye of a holy-mouth-man, as he jabs an awl into an exposed nerve, to suspect that a certain amount of sadism is involved. If this can be established, a very interesting pattern emerges, for most of the population shows definite masochistic tendencies. It was to these that Professor Linton referred in discussing a distinctive part of the daily body ritual which is performed only by men. This part of the rite involves scraping and lacerating the surface of the face with a sharp instrument. Special women's rites are performed only four times during each lunar month, but what they lack in frequency is made up in barbarity. As part of this ceremony, women bake their heads in small ovens for about an hour. The theoretically interesting point is that what seems to be a preponderantly masochistic people have developed sadistic specialists.

The medicine men have an imposing temple, or *latipso*, in every community of any size. The more elaborate ceremonies required to treat very sick patients can only be performed at this temple. These ceremonies involve not only the thaumaturge but a permanent group of vestal maidens who move sedately about the temple chambers in distinctive costume and headdress.

The *latipso* ceremonies are so harsh that it is phenomenal that a fair proportion of the really sick natives who enter the temple ever recover. Small children whose indoctrination is still incomplete have been known to resist attempts to take them to the temple because "that is where you go to die." Despite this fact, sick adults are not only willing but eager to undergo the protracted ritual purification, if they can afford to do so. No matter how ill the supplicant or how grave the emergency, the guardians of many temples will not admit a client if he cannot give a rich gift to the custodian. Even after one has gained admission and survived the ceremonies, the guardians will not permit the neophyte to leave until he makes still another gift.

The supplicant entering the temple is first stripped of all his or her clothes. In every-day life the Nacirema avoids exposure of his body and its natural functions. Bathing and excretory acts are performed only in the secrecy of the household shrine, where they are ritualized as part of the body-rites. Psychological shock results from the fact that body secrecy is suddenly lost upon entry into the *latipso*. A man, whose own wife has never seen him in an excretory act, suddenly finds himself naked and assisted by a vestal maiden while he performs his natural functions into a sacred vessel. This sort of ceremonial treatment is necessitated by the fact that the excreta are used by a diviner to ascertain the course and nature of the client's sickness. Female clients, on the other hand, find their naked bodies are subjected to the scrutiny, manipulation, and prodding of the medicine men.

Few supplicants in the temple are well enough to do anything but lie on their hard beds. The daily ceremonies, like the rites of the holy-mouth-men, involve discomfort and torture. With ritual precision, the vestals awaken their miserable charges each dawn and roll them about on their beds of pain while performing ablutions, in the formal movements of which the maidens are highly trained. At other times they insert magic wands in the supplicant's mouth or force him to eat substances which are supposed to be healing. From time to time the medicine men come to their clients and jab magically treated needles into their flesh. The fact that these temple ceremonies may not cure, and may even kill the neophyte, in no way decreases the people's faith in the medicine men.

There remains one other kind of practitioner, known as a "listener." This witch-doctor has the power to exorcise the devils that lodge in the heads of people who have been bewitched. The Nacirema believe that parents bewitch their own children. Mothers are particularly suspected of putting a curse on children while teaching them the secret body rituals. The counter-magic of the witch-doctor is unusual in its lack of ritual. The patient simply tells the "listener" all his troubles and fears, beginning with the earliest difficulties he can remember. The memory displayed by the Nacirema in these exorcism sessions is truly remarkable. It is not uncommon for the patient to bemoan the rejection he felt upon being weaned as a babe, and a few individuals even see their troubles going back to the traumatic effects of their own birth.

In conclusion, mention must be made of certain practices which have their base in native esthetics but which depend upon the pervasive aversion to the natural body and its functions. There are ritual fasts to make fat people thin and ceremonial feasts to make thin people fat. Still other rites are used to make women's breasts large if they are small, and smaller if they are large. General dissatisfaction with breast shape is symbolized in the fact that the ideal form is virtually outside the range of human variation. A few women afflicted with almost inhuman hypermammary development are so idolized that they make a handsome living by simply going from village to village and permitting the natives to stare at them for a fee.

Reference has already been made to the fact that excretory functions are ritualized, routinized, and relegated to secrecy. Natural reproductive functions are similarly distorted. Intercourse is taboo as a topic and scheduled as an act. Efforts are made to avoid pregnancy by the use of magical materials or by limiting intercourse to certain phases of the moon. Conception is actually very infrequent. When pregnant, women dress so as to hide their condition. Parturition takes place in secret, without friends or relatives to assist, and the majority of women do not nurse their infants.

Our review of the ritual life of the Nacirema has certainly shown them to be a magic-ridden people. It is hard to understand how they have managed to exist so long under the burdens which they have imposed upon themselves. But even such exotic customs as these take on real meaning when they are viewed with the insight provided by Malinowski when he wrote (1948:70):

> Looking from far and above, from our high places of safety in the developed civilization, it is easy to see all the crudity and irrelevance of magic. But without its power and guidance early man could not have mastered his practical difficulties as he has done, nor could man have advanced to the higher stages of civilization.

How Sushi Went Global

THEODORE C. BESTOR

> *A 500-pound tuna is caught off the coast of New England or Spain, flown thousands of miles to Tokyo, sold for tens of thousands of dollars to Japanese buyers . . . and shipped to chefs in New York and Hong Kong? That's the manic logic of global sushi.*

A 40-minute drive from Bath, Maine, down a winding two-lane highway, the last mile on a dirt road, a ramshackle wooden fish pier stands beside an empty parking lot. At 6:00 p.m. nothing much is happening. Three bluefin tuna sit in a huge tub of ice on the loading dock.

Between 6:45 and 7:00, the parking lot fills up with cars and trucks with license plates from New Jersey, New York, Massachusetts, New Hampshire, and Maine. Twenty tuna buyers clamber out, half of them Japanese. The three bluefin, ranging from 270 to 610 pounds, are winched out of the tub, and buyers crowd around them, extracting tiny core samples to examine their color, fingering the flesh to assess the fat content, sizing up the curve of the body.

After about 20 minutes of eyeing the goods, many of the buyers return to their trucks to call Japan by cellphone and get the morning prices from Tokyo's Tsukiji market—the fishing industry's answer to Wall Street—where the daily tuna auctions have just concluded. The buyers look over the tuna one last time and give written bids to the dock manager, who passes the top bid for each fish to the crew that landed it.

The auction bids are secret. Each bid is examined anxiously by a cluster of young men, some with a father or uncle looking on to give advice, others with a young woman and a couple of toddlers trying to see Daddy's fish. Fragments of concerned conversation float above the parking lot: "That's all?" "Couldn't we do better if we shipped it ourselves?" "Yeah, but my pickup needs a new transmission now!" After a few minutes, deals are closed and the fish are quickly loaded onto the backs of trucks in crates of crushed ice, known in the trade as "tuna coffins." As rapidly as they arrived, the flotilla of buyers sails out of the parking lot—three bound for New York's John F. Kennedy Airport, where their tuna will be airfreighted to Tokyo for sale the day after next.

Bluefin tuna may seem at first an unlikely case study in globalization. But as the world rearranges itself—around silicon chips, Starbucks coffee, or sashimi-grade tuna—new channels for global flows of capital and commodities link far-flung individuals and communities in unexpected new relationships. The tuna trade is a prime example of the globalization of a regional industry, with intense international competition and thorny environmental regulations; centuries-old practices combined with high technology; realignments of labor and capital in response to international regulation; shifting markets; and the diffusion of culinary culture as tastes for sushi, and bluefin tuna, spread worldwide.

Growing Appetites

Tuna doesn't require much promotion among Japanese consumers. It is consistently Japan's most popular seafood, and demand is high throughout the year. When the Federation of Japan Tuna Fisheries Cooperative (known as Nikkatsuren) runs ad campaigns for tuna, they tend to be low-key and whimsical, rather like the "Got Milk?" advertising in the United States. Recently, the federation launched "Tuna Day" (Maguro no hi), providing retailers with posters and recipe cards for recipes more complicated than "slice and serve chilled." Tuna Day's mascot is Goro-kun, a colorful cartoon tuna swimming the Australian crawl.

Despite the playful contemporary tone of the mascot, the date selected for Tuna Day carries much heavier freight. October 10, it turns out, commemorates the date that tuna first appeared in Japanese literature, in the eighth-century collection of imperial court poetry known as the *Man'yoshu*—one of the towering classics of Japanese literature. The neat twist is that October 10 today is a national holiday, Sports Day. Goro-kun, the sporty tuna, scores a promotional hat trick, suggesting intimate connections among national culture, healthy food for active lives, and the family holiday meal.

Outside of Japan, tuna, especially raw tuna, hasn't always had it so good. Sushi isn't an easy concept to sell to the uninitiated. And besides, North Americans tend to think of cultural influence as flowing from West to East: James Dean, baseball, Coca-Cola, McDonald's, and Disneyland have all gone over big in Tokyo. Yet Japanese cultural motifs and material—from Kurosawa's *The Seven Samurai* to Yoda's Zen and Darth Vader's armor, from Issey Miyake's fashions to Nintendo, PlayStation, and Pokémon—have increasingly saturated North American and indeed the entire world's consumption and popular culture. Against all odds, so too has sushi.

In 1929, the *Ladies' Home Journal* introduced Japanese cooking to North American women, but discreetly skirted the subject of raw fish: "There have been purposely omitted . . . any recipes using the delicate and raw tuna fish which is sliced wafer thin and served iced with attractive garnishes. [These] . . . might not sound so entirely delicious as they are in reality." Little mention of any Japanese food appeared in U.S. media until well after World War II. By the 1960s, articles on sushi began to show up in lifestyle magazines like *Holiday* and *Sunset*. But the recipes they suggested were canapés like cooked shrimp on caraway rye bread, rather than raw fish on rice.

A decade later, however, sushi was growing in popularity throughout North America, turning into a sign of class and educational standing. In 1972, the *New York Times* covered the opening of a sushi bar in the elite sanctum of New York's Harvard Club. *Esquire* explained the fare in an article titled "Wake up Little Sushi!" Restaurant reviewers guided readers to Manhattan's sushi scene, including innovators like Shalom Sushi, a kosher sushi bar in SoHo.

Japan's emergence on the global economic scene in the 1970s as the business destination du jour, coupled with a rejection of hearty, red-meat American fare in favor of healthy cuisine like rice, fish, and vegetables, and the appeal of the high-concept aesthetics of Japanese design all prepared the world for a sushi fad. And so, from an exotic, almost unpalatable ethnic specialty, then to haute cuisine of the most rarefied sort, sushi has become not just cool, but popular. The painted window of a Cambridge, Massachusetts, coffee shop advertises "espresso, cappuccino, carrot juice, lasagna, and sushi." Mashed potatoes with wasabi (horseradish), sushi-ginger relish, and seared sashimi-grade tuna steaks show Japan's growing cultural influence on upscale nouvelle cuisine throughout North America, Europe, and Latin America. Sushi has even become the stuff of fashion, from "sushi" lip gloss, colored the deep red of raw tuna, to "wasabi" nail polish, a soft avocado green.

Angling for New Consumers

Japan remains the world's primary market for fresh tuna for sushi and sashimi; demand in other countries is a product of Japanese influence and the creation of new markets by domestic producers looking to expand their reach. Perhaps not surprisingly, sushi's global popularity as an emblem of a sophisticated, cosmopolitan consumer class more or less coincided with a profound transformation in the international role of the Japanese fishing industry. From the 1970s onward, the expansion of 200-mile fishing limits around the world excluded foreign fleets from the prime fishing grounds of many coastal nations. And international environmental campaigns forced many countries, Japan among them, to scale back their distant water fleets. With their fishing operations curtailed and their yen for sushi still growing, Japanese had to turn to foreign suppliers.

Jumbo jets brought New England's bluefin tuna into easy reach of Tokyo, just as Japan's consumer economy—a byproduct of the now disparaged "bubble" years—went into hyperdrive. The sushi business boomed. During the 1980s, total Japanese imports of fresh bluefin tuna worldwide increased from 957 metric tons (531 from the United States) in 1984 to 5,235 metric tons (857 from the United States) in 1993. The average wholesale price peaked in 1990 at 4,900 yen (U.S.$34) per kilogram, bones and all, which trimmed out to approximately U.S.$33 wholesale per edible pound.

Stateless Fish

As the bluefin business grows ever more lucrative, the risk of overfishing has become ever more real. The question of who profits from the world's demand for sushi makes for battles among fishers, regulators, and conservationists.

Bluefin tuna have been clocked at 50 miles per hour, and tagged fish have crossed the Atlantic in about two months. Since bluefin swim across multiple national jurisdictions, international regulations must impose political order on stateless fish.

Charged with writing those regulations is the International commission for the Conservation of Atlantic Tunas (ICCAT), which assigns quotas for bluefin tuna and related species in the North Atlantic and the Mediterranean and directs catch reporting, trade monitoring, and population assessments. Based in Madrid since its founding in 1969, ICCAT now has 28 members, including Atlantic and Mediterranean fishing countries and three global fishing powers: South Korea, China, and Japan.

In recent years, conservation groups have criticized ICCAT for not regulating more aggressively to prevent or reverse an apparent bluefin population decline in the Western Atlantic. Some activists have campaigned to have bluefin tuna protected under the Convention on International Trade in Endangered Species, or CITES. At least in part to keep that from happening, Japan and ICCAT have implemented new systems to track and regulate trade; "undocumented fish" from nations that fail to comply with ICCAT regulations are now banned from Japanese markets.

Regulations, though, are complicated by how far and fast these fish can travel: No one can say for certain whether there is one bluefin population in the Atlantic or several. ICCAT, the U.S. National Academy of Sciences, the National Audubon Society, and industry groups disagree over how many bluefin migrate across the Atlantic, and whether or not they are all part of the same breeding stock. What's the big deal? If there are two (or more) stocks, as ICCAT maintains, then conservation efforts can vary from one side of the Atlantic to the other.

When ICCAT registered a dramatic decline in bluefin catches off North America, it imposed stringent quotas on North America's mainly small-scale fishing outfits. On the European side of the Atlantic, however, industrial-strength fishing efforts continued. American fishers, not surprisingly, point to evidence of cross-Atlantic migration and genetic studies of intermingling to argue that Europeans need to conserve bluefin more strenuously as well. ICCAT's regulations, they argue, protect bluefin at America's expense only, and ultimately, fishers from other countries pocket Japanese yen.

—*T.C.B.*

Not surprisingly, Japanese demand for prime bluefin tuna—which yields a firm red meat, lightly marbled with veins of fat, highly prized (and priced) in Japanese cuisine—created a gold-rush mentality on fishing grounds across the globe wherever bluefin tuna could be found. But in the early 1990s, as the U.S. bluefin industry was taking off, the Japanese economy went into a stall, then a slump, then a dive. U.S. producers suffered as their high-end export market collapsed. Fortunately for them, the North American sushi craze took up the slack. U.S. businesses may have written off Japan, but Americans' taste for sushi stuck. An industry founded exclusively on Japanese demand survived because of Americans' newly trained palates and a booming U.S. economy.

A Transatlantic Tussle

Atlantic bluefin tuna ("ABT" in the trade) are a highly migratory species that ranges from the equator to Newfoundland, from Turkey to the Gulf of Mexico. Bluefin can be huge fish; the record is 1,496 pounds. In more normal ranges, 600-pound tuna, 10 feet in length, are not extraordinary, and 250- to 300-pound bluefin, six feet long, are commercial mainstays.

Before bluefin became a commercial species in New England, before Japanese buyers discovered the stock, before the 747, bluefin were primarily sports fish, caught with fighting tackle by trophy hunters out of harbors like Montauk, Hyannis, and Kennebunkport. Commercial fishers, if they caught bluefin at all, sold them for cat food when they could and trucked them to town dumps when they couldn't. Japanese buyers changed all of that. Since the 1970s, commercial Atlantic bluefin tuna fisheries have been almost exclusively focused on Japanese markets like Tsukiji.

In New England waters, most bluefin are taken one fish at a time, by rod and reel, by hand line, or by harpoon—techniques of a small-scale fisher, not of a factory fleet. On the European side of the Atlantic, the industry operates under entirely different conditions. Rather than rod and reel or harpooning, the typical gear is industrial—the purse seiner (a fishing vessel closing a large net around a school of fish) or the long line (which catches fish on baited hooks strung along lines played out for many miles behind a swift vessel). The techniques may differ from boat to boat and from country to country, but these fishers are all angling for a share of the same Tsukiji yen—and in many cases, some biologists argue, a share of the same tuna stock. Fishing communities often think of themselves as close-knit and proudly parochial; but the sudden globalization of this industry has brought fishers into contact—and often into conflict—with customers, governments, regulators, and environmentalists around the world.

Two miles off the beach in Barbate, Spain, a huge maze of nets snakes several miles out into Spanish waters near the Strait of Gibraltar. A high-speed, Japanese-made workboat heads out to the nets. On board are five Spanish hands, a Japanese supervisor, 2,500 kilograms of frozen herring and mackerel imported from Norway and Holland, and two American researchers. The boat is making one of its twice-daily trips to Spanish nets, which contain captured Mediterranean tuna being raised under Japanese supervision for harvest and export to Tsukiji.

Behind the guard boats that stand watch over the nets 24 hours a day, the headlands of Morocco are a hazy purple in the distance. Just off Barbate's white cliffs to the northwest, the light at the Cape of Trafalgar blinks on and off. For 20 minutes, the men toss herring and mackerel over the gunwales of the workboat while tuna the size (and speed) of Harley-Davidsons dash under the boat, barely visible until, with a flash of silver and blue, they wheel around to snatch a drifting morsel.

The nets, lines, and buoys are part of an *almadraba,* a huge fish trap used in Spain as well as Sicily, Tunisia, and Morocco. The *almadraba* consists of miles of nets anchored to the channel floor suspended from thousands of buoys, all laid out to cut across the migration routes of bluefin tuna leaving the strait. This *almadraba* remains in place for about six weeks in June and July to intercept tuna leaving the Mediterranean after their spawning season is over. Those tuna that lose themselves in the maze end up in a huge pen, roughly the size of a football field. By the end of the tuna run through the strait, about 200 bluefin are in the pen.

Two hundred fish may not sound like a lot, but if the fish survive the next six months, if the fish hit their target weights, if the fish hit the market at the target price, these 200 bluefin may be worth $1.6 million dollars. In November and December, after the bluefin season in New England and Canada is well over, the tuna are harvested and shipped by air to Tokyo in time for the end-of-the-year holiday spike in seafood consumption.

The pens, huge feed lots for tuna, are relatively new, but *almadraba* are not. A couple of miles down the coast from Barbate is the evocatively named settlement of Zahara de los Atunes (Zahara of the Tunas) where Cervantes lived briefly in the late 16th century. The centerpiece of the village is a huge stone compound that housed the men and nets of Zahara's *almadraba* in Cervantes's day, when the port was only a seasonally occupied tuna outpost (occupied by scoundrels, according to Cervantes). Along the Costa de la Luz, the three or four *almadraba* that remain still operate under the control of local fishing bosses who hold the customary fishing rights, the nets, the workers, the boats, and the locally embedded cultural capital to make the *almadraba* work—albeit for distant markets and in collaboration with small-scale Japanese fishing firms.

Inside the Strait of Gibraltar, off the coast of Cartagena, another series of tuna farms operates under entirely different auspices, utilizing neither local skills nor traditional technology. The Cartagena farms rely on French purse seiners to tow captured tuna to their pens, where joint ventures between Japanese trading firms and large-scale Spanish fishing companies have set up farms using the latest in Japanese fishing technology. The waters and the workers are Spanish, but almost everything else is part of a global flow of techniques and capital: financing from major Japanese trading companies; Japanese vessels to tend the nets; aquacultural techniques developed in Australia; vitamin supplements from European pharmaceutical giants packed into frozen herring from Holland to be heaved over the gunwales for the tuna; plus computer models of feeding schedules, weight gains, and target market prices developed by Japanese technicians and fishery scientists.

These "Spanish" farms compete with operations throughout the Mediterranean that rely on similar high-tech, high-capital approaches to the fish business. In the Adriatic Sea, for example, Croatia is emerging as a formidable tuna producer. In Croatia's case, the technology and the capital were transplanted by émigré

Tokyo's Pantry

Tsukiji, Tokyo's massive wholesale seafood market, is the center of the global trade in tuna. Here, 60,000 traders come each day to buy and sell seafood for Tokyo's 27 million mouths, moving more than 2.4 million kilograms of it in less than 12 hours. Boosters encourage the homey view that Tsukiji is *Tokyo no daidokoro*—Tokyo's pantry—but it is a pantry where almost $6 billion worth of fish change hands each year. New York City's Fulton Fish Market, the largest market in North America, handles only about $1 billion worth, and only about 13 percent of the tonnage of Tsukiji's catch.

Tuna are sold at a "moving auction." The auctioneer, flanked by assistants who record prices and fill out invoice slips at lightning speed, strides across the floor just above rows and rows of fish, moving quickly from one footstool to the next without missing a beat, or a bid. In little more than half an hour, teams of auctioneers from five auction houses sell several hundred (some days several thousand) tuna. Successful buyers whip out their cellphones, calling chefs to tell them what they've got. Meanwhile, faxes with critical information on prices and other market conditions alert fishers in distant ports to the results of Tsukiji's morning auctions. In return, Tsukiji is fed a constant supply of information on tuna conditions off Montauk, Cape Cod, Cartagena, Barbate, and scores of other fishing grounds around the world.

Tsukiji is the command post for a global seafood trade. In value, foreign seafood far exceeds domestic Japanese products on the auction block. (Tsukiji traders joke that Japan's leading fishing port is Tokyo's Narita International Airport.) on Tsukiji's slippery auction floor, tuna from Massachusetts may sell as action for over $30,000 apiece, near octopus from Senegal, eel from Guangzhou, crab from Sakhalin, salmon from British Columbia and Hokkaido, snapper from Kyushu, and abalone from California.

Given the sheer volume of global trade, Tsukiji effectively sets the world's tuna prices. Last time I checked, the record price was over $200,000 for a particularly spectacular fish from Turkey—a sale noteworthy enough to make the front pages of Tokyo's daily papers. But spectacular prices are just the tip of Tsukiji's influence. The auction system and the commodity chains that flow in and out of the market integrate fishers, firms, and restaurants worldwide in a complex network of local and translocal economies.

As an undisputed hub of the fishing world, Tsukiji creates and deploys enormous amounts of Japanese cultural capital around the world. Its control of information, its enormous role in orchestrating and responding to Japanese culinary tastes, and its almost hegemonic definitions of supply and demand allow it the unassailable privilege of imposing its own standards of quality—standards that producers worldwide must heed.

—*T.C.B.*

Croatians who returned to the country from Australia after Croatia achieved independence from Yugoslavia in 1991. Australia, for its part, has developed a major aquacultural industry for southern bluefin tuna, a species closely related to the Atlantic bluefin of the North Atlantic and Mediterranean and almost equally desired in Japanese markets.

Culture Splash

Just because sushi is available, in some form or another, in exclusive Fifth Avenue restaurants, in baseball stadiums in Los Angeles, at airport snack carts in Amsterdam, at an apartment in Madrid (delivered by motorcycle), or in Buenos Aires, Tel Aviv, or Moscow, doesn't mean that sushi has lost its status as Japanese cultural property. Globalization doesn't necessarily homogenize cultural differences nor erase the salience of cultural labels. Quite the contrary, it grows the franchise. In the global economy of consumption, the brand equity of sushi as Japanese cultural property adds to the cachet of both the country and the cuisine. A Texan Chinese-American restauranteur told me, for example, that he had converted his chain of restaurants from Chinese to Japanese cuisine because the prestige factor of the latter meant he could charge a premium; his clients couldn't distinguish between Chinese and Japanese employees (and often failed to notice that some of the chefs behind his sushi bars were Latinos).

The brand equity is sustained by complicated flows of labor and ethnic biases. Outside of Japan, having Japanese hands (or a reasonable facsimile) is sufficient warrant for sushi competence. Guidebooks for the current generation of Japanese global *wandervogel* sometimes advise young Japanese looking for a job in a distant city to work as a sushi chef; U.S. consular offices in Japan grant more than 1,000 visas a year to sushi chefs, tuna buyers, and other workers in the global sushi business. A trade school in Tokyo, operating under the name Sushi Daigaku (Sushi University) offers short courses in sushi preparation so "students" can impress prospective employers with an imposing certificate. Even without papers, however, sushi remains firmly linked in the minds of Japanese and foreigners alike with Japanese cultural identity. Throughout the world, sushi restaurants operated by Koreans, Chinese, or Vietnamese maintain Japanese identities. In sushi bars from Boston to Valencia, a customer's simple greeting in Japanese can throw chefs into a panic (or drive them to the far end of the counter).

On the docks, too, Japanese cultural control of sushi remains unquestioned. Japanese buyers and "tuna techs" sent from Tsukiji to work seasonally on the docks of New England laboriously instruct foreign fishers on the proper techniques for catching, handling, and packing tuna for export. A bluefin tuna must approximate the appropriate *kata,* or "ideal form," of color, texture, fat content, body shape, and so forth, all prescribed by Japanese specifications. Processing requires proper attention as well. Special paper is sent from Japan for wrapping the fish before burying them in crushed ice. Despite high shipping costs and the fact that 50 percent of the gross weight of a tuna is unusable, tuna is sent to Japan whole, not sliced into salable portions. Spoilage is one reason for this, but form is another. Everyone in the trade agrees that Japanese workers are much more skilled in cutting and trimming tuna than Americans, and no one would want to risk sending botched cuts to Japan.

Not to impugn the quality of the fish sold in the United States, but on the New England docks, the first determination of tuna buyers is whether they are looking at a "domestic" fish or an "export" fish. On that judgment hangs several dollars a pound for the fisher, and the supply of sashimi-grade tuna for fishmongers, sushi bars, and seafood restaurants up and down the Eastern seaboard. Some of the best tuna from New England may make it to New York or Los Angeles, but by way of Tokyo—validated as top quality (and top price) by the decision to ship it to Japan by air for sale at Tsukiji, where it may be purchased by one of the handful of Tsukiji sushi exporters who supply premier expatriate sushi chefs in the world's leading cities.

Playing the Market

The tuna auction at Yankee Co-op in Seabrook, New Hampshire, is about to begin on the second-to-last day of the 1999 season. The weather is stormy, few boats are out. Only three bluefin, none of them terribly good, are up for sale today, and the half-dozen buyers at the auction, three Americans and three Japanese, gloomily discuss the impending end of a lousy season.

In July, the bluefin market collapsed just as the U.S. fishing season was starting. In a stunning miscalculation, Japanese purse seiners operating out of Kesennuma in northern Japan managed to land their entire year's quota from that fishery in only three days. The oversupply sent tuna prices at Tsukiji through the floor, and they never really recovered.

Today, the news from Spain is not good. The day before, faxes and e-mails from Tokyo brought word that a Spanish fish farm had suffered a disaster. Odd tidal conditions near Cartagena led to a sudden and unexpected depletion of oxygen in the inlet where one of the great tuna nets was anchored. Overnight, 800 fish suffocated. Divers hauled out the tuna. The fish were quickly processed, several months before their expected prime, and shipped off to Tokyo. For the Japanese corporation and its Spanish partners, a harvest potentially worth $6.5 million would yield only a tiny fraction of that. The buyers at the morning's auctions in New Hampshire know they will suffer as well. Whatever fish turn up today and tomorrow, they will arrive at Tsukiji in the wake of an enormous glut of hastily exported Spanish tuna.

Fishing is rooted in local communities and local economies—even for fishers dipping their lines (or nets) in the same body of water, a couple hundred miles can be worlds away. Now, a Massachusetts fisher's livelihood can be transformed in a matter of hours by a spike in market prices halfway around the globe or by a disaster at a fish farm across the Atlantic. Giant fishing conglomerates in one part of the world sell their catch alongside family outfits from another. Environmental organizations on one continent rail against distant industry regulations implemented an ocean away. Such instances of convergence are common in a globalizing world. What is surprising, and perhaps more profound, in the case of today's tuna fishers, is the complex interplay between industry and culture, as an esoteric cuisine from an insular part of the world has become a global fad in the span of a generation, driving, and driven by, a new kind of fishing business.

Many New England fishers, whose traditional livelihood now depends on unfamiliar tastes and distant markets, turn to a kind of armchair anthropology to explain Japan's ability to transform tuna from trash into treasure around the world. For some, the quick answer is simply national symbolism. The deep red of tuna served as sashimi or sushi contrasts with the stark white rice, evoking the red and white of the Japanese national flag. Others know that red and white is an auspicious color combination in Japanese ritual life (lobster tails are popular at Japanese weddings for just this reason). Still others think the cultural prize is a fighting spirit, pure machismo, both their own and the tuna's. Taken by rod and reel, a tuna may battle the fisher for four or five hours. Some tuna literally fight to the death. For some fishers, the meaning of tuna—the equation of tuna with Japanese identity—is simple: Tuna is nothing less than the samurai fish!

Of course, such mystification of a distant market's motivations for desiring a local commodity is not unique. For decades, anthropologists have written of "cargo cults" and "commodity fetishism" from New Guinea to Bolivia. But the ability of fishers today to visualize Japanese culture and the place of tuna within its demanding culinary tradition is constantly shaped and reshaped by the flow of cultural images that now travel around the globe in all directions simultaneously, bumping into each other in airports, fishing ports, bistros, bodegas, and markets everywhere. In the newly rewired circuitry of global cultural and economic affairs, Japan is the core, and the Atlantic seaboard, the Adriatic, and the Australian coast are all distant peripheries. Topsy-turvy as Gilbert and Sullivan never imagined it.

Japan is plugged into the popular North American imagination as the sometimes inscrutable superpower, precise and delicate in its culinary tastes, feudal in its cultural symbolism, and insatiable in its appetites. Were Japan not a prominent player in so much of the daily life of North Americans, the fishers outside of Bath or in Seabrook would have less to think about in constructing their Japan. As it is, they struggle with unfamiliar exchange rates for cultural capital that compounds in a foreign currency.

And they get ready for next season.

Being Indigenous in the 21st Century

WILMA MANKILLER

There are more than 300 million indigenous people, in virtually every region of the world, including the Sámi peoples of Scandinavia, the Maya of Guatemala, numerous tribal groups in the Amazonian rainforest, the Dalits in the mountains of Southern India, the San and Kwei of Southern Africa, Aboriginal people in Australia, and, of course the hundreds of Indigenous Peoples in Mexico, Central and South America, as well as here in what is now known as North America.

There is enormous diversity among communities of Indigenous Peoples, each of which has its own distinct culture, language, history, and unique way of life. Despite these differences, Indigenous Peoples across the globe share some common values derived in part from an understanding that their lives are part of and inseparable from the natural world.

Onondaga Faith Keeper Oren Lyons once said, "Our knowledge is profound and comes from living in one place for untold generations. It comes from watching the sun rise in the east and set in the west from the same place over great sections of time. We are as familiar with the lands, rivers, and great seas that surround us as we are with the faces of our mothers. Indeed, we call the earth Etenoha, our mother from whence all life springs."

Indigenous people are not the only people who understand the interconnectedness of all living things. There are many thousands of people from different ethnic groups who care deeply about the environment and fight every day to protect the earth. The difference is that indigenous people have the benefit of being regularly reminded of their responsibilities to the land by stories and ceremonies. They remain close to the land, not only in the way they live, but in their hearts and in the way they view the world. Protecting the environment is not an intellectual exercise; it is a sacred duty. When women like Pauline Whitesinger, an elder at Big Mountain, and Carrie Dann, a Western Shoshone land rights activist, speak of preserving the land for future generations, they are not just talking about future generations of humans. They are talking about future generations of plants, animals, water, and all living things. Pauline and Carrie understand the relative insignificance of human beings in the totality of the planet.

Aside from a different view of their relationship to the natural world, many of the world's Indigenous Peoples also share a fragmented but still-present sense of responsibility for one another. Cooperation always has been necessary for the survival of tribal people, and even today cooperation takes precedence over competition in more traditional communities. It is really quite miraculous that a sense of sharing and reciprocity continues into the 21st century given the staggering amount of adversity Indigenous Peoples have faced. In many communities, the most respected people are not those who have amassed great material wealth or achieved great personal success. The greatest respect is reserved for those who help other people, those who understand that their lives play themselves out within a set of reciprocal relationships.

There is evidence of this sense of reciprocity in Cherokee communities. My husband, Charlie Soap, leads a widespread self-help movement among the Cherokee in which low-income volunteers work together to build walking trails, community centers, sports complexes, water lines, and houses. The self-help movement taps into the traditional Cherokee value of cooperation for the sake of the common good. The projects also build a sense of self-efficacy among the people.

Besides values, the world's Indigenous Peoples are also bound by the common experience of being "discovered" and subjected to colonial expansion into their territories that has led to the loss of an incalculable number of lives and millions and millions of acres of land and resources. The most basic rights of Indigenous Peoples were disregarded, and they were subjected to a series of policies that were designed to dispossess them of their land and resources and assimilate them into colonial society and culture. Too often the policies resulted in poverty, high infant mortality, rampant unemployment, and substance abuse, with all its attendant problems.

The stories are shockingly similar all over the world. When I read Chinua Achebe's Things Fall Apart, which chronicled the systematic destruction of an African tribe's social, cultural, and economic structure, it sounded all too familiar: take the land, discredit the leaders, ridicule the traditional healers, and send the children off to distant boarding schools.

And I was sickened by the Stolen Generation report about Aboriginal children in Australia who were forcibly removed from their families and placed in boarding schools far away from their families and communities. My own father and my Aunt Sally were taken from my This lack of accurate information leaves a void that is often filled with nonsensical stereotypes, which either vilify Indigenous Peoples as troubled descendants of savage peoples, or romanticize them as innocent children of nature, spiritual but incapable of higher thought.

Public perceptions will change in the future as indigenous leaders more fully understand that there is a direct link between public perception and public policies. Indigenous Peoples must frame their own issues, because if they don't frame the issues for themselves, their opponents most certainly will. In the future, as more indigenous people become filmmakers, writers, historians, museum curators, and journalists, they will be able to use a dazzling array of technological tools to tell their own stories, in their own voice, in their own way.

Once, a journalist asked me whether people in the United States had trouble accepting the government of the Cherokee Nation during my tenure as principal chief. I was a little surprised by the question. The government of the Cherokee Nation predated the government of the United States and had treaties with other countries before it executed a treaty with one of the first U.S. colonies.

Cherokee and other tribal leaders sent delegations to meet with the English, Spanish, and French in an effort to protect their lands and people. Traveling to foreign lands with a trusted interpreter, tribal ambassadors took maps that had been painstakingly drawn by hand to show their lands to heads of other governments. They also took along gifts, letters, and proclamations. Though tribal leaders thought they were being dealt with as heads of state and as equals, historical records indicate they were often objects of curiosity, and that there was a great deal of disdain and ridicule of these earnest delegates.

Tribal governments in the United States today exercise a range of sovereign rights. Many tribal governments have their own judicial systems, operate their own police force, run their own schools, administer their own clinics and hospitals, and operate a wide range of business enterprises. There are now more than two dozen tribally controlled community colleges. All these advancements benefit everyone in the community, not just tribal people. The history, contemporary lives, and future of tribal governments is intertwined with that of their neighbors.

One of the most common misperceptions about Indigenous Peoples is that they are all the same. There is not only great diversity among Indigenous Peoples, there is great diversity within each tribal community, just as there is in the larger society. Members of the Cherokee Nation are socially, economically, and culturally stratified. Several thousand Cherokee continue to speak the Cherokee language and live in Cherokee communities in rural northeastern Oklahoma. At the other end of the spectrum, there are enrolled tribal members who have never been to even visit the Cherokee Nation. Intermarriage has created an enrolled Cherokee membership that includes people with Hispanic, Asian, Caucasian, and African American heritage.

So what does the future hold for Indigenous Peoples across the globe? What challenges will they face moving further into the 21st century?

To see the future, one needs only to look at the past. If, as peoples, we have been able to survive a staggering loss of land, of rights, of resources, of lives, and we are still standing in the early 21st century, how can I not be optimistic that we will survive whatever challenges lie ahead, that 100 or 500 years from now we will still have viable indigenous communities? Without question, the combined efforts of government and various religious groups to eradicate traditional knowledge systems has had a profoundly negative impact on the culture as well as the social and economic systems of Indigenous Peoples. But if we have been able to hold onto our sense of community, our languages, culture, and ceremonies, despite everything, how can I not be optimistic about the future?

And though some of our original languages, medicines, and ceremonies have been irretrievably lost, the ceremonial fires of many Indigenous Peoples across the globe have survived all the upheaval. Sometimes indigenous communities have almost had to reinvent themselves as a people but they have never given up their sense of responsibility to one another and to the land. It is this sense of interdependence that has sustained tribal people thus far and I believe it will help sustain them well into the future.

Indigenous Peoples know about change and have proven time and time again they can adapt to change. No matter where they go in the world, they hold onto a strong sense of tribal identity while fully interacting with and participating in the larger society around them. In my state of Oklahoma alone, we have produced an indigenous astronaut, two United States congressmen, a Pulitzer Prize-winning novelist, and countless others who have made great contributions to their people, the state, and the world.

One of the great challenges for Indigenous Peoples in the 21st century will be to develop practical models to capture, maintain, and pass on traditional knowledge systems and values to future generations. Nothing can replace the sense of continuity that a genuine understanding of traditional tribal knowledge brings. Many communities are working on discrete aspects of culture, such as language or medicine, but it is the entire system of knowledge that needs to be maintained, not just for Indigenous Peoples but for the world at large.

Regrettably, in the future the battle for human and land rights will continue. But the future does look somewhat better for tribal people. Last year, after 30 years of advocacy by Indigenous Peoples, the United Nations finally passed a declaration supporting their distinct human rights. The challenge will be to make sure the provisions of the declaration are honored and that the rights of Indigenous Peoples all over the world are protected.

Indigenous Peoples simply do better when they have control of their own lives. In the case of my own people, after we were forcibly removed by the United States military from the southeastern part of the United States to Indian Territory, now Oklahoma, we picked ourselves up and rebuilt our nation, despite the fact that approximately 4,000 Cherokee lives were lost during the forced removal. We started some of the first schools west of the Mississippi, Indian or non-Indian, and built schools for the higher education of women. We printed our own newspapers in Cherokee and English and were more literate than our neighbors in adjoining states. Then, in the early 20th century, the federal government almost abolished the Cherokee Nation, and within two decades, our educational attainment levels dropped dramatically and many of our people were living without the most basic amenities. But our people never gave up the dream of rebuilding the Cherokee Nation. In my grandfather's time, Cherokee men rode horses from house to house to collect dimes in a grandfather by the U.S. government and placed in a government boarding school when they were very young. There is a connection between us. Indigenous Peoples everywhere are connected both by our values and by our oppression.

When contemplating the contemporary challenges and problems faced by Indigenous Peoples worldwide, it is important to remember that the roots of many social, economic, and political problems can be found in colonial policies. And these policies continue today across the globe.

Several years ago Charlie and I visited an indigenous community along the Rio Negro in the Brazilian rainforest. Some of the leaders expressed concern that some environmentalists, who should be natural allies, focus almost exclusively on the land and appear not to see or hear the people at all. One leader pointed out that a few years ago it was popular for famous musicians to wear T-shirts emblazoned with the slogan "Save the Rainforests," but no one ever wore a T-shirt with the slogan "Save the People of the Rainforest," though the people of the forest possess the best knowledge about how to live with and sustain the forests.

With so little accurate information about Indigenous Peoples available in educational institutions, in literature, films, or popular culture, it is not surprising that many people are not even conscious of Indigenous Peoples.

The battle to protect the human and land rights of Indigenous Peoples is made immeasurably more difficult by the fact that so few people know much about either the history or contemporary lives of our people. And without any kind of history or cultural context, it is almost impossible for outsiders to understand the issues and challenges faced by Indigenous Peoples. mason jar so they could send representatives to Washington to remind the government to honor its treaties with the Cherokee people.

Over the past 35 years, we have revitalized the Cherokee Nation and once again run our own school, and we have an extensive array of successful education programs. The youth at our Sequoyah High School recently won the state trigonometry contest, and several are Gates Millennium Scholars. We simply do better when we have control over our own destiny.

Wilma Mankiller was the first female principal chief of the Cherokee Nation. This article is adapted from a talk she gave in October 2008 at Quinnipiac University to celebrate the 60th anniversary of the Universal Declaration of Human Rights.

North America and South America

North America

Topics Covered in Class

Culture and Diversity
Migration to the New World
Culture Areas
Assimilation/ Pluralism
Indian Stereotyping
Controversial Issues
Native American Contributions to Modern Life
US Indian Policies
American Indians as a Minority
Indian Identity
Goals for First Nations Today

About the Readings

Culture contact does not mean just people coming into contact with each other for the first time. They also bring their plants and their animals and their viruses, parasites, and bacteria. Disease plays a very important role in the history of culture contact. A new disease introduced into a population is called a virgin soil epidemic. This can be a new disease that has just evolved or it can be a disease that exists among some human populations, but not among others. If a population has not been exposed to a particular disease, the people have little or no resistance and may get sick and die in large numbers. Native Americans were susceptible to many imported diseases, even childhood diseases, brought to the New World and consequently died in large numbers. Jared Diamond in "The Arrow of Disease," focuses on the role that disease played in the conquest of the Americas. His article stresses the interaction of cultural and biological adaptation. He looks at the spread of disease not only from the human point of view, but also from the perspective of the microbes that cause disease.

In class we learned about forced assimilation and watched a film on the Indian boarding schools. Indian children were taken away from their homes and their relatives to be sent to boarding schools with the hope that they would become assimilated. This is an example of a form of forced assimilation. Usually the children were sent away over the objections of their parents. The article by Rebecca Dobkins documents resistance to these policies by Indian parents. She studies letters from Indian parents, usually mothers, that were sent to the boarding school officials at the Greenville Indian School in California. The letters show that Indian parents showed agency in the form of resistance. They often requested to be able to reestablish contact with their of children. For instance allowing them to come home for the summer or to receive visits from relatives. They were often non-co-operative with school teachers and management and tried to circumvent the schools authority over their children. The Indians are showing agency or power when they do this.

Robert Lake or Medicine Grizzlybear is another letter writer. His son Wind-Wolf has just started school and is not doing well either academically or socially. His father is especially upset that his son is becoming embarrassed to be Indian. The "Indian Father's Plea" is for pluralism. The father wants his son to do well in school so that he will have the opportunity to succeed in the majority culture. He also wants him to be proud of his Indian heritage and identity. Education is the number one goal for Indians today. They recognize that it is vital to a successful future. We will also pursue this theme of education on the units on Africa and Australia.

Most of Americans get their knowledge about Indians from the media. Unless you are a Native American or live near a reservation you probably have a lot of misconceptions about them. First nations Peoples are often stereotyped in our country. The source of these stereotypes are the media, every thing from movies and TV shows to the daily news. In this section I will introduce the concept of stereotype. We will explore our stereotypes of Native Americans using the Native Awareness Inventory in the study guide. First Nations do want to go back to living the way they had hundreds of years in the past. They argue for pluralism. They want to keep what they value of their traditions but to have the same opportunities as other Americans. Just like Robert Lake, They want the opportunities to succeed in this cultures and still be able to celebrate their Indian Identity.

The last article in this section, by Little Finger about the Black Hills in South Dakota, deals with contemporary issues that many native groups are dealing with, land claims, sacred sites, treaties, native rights movements and assimilation.

Although Native Americans are a very small minority in this country, they are not vanishing. They are fighting hard to keep what they value of their traditional way of life. They have survived against incredible odds and are justifiably "proud to be Indian."

Another example of power and agency, is Nunavut. It is the largest land claim ever settled in favor of Native Peoples. Nunavut is a new territory in Canada. Its landmass is twice that of California and the population is 80% Inuit. John Bodely writes about Nunavut's past, present and future.

The Arrow of Disease

Jared Diamond

When Columbus and his successors invaded the Americas, the most potent weapon they carried was their germs. But why didn't deadly disease flow in the other direction, from the New World to the Old?

The three people talking in the hospital waiting room were already stressed out from having to cope with a mysterious illness, and it didn't help at all that they were having trouble communicating. One of them was the patient, a small, timid man, sick with pneumonia caused by an unidentified microbe and with only a limited command of the English language. The second, acting as translator, was his wife, worried about her husband's condition and frightened by the hospital environment. The third person in the trio was an inexperienced young doctor, trying to figure out what might have brought on the strange illness. Under the stress, the doctor was forgetting everything he had been taught about patient confidentiality. He committed the awful blunder of requesting the woman to ask her husband whether he'd had any sexual experiences that might have caused the infection.

As the young doctor watched, the husband turned red, pulled himself together so that he seemed even smaller, tried to disappear under his bed sheets, and stammered in a barely audible voice. His wife suddenly screamed in a rage and drew herself up to tower over him. Before the doctor could stop her, she grabbed a heavy bottle, slammed it onto her husband's head, and stormed out of the room. It took a while for the doctor to elicit, through the man's broken English, what he had said to so enrage his wife. The answer slowly emerged: he had admitted to repeated sexual intercourse with sheep on a recent visit to the family farm; perhaps that was how he had contracted the mysterious microbe.

This episode, related to me by a physician friend involved in the case, sounds so bizarrely one of a kind as to be of no possible significance. But in fact it illustrates a subject of greater importance: human diseases of animal origins. Very few of us may love sheep in the carnal sense. But most of us platonically love our pet animals, like our dogs and cats; and as a society, we certainly appear to have an inordinate fondness for sheep and other livestock, to judge from the vast numbers of them we keep.

Some of us—most often our children—pick up infectious diseases from our pets. Usually these illnesses remain no more than a nuisance, but a few have evolved into far more. The major killers of humanity throughout our recent history—smallpox, flu, tuberculosis, malaria, plague, measles, and cholera—are all infectious diseases that arose from diseases of animals. Until World War II more victims died of microbes than of gunshot or sword wounds. All those military histories glorifying Alexander the Great and Napoleon ignore the ego-deflating truth: the winners of past wars were not necessarily those armies with the best generals and weapons, but those bearing the worst germs with which to smite their enemies.

The grimmest example of the role of germs in history is much on our minds this month, as we recall the European conquest of the Americas that began with Columbus's voyage of 1492. Numerous as the Indian victims of the murderous Spanish conquistadores were, they were dwarfed in number by the victims of murderous Spanish microbes. These formidable conquerors killed an estimated 95 percent of the New World's pre-Columbian Indian population.

Why was the exchange of nasty germs between the Americas and Europe so unequal? Why didn't the reverse happen instead, with Indian diseases decimating the Spanish invaders, spreading back across the Atlantic, and causing a 95 percent decline in *Europe's* human population?

Similar questions arise regarding the decimation of many other native peoples by European germs, and regarding the decimation of would-be European conquistadores in the tropics of Africa and Asia.

Naturally, we're disposed to think about diseases from our own point of view: What can we do to save ourselves and to kill the microbes? Let's stamp out the scoundrels, and never mind what *their* motives are!

In life, though, one has to understand the enemy to beat him. So for a moment, let's consider disease from the microbes' point of view. Let's look beyond our anger at their making us sick in bizarre ways, like giving us genital sores or diarrhea, and ask why it is that they do such things. After all, microbes are as much a product of natural selection as we are, and so their actions must have come about because they confer some evolutionary benefit.

Basically, of course, evolution selects those individuals that are most effective at producing babies and at helping those babies find suitable places to live. Microbes are marvels at this requirement. They have evolved diverse ways of spreading from one person to another, and from animals to people. Many of our symptoms of disease actually represent ways in which some clever bug modifies our bodies or our behavior such that we become enlisted to spread bugs.

The most effortless way a bug can spread is by just waiting to be transmitted passively to the next victim. That's the strategy practiced by microbes that wait for one host to be eaten by the next—salmonella bacteria, for example, which we contract by eating already infected eggs or meat; or the worm responsible for trichinosis, which waits for us to kill a pig and eat it without properly cooking it.

As a slight modification of this strategy, some microbes don't wait for the old host to die but instead hitchhike in the saliva of an insect that bites the host and flies to a new one. The free ride may be provided by mosquitoes, fleas, lice, or tsetse flies, which spread malaria, plague, typhus, and sleeping sickness, respectively. The dirtiest of all passive-carriage tricks is perpetrated by microbes that pass from a woman to her fetus—microbes such as the ones responsible for syphilis, rubella (German measles), and AIDS. By their cunning these microbes can already be infecting an infant before the moment of birth.

Other bugs take matters into their own hands, figuratively speaking. They actively modify the anatomy or habits of their host to accelerate their transmission. From our perspective, the open genital warts caused by venereal diseases such as syphilis are a vile indignity. From the microbes' point of view, however, they're just a useful device to enlist a host's help in inoculating the body cavity of another host with microbes. The skin lesions caused by smallpox similarly spread microbes by direct or indirect body contact (occasionally very indirect, as when U.S. and Australian whites bent on wiping out "belligerent" native peoples sent them gifts of blankets previously used by smallpox patients).

More vigorous yet is the strategy practiced by the influenza, common cold, and pertussis (whooping cough) microbes, which induce the victim to cough or sneeze, thereby broadcasting the bugs toward prospective new hosts. Similarly the cholera bacterium induces a massive diarrhea that spreads bacteria into the water supplies of potential new victims. For modification of a host's behavior, though, nothing matches the rabies virus, which not only gets into the saliva of an infected dog but drives the dog into a frenzy of biting and thereby infects many new victims.

Thus, from our viewpoint, genital sores, diarrhea, and coughing are "symptoms" of disease. From a bug's viewpoint, they're clever evolutionary strategies to broadcast the bug. That's why it's in the bug's interests to make us "sick." But what does it gain by killing us? That seems self-defeating, since a microbe that kills its host kills itself.

Though you may well think it's of little consolation, our death is really just an unintended by-product of host symptoms that promote the efficient transmission of microbes. Yes, an untreated cholera patient may eventually die from producing diarrheal fluid at a rate of several gallons a day. While the patient lasts, though, the cholera bacterium profits from being massively disseminated into the water supply of its next victims. As long as each victim thereby infects, on average, more than one new victim, the bacteria will spread, even though the first host happens to die.

So much for the dispassionate examination of the bug's interests. Now let's get back to considering our own selfish interests: to stay alive and healthy, best done by killing the damned bugs. One common response to infection is to develop a fever. Again, we consider fever a "symptom" of disease, as if it developed inevitably without serving any function. But regulation of body temperature is under our genetic control, and a fever doesn't happen by accident. Because some microbes are more sensitive to heat than our own bodies are, by raising our body temperature we in effect try to bake the bugs to death before we get baked ourselves.

Another common response is to mobilize our immune system. White blood cells and other cells actively seek out and kill foreign microbes. The specific antibodies we gradually build up against a particular microbe make us less likely to get infected once we are cured. As we all know, there are some illnesses, such as flu and the common cold, to which our resistance is only temporary; we can eventually contract the illness again. Against other illnesses, though—including measles, mumps, rubella, pertussis, and the now defeated menace of smallpox—antibodies stimulated by one infection confer lifelong immunity. That's the principle behind vaccination—to stimulate our antibody production without having to go through the actual experience of the disease.

Alas, some clever bugs don't just cave in to our immune defenses. Some have learned to trick us by changing their antigens, those molecular pieces of the microbe that our antibodies recognize. The constant evolution or recycling of new strains of flu, with differing antigens, explains why the flu you got two years ago didn't protect you against the different strain that arrived this year. Sleeping sickness is an even more slippery customer in its ability to change its antigens rapidly.

Among the slipperiest of all is the virus that causes AIDS, which evolves new antigens even as it sits within an individual patient, until it eventually overwhelms the immune system.

Our slowest defensive response is through natural selection, which changes the relative frequency with which a gene appears from generation to generation. For almost any disease some people prove to be genetically more resistant than others. In an epidemic, those people with genes for resistance to that particular microbe are more likely to survive than are people lacking such genes. As a result, over the course of history human populations repeatedly exposed to a particular pathogen tend to be made up of individuals with genes that resist the appropriate microbe just because unfortunate individuals without those genes were less likely to survive to pass their genes on to their children.

Fat consolation, you may be thinking. This evolutionary response is not one that does the genetically susceptible dying individual any good. It does mean, though, that a human population as a whole becomes better protected.

In short, many bugs have had to evolve tricks to let them spread among potential victims. We've evolved countertricks, to which the bugs have responded by evolving counter-countertricks. We and our pathogens are now locked in an escalating evolutionary contest, with the death of one contestant the price of defeat, and with natural selection playing the role of umpire.

The form that this deadly contest takes varies with the pathogens: for some it is like a guerilla war, while for others it is a blitzkrieg. With certain diseases, like malaria or hookworm, there's a more or less steady trickle of new cases in an affected area, and they will appear in any month of any year. Epidemic diseases, though, are different: they produce no cases for a long time, then a whole wave of cases, then no more cases again for a while.

Among such epidemic diseases, influenza is the most familiar to Americans, this year having been a particularly bad one for us (but a great year for the influenza virus). Cholera epidemics come at long intervals, the 1991 Peruvian epidemic being the first one to reach the New World during the twentieth century. Frightening as today's influenza and cholera epidemics are, though they pale beside the far more terrifying epidemics of the past, before the rise of modern medicine. The greatest single epidemic in human history was the influenza wave that killed 21 million people at the end of the first World War. The black death, or bubonic plagued, killed one-quarter of Europe's population between 1346 and 1352, with death tolls up to 70 percent in some cities.

The infectious diseases that visit us as epidemics share several characteristics. First, they spread quickly and efficiently from an infected person to nearby healthy people, with the result that the whole population gets exposed within a short time. Second, they're "acute" illnesses: within a short time, you either die or recover completely. Third, the fortunate ones of us who do recover develop antibodies that leave us immune against a recurrence of the disease for a long time, possibly our entire lives. Finally, these diseases tend to be restricted to humans; the bugs causing them tend not to live in the soil or in other animals. All four of these characteristics apply to what Americans think of as the once more-familiar acute epidemic diseases of childhood, including measles, rubella, mumps, pertussis, and smallpox.

It is easy to understand why the combination of those four characteristics tends to make a disease run in epidemics. The rapid spread of microbes and the rapid course of symptoms mean that everybody in a local human population is soon infected, and thereafter either dead of else recovered and immune. No one is left alive who could still be infected. But since the microbe can't survive except in the bodies of living people, the disease dies out until a new crop of babies reaches the susceptible age—and until an infectious person arrives from the outside to start a new epidemic.

A classic illustration of the process is given by the history of measles on the isolated Faeroe Islands in the North Atlantic. A severe epidemic of the disease reached the Faeroes in 1781, then died out, leaving the islands measles-free until an infected carpenter arrived on a ship from Denmark in 1846. Within three months almost the whole Faeroes population—7,782 people—had gotten measles and then either died or recovered, leaving the measles virus to disappear once again until the next epidemic. Studies show that measles is likely to die out in any human population numbering less than half a million people. Only in larger populations can measles shift from one local area to another, thereby persisting until enough babies have been born in the originally infected area to permit the disease's return.

Rubella in Australia provides a similar example, on a much larger scale. As of 1917 Australia's population was still only 5 million, with most people living in scattered rural areas. The sea voyage to Britain took two months, and land transport within Australia itself was slow. In effect, Australia didn't even consist of a population of 5 million, but of hundreds of much smaller populations. As a result, Rubella hit Australia only as occasional epidemics, when an infected person happened to arrive from overseas and stayed in a densely populated area. By 1938, though, the city of Sydney alone had a population of over one million, and people moved frequently and quickly by air between London, Sydney, and other Australian cities. Around then, rubella for the first time was able to establish itself permanently in Australia.

What's true for rubella in Australia is true for most familiar acute infectious diseases throughout the world. To sustain themselves, they need a human population that is sufficiently numerous and densely packed that a new crop of susceptible children is available for infection by the time the disease would otherwise be waning. Hence measles and other such diseases are also known as "crowd diseases."

Crowd diseases could not sustain themselves in small bands of hunter-gatherers and slash-and-burn farmers. As tragic recent experience with Amazonian Indians and Pacific Islanders confirms, almost an entire tribelet may be wiped out by an epidemic brought by an outside visitor, because no one in the tribelet has any antibodies against the microbe. In addition, measles and some other "childhood" diseases are more likely to kill infected adults than children, and all adults in the tribelet are susceptible. Having killed most of the tribelet, the epidemic then disappears. The small population size explains why tribelets can't sustain epidemics introduced from the outside; at the same time it explains why they could never evolve epidemic diseases of their own to give back to the visitors.

That's not to say that small human populations are free from all infectious diseases. Some of their infections are caused by microbes capable of maintaining themselves in animals or in soil, so the disease remains constantly available to infect people. for example, the yellow fever virus is carried by African wild monkeys and is constantly available to infect rural human populations of Africa. It was also available to be carried to New World monkeys and people by the transatlantic slave trade.

Other infections of small human populations are chronic diseases, such as leprosy and yaws, that may take a very long time to kill a victim. The victim thus remains alive as a reservoir of microbes to infect other members of the tribelet. Finally, small populations are susceptible to nonfatal infections against which we don't develop immunity, with the result that the same person can become reinfected after recovering. That's the case with hookworm and many other parasites.

All these types of diseases, characteristic of small, isolated populations, must be the oldest diseases of humanity. They were the ones that we could evolve and sustain through the early millions of years of our evolutionary history, when the total human population was tiny and fragmented. They are also shared with, or as similar to the diseases of, our closest wild relatives, the African great apes. In contrast, the evolution of our crowded diseases could only have occurred with buildup of large, dense human populations, first made possible by the rise of agriculture about 10,000 years ago, then by the rise of cities several thousand years ago. Indeed, the first attested dates for many familiar infectious diseases are surprisingly recent: around 1600 B.C. for smallpox (as deduced from pockmarks on an Egyptian mummy), 400 B.C. for mumps, 1840 for polio, and 1959 for AIDS.

Agriculture sustains much higher human population densities than does hunting and gathering—on average, 10 to 100 times higher. In addition, hunter-gatherers frequently shift camp, leaving behind their piles of feces with their accumulated microbes and worm larvae. But farmers are sedentary and live amid their own sewage, providing microbes with a quick path from one person's body into another person's drinking water. Farmers also become surrounded by disease-transmitting rodents attracted by stored food.

Some human populations make it even easier for their own bacteria and worms to infect new victims, by intentionally gathering their feces and urine and spreading it as fertilizer on the fields where people work. Irrigation agriculture and fish farming provide ideal living conditions for the snails carrying schistosomes, and for other flukes that burrow through our skin as we wade through the feces-laden water.

If the rise of farming was a boon for our microbes, the rise of cities was a veritable bonanza, as still more densely packed human populations festered under even worse conditions. (Not until the beginning of the twentieth century did urban populations finally become self-sustaining; until then, constant immigration of healthy peasants from the countryside was necessary to make good the constant deaths of city dwellers from the crowd diseases.) Another bonanza was the development of world trade routes, which by the late Roman times effectively joined the populations of Europe, Asia, and North Africa into one giant breeding ground for microbes. That's when smallpox finally reached Rome as the "plague of Antonius," which killed millions of Roman citizens between A.D. 165 and 180.

Similarly, bubonic plague first appeared in Europe as the plague of Justinian (A.D. 542-543). But plague didn't begin to hit Europe with full force, as the black death epidemics, until 1346, when new overland trading with China provided rapid transit for flea-infested furs from plague-ridden areas of Central Asia. Today our jet planes have made even the longest continental flights briefer than the duration of any infectious disease. That's how an Aerolineas Argentinas airplane, stopping in Lima, Peru, earlier this year, managed to deliver dozens of cholera-infected people the same day to my city Los Angeles, over 3,000 miles away. The explosive increase in world travel by Americans, and in turning us into another melting pot—this time of microbes that we previously dismissed as just causing exotic diseases in far-off countries.

When the human population became sufficiently large and concentrated, we reached the stage in our history when we could at last sustain crowd diseases confined to our species. But that presents a paradox: such diseases could never have existed before. Instead they had to evolve as new diseases. Where did those new diseases come from?

Evidence emerges from studies of the disease-causing microbes themselves. In many cases molecular biologists have identified the microbe's closest relative. Those relatives also prove to be agents of infectious crowd diseases—but ones confined to various species of domestic animals and pets! Among animals too, epidemic diseases require dense populations, and they're mainly confined to social animals that provide the necessary large populations. Hence when we domesticated social animals such as cows and pigs, they were already afflicted by epidemic diseases just waiting to be transferred to us.

For example, the measles virus is most closely related to the virus causing rinderpest, a nasty epidemic disease of cattle and many wild cud-chewing mammals. Rinderpest doesn't affect humans. Measles, in turn, doesn't affect cattle. The close similarity of the measles and rinderpest viruses suggests that the rinderpest virus transferred from cattle to humans, then became the measles virus by changing its properties to adapt to us. That transfer isn't surprising, considering how closely many peasant farmers live and sleep next to cows and their accompanying feces, urine, breath, sores, and blood. Our intimacy with cattle has been going on for the 8,000 years since we domesticated them—ample time for the rinderpest virus to discover us nearby. Other familiar infectious diseases can similarly be traced back to diseases of our animal friends.

Given our proximity to the animals we love, we must constantly be getting bombarded by animal microbes. The invaders get winnowed by natural selection, and only a few succeed in establishing themselves as human diseases. A quick survey of current diseases lets us trace four stages in the evolution of a specialized human disease from an animal precursor.

In the first stage, we pick up animal-borne microbes that are still at an early stage in their evolution into specialized human pathogens. They don't get transmitted directly from one person to another, and even their transfer from animal to us remains uncommon. There are dozens of diseases like this that we get directly from pets and domestic animals. They include cat scratch fever from cats, leptospirosis from dogs, psittacosis from chickens and parrots, and brucellosis from cattle. We're similarly susceptible to picking up diseases from wild animals, such as the tularemia that hunters occasionally get from skinning wild rabbits.

In the second stage, a former animal pathogen evolves to the point where it does get transmitted directly between people and causes epidemics. However, the epidemic dies out for several reasons—being cured by modern medicine, stopping when everybody has been infected and died, or stopping when everybody has been infected and become immune. For example, a previously unknown disease termed *o'nyong-nyong* fever appeared in East Africa in 1959 and infected several million Africans. It probably arose from a virus of monkeys and was transmitted to humans by mosquitoes. The fact that patients recovered quickly and became immune to further attack helped cause the new disease to die out quickly.

The annals of medicine are full of diseases that sound like no known disease today but that once caused terrifying epidemics before disappearing as mysteriously as they had come. Who alive remembers the "English sweating sickness" that swept and terrified Europe between 1485 and 1578, or the "Picardy sweats" of eighteenth- and nineteenth-century France?

A third stage in the evolution of our major diseases is represented by former animal pathogens that establish themselves in humans and that do not die out; until they do, the question of whether they will become major killers of humanity remains up for grabs. The future is still very uncertain for Lassa fever, first observed in 1969 in Nigeria and caused by a virus probably derived from rodents. Better established is Lyme disease, caused by a spirochete that we get from the bite of a tick. Although the first known human cases in the United States appeared only as recently as 1962, Lyme disease is already reaching epidemic proportions in the Northeast, on the West Coast, and in the upper Midwest. The future of AIDS, derived from monkey viruses, is even more secure, from the virus's perspective.

The final stage of this evolution is represented by the major, long-established epidemic diseases confined to humans. These diseases must have been the evolutionary survivors of far more pathogens that tried to make the jump to us from animals—and mostly failed.

Diseases represent evolution in progress, as microbes adapt by natural selection to new hosts. Compared with cows' bodies, though, our bodies offer different immune defenses and different chemistry. In that new environment, a microbe must evolve new ways to live and propagate itself.

The best-studied example of microbes evolving these new ways involves myxomatosis, which hit Australian rabbits in 1950. The myxoma virus, native to a wild species of Brazilian rabbit, was known to cause lethal epidemic in European domestic rabbits, which are a different species. The virus was intentionally introduced to Australia in the hopes of ridding the continent of its plague of European rabbits, foolishly introduced in the nineteenth century. In the first year, myxoma produced a gratifying (to Australian farmers) 99.8 percent mortality in infected rabbits. Fortunately for the rabbits and unfortunately for the farmers, the death rate then dropped in the second year to 90 percent and eventually to 25 percent, frustrating hopes of eradicating rabbits completely from Australia. The problem was that the myxoma virus evolved to serve its own interests and those of the rabbits. The virus changed to kill fewer rabbits and to permit lethally infected ones to live longer before dying. The result was bad for Australian farmers but good for the virus: a less lethal myxoma virus spreads baby viruses to more rabbits than did the original, highly virulent myxoma.

For a similar example in humans, consider the surprising evolution of syphilis. Today we associate syphilis with genital sores and a very slowly developing disease, leading to the death of untreated victims only after many years. However, when syphilis was first definitely recorded in Europe in 1495, its postules often covered the body from head to the knees, caused flesh to fall off people's faces, and led to death within a few months. By 1546 syphilis had evolved into the disease with the symptoms known to us today. Apparently, just as with myxomatosis, those syphilis spirochetes evolved to keep their victims alive longer in order to transmit their spirochete offspring into more victims.

How, then, does all this explain the outcome of 1492—the Europeans conquered and depopulated the New World, instead of Native Americans conquering and depopulating Europe?

Part of the answer, of course, goes back to the invaders' technological advantages. European guns and steel swords were more effective weapons than Native American stone axes and wooden clubs. Only Europeans had ships capable of crossing the ocean and horses that could provide a decisive advantage in battle. But that's not the whole answer. Far more Native Americans died in bed than on the battlefield—the victims of germs, not of guns and swords. Those germs undermined Indian resistance by killing most Indians and their leaders and by demoralizing the survivors.

The role of disease in the Spanish conquests of the Aztec and Inca empires is especially well documented. In 1519 Cortés landed on the coast of Mexico with 600 Spaniards to conquer the fiercely militaristic Aztec Empire, which at the time had a population of many millions. That Cortés reached the Aztec capitol of Tenochtitlán, escaped with the loss of "only" two-thirds of his force, and managed to fight his way back to the coast demonstrates both Spanish military advantages and the initial naïveté of the Aztecs. But when Cortés's next onslaught came, in 1521, the Aztecs were no longer naïve, they fought street by street with the utmost tenacity.

What gave the Spaniards a decisive advantage this time was smallpox, which reached Mexico in 1520 with the arrival of one infected slave from Spanish Cuba. The resulting epidemic proceeded to kill nearly half the Aztecs. The survivors were demoralized by the mysterious illness that killed Indians and spared Spaniards, as if advertising the Spaniards' invincibility. By 1618 Mexico's initial population of 20 million had plummeted to about 1.6 million.

Pizarro had similarly grim luck when he landed on the coast of Peru in 1531 with about 200 men to conquer the Inca Empire. Fortunately for Pizarro, and unfortunately for the Incas, smallpox had arrived overland around 1524, killing much of the Incan population, including both Emperor Huayna Capac and his son and designated successor, Ninan Cuyoche. Because of the vacant throne, two other sons of Huayna Capac, Atahuallpa and Huascar, became embroiled in a civil war that Pizarro exploited to conquer the divided Incas.

When we in the United States think of the most populous New World societies existing in 1492, only the Aztecs and Incas come to mind. We forget that North America also supported populous Indian societies in the Mississippi Valley. Sadly, these societies too would disappear. But in the case conquistadores contributed nothing directly to the societies' destruction; the conquistadores' germs, spreading in advance, did everything. When De Soto marched through the Southeast in 1540, he came across Indian towns abandoned two years previously because nearly all the inhabitants had died in epidemics. However, he was still able to see some of the densely populated towns lining the lower Mississippi. By a century and a half later, though, when French settlers returned to the lower Mississippi, almost all those towns had vanished. Their relics are the great mound sites of the Mississippi valley. Only recently have we come to realize that the mound-building societies were largely intact when Columbus arrived, and that they collapsed between 1492 and the systematic European exploration of the Mississippi.

When I was a child in school, we were taught that North America had originally been occupied by about one million Indians. That low number helped justify the white conquest of what could then be viewed as an almost empty continent. However, archeological excavations and descriptions left by the first European explorers on our coasts now suggests an initial number of around 20 million. In the century or two following Columbus's arrival in the New World, the Indian population is estimated to have declined by about 95 percent.

The main killers were European germs, to which the Indians had never been exposed and against which they therefore had neither immunologic nor genetic resistance. Smallpox, measles, influenza, and typhus competed for top rank among the killers. As if those were not enough, pertussis, plague, tuberculosis, diphtheria, mumps, malaria, and yellow fever came close behind. In countless cases Europeans were actually there to witness the decimation that occurred when the germs arrived. For example, in 1837 the Mandan Indian tribe, with one of the most elaborate cultures in the Great Plains, contracted smallpox thanks to a steamboat traveling up the Missouri River form St. Louis. The population of one Mandan village crashed from 2,000 to less than 40 within a few weeks.

The one-sided exchange of lethal germs between the Old and New Worlds is among the most striking and consequence-laden facts of recent history. Whereas over a dozen major infectious diseases of Old World origins became established in the New World, not a single major killer reached Europe from the Americas. The sole possible exception is syphilis, whose origin still remains controversial.

That one-sidedness is more striking with the knowledge that large, dense human populations are a prerequisite for the evolution of crowd diseases. If recent reappraisals of the pre-Columbian New World population are correct, that population was not far below the contemporaneous population of Eurasia. Some New World cities, like Tenochtitlán, were among the world's most populous cities at that time. Yet Tenochtitlán didn't have awful germs waiting in store for the Spaniards. Why not?

One possible factor is that the rise of dense human populations began somewhat later in the New World than in the Old. Another is that the three most populous American centers—the Andes, Mexico, and the Mississippi Valley—were never connected by regular fast trade into one gigantic breeding ground for microbes, in the way that Europe, North Africa, India, and China became connected in late Roman times.

The main reasons becomes clear, however, if we ask a simple question: From what microbes could any crowd diseases of the Americas have evolved? We've seen that Eurasian crowd diseases evolved from diseases of domesticated herd animals. Significantly, there were many such animals in Eurasia. But there were only five animals that became domesticated in the Americas: the turkey in Mexico and parts of North America, the guinea pig and llama/alpaca (probably derived form the same original wild species) in the Andes, the Muscovy duck in tropical South America, and the dog throughout the Americas.

That extreme paucity of New World domestic animals reflects the paucity of wild starting material. About 80 percent of the big wild mammals of the Americas became extinct at the end of the last ice age, around 11,000 years ago, at approximately the same time that the first well-attested wave of Indian hunters spread over the Americas. Among the species that disappeared were ones that would have yielded useful domesticates, such as American horses and camels. Debate still rages as to whether those extinctions were due to climatic changes or to the impact of Indian hunters on prey that had never seen hunters. Whatever the reason, the extinctions removed most of the basis for Native American animal domestication—and for crowd diseases.

The few domesticates that remained were not likely sources of such diseases. Muscovy ducks and turkeys don't live in enormous flocks, and they're not naturally endearing species (like young lambs) with which we have much physical contact. Guinea pigs may have contributed a trypanosome infection like Chagas' disease or leishmaniasis to our catalog of woes, but that's uncertain.

Initially the most surprising absence is of any human disease derived from llamas (or alpacas), which are tempting to consider as Andean equivalent of Eurasian livestock. However, llamas had three strikes against them as a source of human pathogens: their wild relatives don't occur in big herds as do wild sheep, goats, and pigs; their total numbers were never remotely as large as the Eurasian populations of domestic livestock, since llamas never spread beyond the Andes; and llamas aren't as cuddly as piglets and lambs and aren't kept in such close association with people. (You may not think of piglets as cuddly, but human mothers in the New Guinea highlands often nurse them, and they frequently live right in the huts of peasant farmers.)

The importance of animal-derived diseases for human history extends far beyond the Americas. Eurasian germs played a key role in decimating native peoples in many parts of the world as well, including the Pacific islands, Australia, and southern Africa. Racist Europeans used to attribute those conquests to their supposedly better brains. But no evidence for such better brains has been forthcoming. Instead, the conquests were made possible by Europeans nastier germs, and by the technological advances and denser populations that Europeans ultimately acquired by means of their domesticated plants and animals.

So on the 500th anniversary of Columbus's discovery, let's try to regain our sense of perspective about his hotly debated achievements. There's no doubt that Columbus was a great visionary, seaman, and leader. There's also no doubt that he and his successors often behaved as bestial murderers. But those facts alone don't fully explain why it took so few European immigrants to initially conquer and ultimately supplant so much of the native population of the Americas. Without the germs Europeans brought with them—germs that were derived from their animals—such conquests might have been impossible.

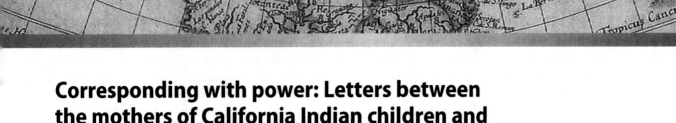

Corresponding with power: Letters between the mothers of California Indian children and federal boarding-school officials, 1916-19221

REBECCA DOBKINS

Department of Anthropology University of California, Berkeley

> *These old times have changed and [the Indians] should be taught in strong language and actions that the Government insists on their children going to some school and staying there. (National Archives 1921, Superintendent Edward K. Miller)*

> *My life is very disagreeable without [my daughter] at home. I wish you would please send her home, with her father. I remain in great anxiety. (National Archives 1918a, Lola Peters)*

"Strong language and actions" are the focus of my analysis of the correspondence between California Indian parents and the superintendent of the Greenville Indian School, a federal boarding school in operation in the Sierra Mountains of Plumas County, California, from 1888 to 1922. Over 200 letters that were restricted, as are all personal documents, for a seventy-two-year period have been newly released by the Pacific Sierra Region of the National Archives. In this paper, I discuss only a small selection of California Indian women's letters and the replies from Greenville School superintendent Edward Miller in the period 1916–22.

A general profile of the letter-writers indicates that most are parents of children attending Greenville Indian School, although other relatives also write, and sometimes reservation agency personnel write to inquire about the children's conditions. Women write somewhat more often than men, which raises the question whether this is because women were more frequently responsible for children or because of differential literacy rates between women and men. Because the letters are a random rather than a representative sample of California Indian life and concerns at the time, there is no way of answering these questions from the letters alone. Most letters appear to be written by the authors themselves, although a few have an amanuensis, usually an Indian agency "matron" or agent writing on behalf of a family who cannot.

The letters provoke many questions about Indian-white relations, cross-cultural communication, gender, authority, and resistance. From my experience working with contemporary California Indians who themselves or whose relatives attended Indian boarding schools, I am wary of creating an easy opposition between school authority and domination on the one hand and parental and student resistance and subordination on the other. Hence my purposely multivalent title, "Corresponding with Power."

I base my approach to these texts on an understanding of the relationship of resistance to power articulated by anthropologist Lila Abu-Lughod (1990). In attending to Bedouin women's narratives, Abu-Lughod inverts Foucault's proposition that "where there is power, there is resistance" to argue that resistance should be used as a diagnostic of power. She cautions against romanticizing resistance, in part because doing so can obscure the very real workings of power relations and the ways in which people are embedded within them.

The question then becomes: What do we identify as acts of resistance, and what do these acts reveal about local and global power structures? Keeping in mind that the boarding schools were total institutions, I argue that virtually any action that exerted maternal or familial influence on Indian children resisted the school's project of transforming the Indian child into an assimilated American. A range of actions revealed in the women's correspondence can thus be identified as resistance, first, those actions that were acceptable to boarding-school authorities but achieved the women's goal of reestablishing contact with their children; second, those actions intended to circumvent but not overturn authority; and third, those actions, that were out-right refusals to cooperate with the routines of power. The federal boarding schools were composite cultural institutions, mutually constituted by students, school officials, and, somewhat peripherally, parents. While I am initially concerned with identifying the strategies, both rhetorical and actual that women employed to resist boarding-school control of their children, I am secondly concerned with scrutinizing these strategies to see what they reveal about the mechanics of—as well as the ruptures in—official school authority.

The Greenville Indian School began in 1888 as a mission endeavor operated at first as an open-air revival; by 1891, the school came under the sponsorship of the Women's National Indian Association. Beginning in 1894, the federal government provided funds for the school's maintenance, and by 1899 the Women's Association had completely transferred the school to the federal government.[2]

Greenville was an example of the non-reservation boarding school favored by the Bureau of Indian Affairs (BIA) to "prepare Indian youth for the duties privileges and responsibilities of American citizenship," away from the communal values practiced in the everyday life of traditional Indian communities (National Archives 1919). Beginning in the 1870s, the federal government promoted education as a central strategy for assimilating Indians into mainstream American life. The first federal boarding school, the Carlisle Indian Training and Industrial School in Pennsylvania, was run by Colonel Richard H. Pratt, who got his start in Indian education while supervising Indian prisoners at Fort Marion in Florida Based on a military system, complete with uniforms, companies, and ranks, the schools were designed to transform the Indian child via a program of vocational training, moral instruction, physical discipline, and English-language learning Native languages were strictly prohibited, and children were punished if caught speaking their tribal tongues.[3] One of the purported aims of the schools was to make Indians self-reliant, and this self-reliance was deeply gendered: boys were to learn manual skills needed for agriculture, forestry, or trades, and girls were to learn the domestic skills necessary for working in white households or for establishing their own households upon a white middle-class model (Prucha 1984:233).[4]

The Greenville Indian School, with an enrollment of about eighty students, was one of five such boarding schools in California by 1900. Its student body was extremely diverse linguistically, with Yokuts, Mono, and Miwok children drawn from as far south as the Tule River Reservation near Bakersfield, and Maidu, Northern Paiute, and Achumawi children from northern California tribes. In accordance with federal policy, students were enrolled at Greenville for terms of three to five years, during which time they were not to return home unless their parents paid the costs of transportation. Superintendents actively discouraged this practice, because of the possibility students would not come back to school at all, and because of the threat a visit home represented to the child's assimilation process. Parents were also responsible for other costs and had to deposit a sum with the school upon the child's enrollment. If the child did not return to school after a trip home, the sum was forfeited to the government (National Archives 1918b). In a 1921 letter to the Bureau of Indian Affairs agent of the Porterville district near the Tule River Reservation, Superintendent Edward Miller of the Greenville Indian School and Agency outlined this policy:

> . . . These old times have changed and [the Indians] should be taught in strong language and actions that the Government insists on their children going to some school and staying there.
>
> We have had trouble with those old Indians under you because I have stood firm for getting expense money on students going home, according to regulations. In several cases students went home and never came back, I depositing to the credit of the Government those moneys held. I do not believe one singel students returned here as per their promise. . . . On this account you will find some critical sentiment [on the part of Indians] against this school. I am sorry for it, but rather than have a lot of Indians dictating to me what should and should not be done I will get oyt of the work. . . .
>
> My idea is to hold children in school as long as I can, where they are progressing and in good health. I have transferred them direct to other larger [boarding] schools after they finish here, in some cases without the consent of the parents, or where parents, and guardians, objected, with the consent of the Office [the BIA], after putting the matter up to it. (National Archives 1921; original spelling and grammar retained)

This letter clearly identifies the key area of contention between the school and the parents: controlling the education—and the bodies—of Indian children. Miller makes explicit the tools of this control: "strong language and actions."

In letters from Indian women addressed to the superintendent, two specific arenas of negotiation emerge: control over children's ability to return home and control over information about and treatment of children's health. The boarding school exerted almost exclusive control over the children's health care, rarely releasing children to parents unless they were extremely ill or posed a threat to other children's health. Many children became ill from infectious diseases, and an alarming number died. But the school's control over children's attendance was weaker; children could and did run away or simply never return to school after a vacation home.

Mothers and maternal relatives negotiated for their children to come home, often within the regulations established by the school. In this letter from Jennie Frease, aunt of two Greenville School girls, we glimpse the sorts of hard work women and children performed in order to raise the funds needed to bring students home during vacations:

> Marshall, Calif
> June 7, 1918
>
> Mr. Edgar Miller
> Dear Sir
>
> I will just drope you this fue lines to ask you if there is any chance of getting my girls home on the government expenc as Annie Frease wrote to her mother and told her that she could come home on the government expense but I don't see how that can be so that is the reason I am droping you this lines and fine out as I don't leve, on less it is in account of the war of corse if I could get the girls home paying one way I could make them pick berries and others fruits as there is lots of that work around Sebestopol as I am going out picking berries in two or thee week more so please let me know at once.
>
> From your truly
> Jennie Frease
> Marshall Cal (National Archives 1918c)

In other letters, we read of women working in Sacramento canneries, as chamber maids in hotels, and as domestic servants in households.

Miller replied, restating the policy that children could not return home except when parents paid in advance the roundtrip fare from school to home. Jennie Frease was unable to raise those funds in 1918; however, the correspondence reveals that by the following year, she apparently saved enough money, and the girls went home for summer vacation. Though working within terms set by the school, Jennie Frease insistently reasserted familial ties by finding a way to bring her nieces home.

One set of letters from a file marked "The Thompson Girls" reflects a mother's concern about a child's health and her desire to bring the child home. It illustrates the second category of resistance, acts that attempt to circumvent school anthority Mrs. Thompson first writes September 27, 1916:

> Dear Mr. Miller:
>
> I take the pleasure in droping you this few lines to ask you if you will send Myrtle home for a few weeks she wrote to me and she said she is not feeling well I will send you her fair so you can send her home she's got to be doctor by an indian doctor the sickness she's got can't be cure by a white doctor so I wish you would let me know wright away so I can send you the money she must come home because her father wants to have her doctored she will come back just as soon as she gets well she is bother with her head and when a child is that way they can't study much she was sick with the same sickness and we had an indian doctor and she got alwright we took her to a white doctor and he said he couldn't do any thing for her so I wish you would let me know wright away I remain as ever yours truely
>
> Mrs. A. Thompson
>
> PS please answer soon (National Archives 1916a)

This letter is remarkable in several ways. Appearing in several variations in other writers' letters, the formulaic opening, *I take the pleasure in droping you this few lines,* and closing, *I remain as ever yours truly,* signal a familiarity with the letter-writing conventions of the day. There is no punctuation whatsoever throughout the letter and no evidence of an amanuensis (as is true of other letters), suggesting that Mrs. Thompson wrote the letter herself.

Mrs. Thompson's letter to Superintendent Miller was prompted by her daughter Myrtle's writing to say she was not well, and although that letter is not extant, it must have been alarming enough for the mother to write requesting her release. What is most compelling about Mrs. Thompson's letter is her insistence that an Indian doctor treat her daughter, an adamant assertion of her parental right to care in culturally appropriate ways for her child.

The superintendent replied on October 2, 1916:

Dear Mrs. Thompson:

I have your letter in which you ask that Myrtle Thompson be allowed to go home.

I am sorry you ask this and am sorry that it is against the rules to allow her to go unless your agent, Mr. Shafer, makes the request. It is for some extraordinary reason that we allow students to leave the school after entering.

Myrtle has never been ill. She has no hospital record and her card shows that she is in good health. I can see no reason for her wanting to leave. In fact, nothing has ever been said to her matron or to me that would lead one to believe that she wanted to go home.

Under the circumstances I believe Myrtle is better off here with her sisters. I will talk with her and tell her what I told you in this letter. We will take good care of her and she will be cared for in every way. There is no use in worrying about her for she is in good health.

She has complained of dreaming some in the night time, but that is nothing to worry over at all. If there should anything get the matter with any of the girls you would hear from me.

I will send a copy of this letter to Miss Tibbetts and to Mr. Shafer and I am sure they will advise you to not worry and that it will be best for Myrtle to not think of coming home.

> Very truly yours,
> Superintendent

(National Archives 1916b)

What Miller intended as words of assurance, *If there should anything get the matter with any of the girls you would hear from me,* must have confirmed Mrs. Thompson's worst fears, for to her, the superintendent unintentionally verified that something was definitely wrong with Myrtle by *writing She has complained of dreaming some in the night time.* For many California Indian people, and many peoples worldwide, dreams are indications of health, illness, or power. Miller either did not realize the significance of dreams, or did realize and chose to stress that dreams are "nothing to worry over at all." Parents' concerns about their children's health went unaddressed if the illness they feared their children had was unrecognized—or purposely ignored—by the school administration. This correspondence must have reinforced Mrs. Thompson's concern that communication from the school was partial and obscured her daughter's actual condition. We do not know whether Myrtle was ever allowed to go home the remaining letters in the file concern other matters involving her two sisters. What is clear is that the school not only controlled information about and treatment of children's health, but also defined health and illness in terms that conflicted with Native definitions.

Another case study of parental concern about children's health is the series of letters written by Lola Peters and her husband Francisco about their daughter Philomena in 1918, during the great flu epidemic. From the Tule River Reservation the Peterses inquired about their daughter's health; Superintendent Miller replied that she "seems to be getting along all right" although he also wrote that she had malaria just after getting over the flu! Her parents wired back for Philomena to be sent home immediately; Superintendent Miller wrote back, saying, "We have no money to advance to her or for her fare. She is all right here, a little lonesome at times, but getting along nicely. She is a girl that will like it better as she gets more acquainted and talks more.

. . . I will be unwilling to send her home unless Mr. Virtue [the Indian agent at Tule River Reservation] says so or her health is not good here" (Nov. 2, 1918). Miller's main aim is clearly not to comfort the parents, he is asserting the authority of the school, the school hospital, and even that of the Indian agent at the reservation.

But the Peterses did not accept this control over their daughter. After meeting with another Indian, Jose Vera, who had visited the school and brought back firsthand accounts of the child's condition, Lola Peters writes on November 7 1918:

> Edgar K. Miller, Greenville, Cal
>   We are informed that our daughter is sick at the Greenville School. Jose Vera, states that your clerk at the school told him that the girl was sick internally. My life is very disagreeable without her at home. I wish you would please send her home, with her father.
>   I remain in great anxiety
>   Lola Peters (National Archives 1918a).

Superintendent Miller notes at the bottom: "Philomena left Sat. Nov. 9th with her father." There is no further correspondence in the file.

The intervention of the parents is made all the more astonishing when one realizes that the journey between Tule River and Greenville is over 400 miles and in 1918 would have taken great effort, by train and other means of transportation. In the face of the school's refusal to send the child home, the Peterses took matters into their own hands and retrieved her, a clear example of the third category of resistance, Indian non-cooperation with school authority.

The Greenville Indian School burned down in December 1921 in a mysterious fire. Alumni of the school, interviewed in the 1970s, were certain that the fire was set by disgruntled students (Jewell 1987:87–92). Over the years, other fires had been set by students, and superintendents had complained of such incidents in correspondence to Washington.

But even the destruction of the school did not bring freedom for the students. They were still under the control of the federal Indian education system and were sometimes sent to other boarding schools without parental permission. Mrs. Clara Symmes inquired about her son:

> Independence Cal
> Jan 2, 1922
>
> Dear sir
>   Mr. Miller
>   recived your letter last wekk—on Saturday evening—about your burned down. I am very sorry to hear about that—then I went to Mr. Parrot supt. office [the Indian agent] and heard he telegraph already and heard 4th grade are coming home and never heard they coming or not. because my boy— Arthur Richard is 4th grade. That why I am wainting him to come home. Then I can send him school here. Till your school open again. I am worry abuot him all the time. Wil you please send him home with other boys, or lone if to late, send him in Bishop, please.
>
> From yours truly
> Mrs. Clara Symmes (National Archives 1922a)

In the reply, Superintendent Miller cuts off any negotiation:

> January 6,1922
>
> Dear Madam:
>   I have your letter about ARTHUR RICHARDS going home and would advise you it came too late. We transferred him to the Chemawa, Oregon, School at his own request. He is there now. It is a fine school and he will have wonderful opportunities there to get a good education.
> He was well and happy when he left here. He did not want to go home at all
>
> Sincerely yours,
> Supt. (National Archives 1922b)

One wonders how a fourth grader could have requested being transferred, without parental knowledge, to a school several hundred miles farther north from home. The desire to remain with his peers could have played a role, or the child may have protested and had no avenue to express his dissent. The correspondence file does not reveal any further negotiation between the mother and the school.

Yet when the Greenville Indian School closed, the federal boarding school project was increasingly seen as an expensive failure. By the 1930s, federal Indian policy shifted from advocating total assimilation to limited autonomy. As Superintendent Miller lamented in his 1921 letter, many children simply did not return to school after vacations home, and his personal complaint, "rather than have a lot of Indians dictating to me what should and should not be done I will get [out] of the work," became de facto BIA policy. Boarding-school officials indeed got out or were put out of "the work," in large measure because Indian people refused some overtly and some quietly, to undergo the transformation demanded of them. While many children continued to attend boarding schools, particularly Sherman Institute in Riverside, Stewart in Reno, and Chemawa in Oregon, most Indian pupils in California enrolled in local public schools and the BIA began actively seeking agreements with public schools so that Indian children could attend, with the federal government paying the cost. Rural school districts in California saw the benefit of increasing Indian enrollment if only to receive additional funding However, integrated schooling did not translate into equitable conditions, and today California Indian students continue to have a high-school graduation rate that dips to less than 20% in some rural areas.

These letters illuminate a previously obscured intersection of culture, gender and power. They give texture to the mechanisms of federal authority and give voice to the California Indian women who strategized ways to weaken the tools of that authority, "strong language and actions," with corresponding tools of their own.

NOTES

1. The research upon which this article is based was supported by the Sourisseau Academy of San Jose State University. I would like to thank Kathleen O'Connell of the National Archives Pacific Sierra Region for her assistance and Francesca Freccero for her editorial insights and constant support.
2. See Jones (1978) for the most complete history of the Greenville Indian School to date.
3. See Hinton (1994:173–80) for a discussion of the impact of the Indian boarding-school experience on California Indian languages.
4. See Lomawaima (1993) for an extended discussion of gender and authority in the federal Indian boarding schools.

REFERENCES

Abu-Lughod, Lila (1990). The romance of resistance: Tracing transformations of power through Bedouin women's lives. *American Ethnologist* 17:41–55.

Hinton, Leanne (1994). *Flutes of fire.* Berkeley, CA: Heyday Books.

Jewell, Donald P. (1987). *Indians of the Feather River: Tales and legends of the Concow Maidu of California.* Menlo Park, CA: Ballena Press.

Jones, William Allan (1978). *The historical development of the Greenville Indian Industrial School: Greenville, Plumas County, California.* Unpublished M.A. thesis. California State University, Chico, Department of History.

Lomawaima, Tsianina (1993). Domesticity in the federal Indian schools: The power of authority over mind and body. *American Ethnologist* 20:227–40.

Prucha, Francis Paul (1984). *The great father: The United States government and the American Indian.* Abridged ed. Lincoln: University of Nebraska Press.

National Archives, Pacific Sierra Region, San Bruno, CA (1916a). Letter from Mrs. A. Thompson to Superintendent Edward K. Miller. Sept. 27. Record group 75, series 42, box 122, folder Thompson Girls.

_____ (1916b). Letter from Superintendent Edward K. Miller to Mrs. A. Thompson. Oct. 2. Record group 75, series 42, box 122, folder Thompson Girls.

_____ (1918a). Letter from Lola Peters to Superintendent Edward K. Miller.

_____ (1918b). Application for enrollment in a nonreservation school. Record group 75, series 42, box 120, folder Copeland Children.

_____ (1918c). Letter from Jennie Frease to Superintendent Edward K. Miller. June 7. Record group 75, series 42, box 120, folder Frease.

_____ (1919). Annual calendar of the Greenville Indian School. Record group 75, series 30, box 86, folder Calendars, 1913–1920.

_____ (1921). Letter from Superintendent Edward K. Miller to Agent Joe Taylor. Record group 75, series 42, box 120, folder L. Chambers.

_____ (1922a). Letter from Mrs. Clara Symmes to Superintendent Edward K. Miller. Jan. 2. Record group 75, series 42, box 120, folder Richards, Arthur.

_____ (1922b). Letter from Superintendent Edward K. Miller to Mrs. Clara Symmes. Jan. 6. Record group 75, series 42, box 120, folder Richards, Arthur.

An Indian Father's Plea

Robert Lake (Medicine Grizzlybear)

Dear teacher, I would like to introduce you to my son, Wind-Wolf. He is probably what you consider a typical Indian kid. He was born and raised on the reservation. He has black hair, dark brown eyes, and an olive complexion. And like so many Indian children his age, he is shy and quiet in the classroom. He is 5 years old, in kindergarten, and I can't understand why you have already labeled him a "slow learner."

At the age of 5, he has already been through quite an education compared with his peers in Western society. As his introduction into this world, he was bonded to his mother and to the Mother Earth in a traditional native childbirth ceremony. And he has been continuously cared for by his mother, father, sisters, cousins, aunts, uncles, grandparents, and extended tribal family since this ceremony.

From his mother's warm and loving arms, Wind-Wolf was placed in a secure and specially designed Indian baby basket. His father and the medicine elders conducted another ceremony with him that served to bond him with the essence of his genetic father, the Great Spirit, the Grandfather Sun, and the Grandmother Moon. This was all done in order to introduce him properly into the new and natural world, not the world of artificiality, and to protect his sensitive and delicate soul. It is our people's way of showing the newborn respect, ensuring that he starts his life on the path of spirituality.

The traditional Indian baby basket became his "turtle's shell" and served as the first seat for his classroom. He was strapped in for safety, protected from injury by the willow roots and hazel wood construction. The basket was made by a tribal elder who had gathered her materials with prayer and in a ceremonial way. It is the same kind of basket that our people have used for thousands of years. It is specially designed to provide the child with the kind of knowledge and experience he will need in order to survive in his culture and environment.

Wind-Wolf was strapped in snugly with a deliberate restriction upon his arms and legs. Although you in Western society may argue that such a method serves to hinder motor-skill development and abstract reasoning, we believe it forces the child to first develop his intuitive faculties, rational intellect, symbolic thinking, and five senses. Wind-Wolf was with his mother constantly, closely bonded physically, as she carried him on her back or held him in front while breast-feeding. She carried him everywhere she went, and every night he slept with both parents. Because of this, Wind-Wolf's educational setting was not only a "secure' environment, but it was also very colorful, complicated, sensitive, and diverse. He has been with his mother at the ocean at daybreak when she made her prayers and gathered fresh seaweed from the rocks, he has sat with his uncles in a rowboat on the river while they fished with gillnets, and he has watched and listened to elders as they told creation stories and animal legends and sang songs around campfires.

He has attended the sacred and ancient White Deerskin Dance of his people and is well acquainted with the cultures and languages of other tribes. He has been with his mother when she gathered herbs for healing and watched his tribal aunts and grandmothers gather and prepare traditional foods such as acorn, smoked salmon, eel, and deer meat. He has played with abalone shells, pine nuts, iris grass string, and leather while watching the women make beaded jewelry and traditional native regalia. He has had many opportunities to watch his father, uncles, and ceremonial leaders use different kinds of songs while preparing for the sacred dances and rituals.

As he grew older, Wind-Wolf began to crawl out of the baby basket, develop his motor skills, and explore the world around him. When frightened or sleepy, he could always return to the basket, as a turtle withdraws into its shell. Such an inward journey allows one to reflect in privacy on what he has learned and to carry the new knowledge deeply into the unconscious and the soul. Shapes, sizes, colors, texture, sound, smell, feeling, taste, and the learning process are therefore, integrated—the physical and spiritual, matter and energy, conscious and unconscious, individual and social.

This kind of learning goes beyond the basics of distinguishing the difference between rough and smooth, square and round, hard and soft, black and white, similarities and extremes.

For example, Wind-Wolf was with his mother in South Dakota while she danced for seven days straight in the hot sun, fasting, and piercing herself in the sacred Sun Dance Ceremony of a distant tribe. He has been doctored in a number of different healing ceremonies by medicine men and women from diverse places ranging from Alaska and Arizona to New York and California. He has been in more than 20 different sacred sweat-lodge rituals—used by native tribes to purify mind, body, and soul—since he was 3 years old, and he has already been exposed to many different religions of his racial brothers: Protestant, Catholic, Asian Buddhist, and Tibetan Lamaist.

It takes a long time to absorb and reflect on these kinds of experiences, so maybe that is why you think my Indian child is a slow learner. His aunts and grandmothers taught him to count and know his numbers while they sorted out the complex materials used to make the abstract designs in the native baskets. He listened to his mother count each and every bead and sort out numerically according to color while painstakingly made complex beaded belts and necklaces. He learned his basic numbers by helping his father count and sort the rocks to be used in the sweat lodge—seven rocks for a medicine sweat, say, or 13 for the summer solstice ceremony. (The rocks are later heated and doused with water to create purifying steam.) And he was taught to learn mathematics by counting the sticks we use in our traditional native hand game. So I realize he may be slow in grasping the methods and tools that you are now using in your classroom, ones quite familiar to his white peers, but I hope you will be patient with him. It takes time to adjust to a new cultural system and learn new things.

He is not culturally "disadvantaged," but he is culturally "different." If you ask him how many months there are in a year, he will probably tell you 13. He will respond this way not because he doesn't know how to count properly, but because he has been taught by our people that there are 13 full moons in a year according to the native tribal calendar and that there are really 13 planets in our solar system and 13 tail feathers on a perfectly balanced eagle, the most powerful kind of bird to use in ceremony and healing. But he also knows that some eagles may only have 12 tail feathers, or seven, that they do not all have the exact number. He knows that the flicker has exactly 10 tail feathers; that they are red and black, representing the directions of east and west, life and death; and that this bird is considered a "fire" bird, a power used in native doctoring and healing, he can probably count more than 40 different kinds of birds, tell you and his peers what kind of bird each is and where it lives, the seasons in which if appears, and how it is used in a sacred ceremony. He may have trouble writing his name on a piece of paper, but he knows how to say it and many other things in several different Indian languages. He is not fluent yet because he is only 5 years old and required by law to attend your educational system, learn your language, your values, your ways of thinking, and your methods of teaching and learning.

So you see, all of these influences together make him somewhat shy and quiet—perhaps "slow" according to your standards. But if Wind-Wolf was not prepared for his first tentative foray into your world, neither were you appreciative of his culture. On the first day of class, you had difficulty with his name. You wanted to call him Wind, insisting that Wolf somehow must be his middle name. The students in the class laughed at him, causing further embarrassment.

While you are trying to teach him your new methods, helping him learn new tools for self-discovery and adapt to his new learning environment, he may be looking out the window as if daydreaming. Why? Because he has been taught to watch and study the changes in nature. It is hard for him to make the appropriate psychic switch from the right to the left hemisphere of the brain when he sees the leaves turning bright colors, the geese heading south, and the squirrels scurrying around for nuts to get ready for a harsh winter. In his heart, in his young mind, and almost by instinct, he knows that this is the time of year he is supposed to be with his people gathering and preparing fish, deer meat, and native plants and herbs, and learning his assigned tasks in this role. He is caught between two worlds, torn by two distinct cultural systems.

Yesterday, for the third time in two weeks he came home crying and said he wanted to have his haircut. He said he doesn't have any friends at school because they make fun of his long hair. I tried to explain to him that in our culture, long hair is a sign of masculinity and balance and is a source of power. But he remained adamant in his position.

To make matters worse, he recently encountered his first harsh case of racism. Wind-Wolf had managed to adopt at least one good school friend. On the way home from school one day, he asked his new pal if he wanted to come home to play with him until supper. That was OK with Wind-Wolf's mother, who was walking with them. When they all got to the little friend's house, the two boys ran inside to ask permission while Wind-Wolf's mother waited. But the other boy's mother lashed out: "It is OK if you have to play with him at school, but we don't allow those kind of people in our house!" When my wife asked why not, the other boy's mother answered, "Because you are Indians and we are white, and I don't want my kids growing up with your kind of people."

So now my young Indian child does not want to go to school anymore (even though we cut his hair). He feels that he does not belong. He is the only Indian child in your class, and he is well-aware of this fact. Instead of being proud of his race, heritage, and culture, he feels ashamed. When he watches television, he asks why the white people hate us so much and always kill our people in the movies and why they take everything away from us. He asks why the other kids in school are not taught about power, beauty, and essence of nature or provided with an opportunity to experience the world around them firsthand. He says he hates living in the city and that he misses his Indian cousins and friends. He asks why one young white girl at school who is his friend always tells him, "I like you, Wind-Wolf, because you are a good Indian."

Now he refuses to sing his native songs, play with his Indian artifacts, learn his language, or participate in his sacred ceremonies. When I ask him to go to an urban powwow or help me with a sacred sweat-lodge ritual, he says no because "that's weird" and he doesn't want his friends at school to think he doesn't believe in God.

So, dear teacher, I want to introduce you to my son, Wind-Wolf, who is not really a "typical" little Indian kid after all. He stems from a long line of hereditary chiefs, medicine men and women, and ceremonial leaders whose accomplishments and unique forms of knowledge are still being studied and recorded in contemporary books. He has seven different tribal systems flowing through his blood; he is even part white. I want my child to succeed in school and life. I don't want him to be a dropout or juvenile delinquent or to end up on drugs and alcohol because he is made to feel inferior or because of discrimination. I want him to be proud of his rich heritage and culture, and I would like him to develop the necessary capabilities to adapt to, and succeed in, both cultures. But I need your help.

What you say and what you do in the classroom, what you teach and how you teach it, and what you don't say and don't teach will have a significant effect on the potential success or failure of my child. Please remember that this is the primary year of his education and development. All I ask is that you work with me, not against me, to help educate my child in the best way. If you don't have the knowledge, preparation, experience, or training to effectively deal with culturally different children, I am willing to help you with the few resources I have available or direct you to such resources.

Millions of dollars have been appropriated by Congress and are being spent each year for "Indian Education." All you have to do is take advantage of it and encourage your school to make an effort to use it in the name of "equal education." My Indian child has a constitutional right to learn, retain, and maintain his heritage and culture. By the same token, I strongly believe that non-Indian children also have a constitutional right to learn about our Native American heritage and culture, because Indians play a significant part in the history of Western society. Until this reality is equally understood and applied in education as a whole, there will be a lot more schoolchildren in grades K-2 identified as "slow learners."

My son, Wind-Wolf, is not an empty glass coming into your class to be filled. He is a full basket coming into a different environment and society with something special to share. Please let him share his knowledge, heritage, and culture with you and his peers.

Creating Nunavut

BODLEY

One of the most comprehensive recent agreements negotiated by indigenous peoples was the establishment of the Inuit-governed Canadian territory of Nunavut in 1999 in combination with the comprehensive settlement of Inuit land claims signed in 1993. In this exceptional case most of the demands of the indigenous group were met. The negotiation process began in 1976 when the Inuit Tapirisat of Canada presented the Canadian government with a proposal for the establishment of a special territory to be known as Nunavut, which means "our land" in the Inuit language. Nunavut would consist of the nearly two million square kilometers of land that the Inuit had never surrendered by treaty, where the Inuit continued to be the dominant inhabitants. The Inuit wanted full ownership of some 648,000 square kilometers and exclusive hunting and fishing rights over the remainder. They also proposed that they should, as the majority population, control the regional government as well as the regulation of any resource development of Nunavut. Such ownership and control would ensure their primary objective of self-sufficiency.

In their 1982 letter to the provincial prime ministers of Canada, the Inuit Committee on National Issues (ICNI) eloquently presented their position on the constitutional guarantees they required as the minimum conditions for the recognition of their basic rights and to set the stage for the creation of Nunavut. Specifically, they wanted the following principles to be protected:

  a. The collective recognition of the aboriginal peoples as distinct peoples in Canada due to our occupation of our lands since time immemorial, including the protection of our cultures, histories and lifestyles, and flowing from this principle:
  b. The recognition of our political rights to self-governing institutions (structures) of various kinds within the Canadian Confederation; and
  c. The recognition of our economic rights to our lands and waters, their resources and their benefits, as a base for self-sufficiency and the development of native communities and families, including the protection of our traditional livelihoods.

In 1982 the Inuit voted overwhelmingly in a plebiscite in favor of the establishment of Nunavut as a politically separate Inuit territory. Shortly thereafter, the Nunavut Constitutional Forum (NCF) and the Canadian federal government agreed in principle to the establishment of Nunavut.16 The forum made it clear that what they were seeking was not an ethnically or racially based political division, but rather a division based on peoples who were permanent residents of a natural region and who practiced a self-sufficient economy based on renewable resources. Additional and more detailed proposals for the design of Nunavut were presented by Inuit representatives at a constitutional conference held in 1983, in which the Inuit emphasized that Nunavut was to be a form of self-government within the Canadian federal tradition. Final agreements on the specific boundaries of Nunavut were not completed until 1988. Nunavut Territory became official in April 1999 (see figure 10.1). At that time Nunavut contained 26,000 people, 85 percent of whom were Inuit, and a total of 770,000 square miles (1,993,530 square kilometers), an area larger than Mexico. The Inuit received a cash settlement of 840 million dollars over 14 years, as well as mineral rights to 14,000 square miles (35,250 square kilometers), and direct title to 136,000 square miles (352,104 kilometers), which was substantially more than the Alaska natives received in their claims settlement.

Nunavut is a small nation within a nation, with its own government, the Government of Nunavut, which has a full complement of government agencies, including a premier, seven ministerial departments, and a nineteen-person assembly to represent three regional communities. Nunavut also sends a representative to the Canadian Parliament. A special organization. Nunavut Tunngavik Inc. (NTI), manages the land and resources collectively owned by the Inuit and promotes Inuit well-being generally, according to the terms of the Nunavut Land Claims Agreement Act. The NTI also issues the annual "State of Inuit Culture and Society" report18 and maintains a registry of Inuit-owned business corporations operating in Nunavut.

Nunavut is a unique experiment in which indigenous peoples are attempting to create a truly sustainable society in the commercial world based on social and cultural principles that proved successful in the tribal world. A formal Nunavut Economic Development Strategy was issued in 2003 by the newly formed Sivummut Economic Development Strategy (SEDS) Group, a coalition of some twenty Inuit organizations convened by the Nunavut Economic Forum (NEF). The SEDS Group's goal was "a high and sustainable quality of life," to be achieved "without compromising the unique culture, values, and connections to the land that have supported Inuit society over countless generations."The Nunavut Development Strategy emphasizes sustainability and self-reliance, environmental stewardship, traditional knowledge, and social equity based on four principles: cultural integrity, determination and realism, community control, and cooperation and coordination.The Inuit envision a mixed economy that balances a wage and salary sector with a strong "land-based economy" drawing on natural resources. Hunting, fishing, and foraging are dominant features of Inuit culture and identity, but also provide at least half of Nunavut's food and are important sources of income.

Nunavut's development goals are more achievable because Nunavut is a small-scale society. There are only 28 communities, averaging just 820 persons. Iqaluit, the capital, is the largest settlement, with an Inuit population of 2,956 in 1999. In 1995 there were about 100 Inuit-owned commercial businesses, most very small, operating in the territory, but by 2007 there were 243 businesses. Nunasi Corporation, headquartered in Iqaluit, produced revenues of over $200 million (US) in 2005 and was probably the largest Inuit business in Nunavut. Nunasi is collectively owned by all the Nunavut Inuit.Nunasi owns a holding company, NorTerra, jointly with the Inuit of the Western Arctic. In turn, NorTerra owns Canadian North, an airline operating Boeing 737 jetliners in the Arctic; the Northern. Transportation Company Limited, (NTCL), which operates maritime shipping in the Canadian Arctic; and Weldco-Beales (WBM), a heavy equipment manufacturing company with plants in Alberta, British Columbia, and Washington State. The political and commercial development of Nunavut is certainly a dramatic transformation of Inuit society and culture as it existed a century ago, but many problems remain to be resolved.

We Walk on Our Ancestors: The Sacredness of the Black Hills

Michael Dorris, I'm Not Thankful for TG.

LEONARD LITTLE FINGER

In 1883, my grandfather, Saste, was a child of seven years. With his parents, he traveled in a group into the Black Hills in South Dakota for a sacred prayer journey to Washun Niye, a site from which Mother Earth breathes. They were following a path that had been a journey for his people for thousands of years. In preparation for the ceremony, the women dried the hide of apte, or tatanka (buffalo), which was carried to this site for the sacred ceremony. The cannupa (sacred pipe) acknowledged apte by returning the hide to the world; upon completion of the prayers, the hide would be dropped into the hole. As my grandfather watched, Washun Niye carried the hide downward in a spiraling motion, soon to be enveloped into the darkness. The power of the sacred circle which has no ending was affirmed.

I heard this story in 1947, in Lakota, at the age of eight, seven years before he was to make his spirit journey—from which we all come as a spirit or soul. It took me many years to understand the importance of his story, because we must revisit anything of importance many times before we can fully understand its significance. When one finally understands, then begins the process of interpretation. The spiritual quest of truth, especially for Indigenous people, is in this process.

My grandfather and I are from a sub-band of the Teton, a member of the Nation of the Seven Council Fires. We are called the Mniconjou, or People Who Plant Near the Water. In the 1500s, one of our villages was the location of present day Rapid City along the streams of Mniluzahan Creek, or Rapid Creek, which is today's northern gateway to the Black Hills of South Dakota. Our family has had a spiritual relationship with this special land for over 500 years.

The Black Hills were recognized as the Black Hills because of the darkness from the distance. The term also referred to a container of meat; in those days people used a box made out of dried buffalo hide to carry spiritual tools, like the sacred pipe, or the various things that were used in prayers or to carry food. That's the term that was used for the Black Hills: they were a container for our spiritual need as well as our needs of food and water, whatever it is that allows survival.

A Legacy of Threats

The story of the Black Hills is an age-old conflict between imperialism and the understanding of their spiritual significance as a sacred site. The threats to our sacred lands began when the first two treaties were drawn up with the federal government. The first was in 1851 recognizing several tribes, including the People of the Seven Council Fires, and identified the territories of each tribe. In 1868 the Fort Laramie treaty designated an area that included the entire western half of South Dakota, with the eastern line marked by the Missouri River and a portion of North Dakota and Wyoming. We would not, as a nation, be recognized.

When gold was discovered in Montana, the trails leading to it came into the territory of the Sioux. In 1872, General Custer led a contingent of gold mining experts, theologists, and botanists into the Black Hills. Although just traces of gold were found in the streams, it was an indication that there was probably gold, veins of gold in the hills, so the US government sent two commissions to renegotiate the treaty. One of the articles stated that three-fourths of the male population had to agree to any amendments. Both commissions failed to achieve an agreement, so in 1874 Congress declared that treaties would no longer be used. Following this action (which nullified Article 6 of the US Constitution), more than 25,000 gold seekers came into the Black Hills over a very short period of time, essentially claiming that land. It's been estimated that during that time up until 2005, when the last gold mine was shut down, approximately 500 billion ounces, or $9 trillion worth, of gold were extracted.

Problems continued in 1888 when North and South Dakota were admitted into the union and the Sioux were forced onto reservations to become US citizens. In 1876 the Sioux had wiped out General Custer and the entire 7th Cavalry in Montana, becoming the only nation to ever defeat the United States in battle. That really marked us for violation, leading to the massacre at Wounded Knee in 1890. All of these things led to the people moving away from the Black Hills, away from the sacred sites for their spiritual journeys; we could no longer go back without the threat of being jailed or killed.

In the early 1920s the Sioux filed a complaint with the Indian Claims Commission alleging that the United States had illegally taken the land that had been designated to us by the treaties of 1851 and 1868. The claim entered the Supreme Court in 1962 and took nearly 20 years to settle, enduring as the longest court case in US history. On June 30, 1980 the Supreme Court determined that the United States had indeed violated the treaty of the People of the Seven Council Fires: not just the Sioux, but the original title that we were known by. However, the federal government argued that it could not give back the land since it is occupied and includes the national monument of Mount Rushmore, a sculpture on a sacred site. The government offered compensation—for the value of the land in 1876, prior to its occupation and the gold that was extracted, including interest—of $350 million. Of course the People of the Seven Council Fires rejected that offer. The Black Hills is a sacred grandmother to us, filled with sacred power sites. How can one sell a sacred grandmother?

Now we have an opportunity to sit down in a unified way to discuss the Black Hills and the threat that is coming from ourselves as a people, as we have begun to travel the road of assimilation. Less and less people speak our native language, Lakota. Less and less adhere to the spiritual significance because of the introduction of Christianity to the reservations. One of my fears is that there is a day coming that the Bureau of Indian Affairs will sit down at a table with the offer and our people will accept the money. At that point, thousands and thousands of years of spiritual significance of the Black Hills will be left to the wayside because the new culture of the new people that have come onto the reservation will see the same meaning in the value of the money.

Our Place in History

Recently we were asked as elders to look at some aerial photos of the southern Black Hills. We looked at them as sacred circles, and in an aerial photo we saw the image of the big dipper. This is an image of what we are, the journey of the Black Hills, the sacred journey known as "seeking sacred goodness" and the pipe that is used, the cannupa. Today the UN Declaration on the Rights of Indigenous Peoples gives us the modern tools to stand up and declare our rights. We have come back to the table on the basis of what is recognized for Indigenous Peoples' rights and on the basis of what sacredness is. Our beliefs are substantiated by the image of the aerial rock formations in the sacred circle that were left by our ancestors thousands of years ago.

The desecration of the Black Hills is indicative of the violation of the sacredness of who we are as a people. The insides of Grandmother Earth are being taken; the atmosphere, the area that's there to protect us and all things is being destroyed. Earth is our grandmother, as animate as we all are, because she provides us with all of our needs to live. From the time of birth until now I look at that relationship as sacred. When our life ends here on Grandmother Earth, we become as one. This sacredness means that we walk on our ancestors. As Indigenous Peoples we are guided by the spiritualism of greater powers than we humans. We don't seek equality, we seek justice. This is who we are, and this is where we come from.

North America and South America

South America

▼

Topics Covered in Class

Areas after Contact and Today
Three Culture Areas of South America
Grasslands, Lowlands, Highlands
Onion Model

About the Readings

A lot of the information and terminology that I introduced in the beginning of this section also applies to South America. There are three culture areas in South America. Using a combination of maps and charts we will learn about each of these areas with a focus on the cultures that existed at contact, what happened at contact and what the situation is today.

In the final article in this section we look at the impact of culture change on the Shavante living in the Lowlands. Like the Yanomamo, they have only been contacted recently. Pia Mayberry-Lewis and her husband visited the Shavante in 1958 and again in 1982. Over those three decades the tribe had experienced a lot of change.

This article addresses an issue that has not been discussed yet. Change and development don't always impact all the members of a society in the same way. Sometimes there is a difference between how different ranks in society are affected. The elite may benefit when the vast majority of people see no change or life even gets more difficult. In the article, "One Step Forward-Two Steps Back", gender plays an important role. According to Mayberry-Lewis the lives of men among the Shavante of Brazil have gotten better and the lives of women have gotten worse. She makes two visits to the Shavante, the first in 1958 and the second in 1982. Remember that anthropologists are products of their own culture. We cannot overlook changes in our society that may have had an influence on how the anthropologist viewed the lives of the Shavante women. These changes would be the Woman's Liberation Movement and the rise of feminism.

One Step Forward—Two Steps Back
Shavante Women of Central Brazil, 1958–1982

PIA MAYBURY-LEWIS

Twenty-five years ago the only way to reach the Shavante Indians near the Rio das Mortes in central Brazil was by plane or boat. By boat the journey took weeks, through territory inhabited only by nomadic Indians. Luckily, my husband, baby son and I went by plane, but even so it was days before we were finally deposited at a roughly cleared landing strip near a Shavante village. The dilapidated two-engine plane took off, leaving us in a sea of naked and semi-naked people whose language we could barely understand.

Our first visit to the village was quite ceremonious. The chief's sons solemnly walked us—one in the front and one behind—to their father's hut, which was occupied by the chief, his daughters, their husbands and their children. We were led to a tall beehive-shaped hut which we stooped to enter through a tunnel-like doorway. Once our eyes had become accustomed to the darkness we identified the chief, lying on his mat to the right of the entry, using his hardwood club as a headrest. He was naked, but his wife, who sat next to him, was dressed in a shapeless shift made from cheap cloth donated by people who felt that nakedness was sinful.

We sat down, presents were given and a halting conversation ensued. Suddenly the women carried our little son into the recesses of the hut. I could hear them giggling as they gathered around him, and went over to see what was going on. Their curiosity had been too much for them, so they had taken off his diaper to see what sex he was. The good humor continued as I dressed him again, while the men ignored us and carried on their solemn conversation about such trivia as the weather, what they saw and said on the last hunting trip and whether there were enough feathers to make new arrows.

The Shavante built "our" hut next door to the chiefs. Men cut the trees for it and lashed them into the bee-hive frame. Women brought in the palm leaves and put them over the frame to provide the thatch cover. Once we were installed in the village, I sat like the other women outside the doorway of my hut in the evenings, looking at the sweeping semi-circle of dwellings that comprised the village and listening to the men making speeches in the center of it. The men discussed everything from the day's gossip to matters of life and death, while the women talked among themselves and occasionally shouted comments and objections to the men in the middle.

In the mornings, often before sunrise, I would be woken by one of my neighbors who whispered that we had to be off hunting for berries and especially for roots. We would file off with our boat-shaped baskets slung from our foreheads and resting on our backs. Several of the baskets weren't empty, but contained sleeping babies who would soon have to share their cribs with the day's produce, for the women always found something to eat.

As we trudged through open savannah or dense undergrowth we would occasionally get glimpses of parties of men out after boar, or lone hunters setting out for days at a time in quest of deer. There would be huge excitement in the village when the men came staggering in under loads of meat; but most returned empty-handed. Then it was the "women's food" that kept everybody going.

On other days I would take my little son and walk a few miles to one of the clearings where Shavante planted their traditional crops of corn, beans and squash. They were only just beginning to plant manioc, the staple of their Brazilian neighbors, and they did so with some reluctance, for they feared it required too much care and would interfere with the nomadic lifestyle which they prized so highly. Men cut and burned the trees and undergrowth, leaving the women to plant, weed and harvest the crops in the rough clearings. Men would often accompany their wives to the gardens, ostensibly to help them but also because they were places where a couple could make love in relative privacy.

Shavante neither sought nor enjoyed much privacy in their villages and looked on chronic loners with suspicion. Loneliness was a characteristic they associated with malevolent spirits. Human beings were by contrast gregarious. Yet men and women, though they did not avoid each other, spent little time in each other's company. Almost every day the men's groups, age-sets composed of individuals of roughly the same age, danced around the village or busied themselves with the elaborate ritual ceremonies. The women might help the men get painted but they themselves neither painted nor took part in the ceremonies. We sat by the huts at the periphery and witnessed the essentially male goings-on in the center.

In the 1950s Shavante technology was very simple. The most used utensil—apart from the shotgun we brought—was the digging stick, which served as a club to break an enemy's head, a tool for knocking down bee's nests on the savannah, a hoe for clearing and planting, a head rest for sleeping, and a host of other things. Women wove beautiful baskets for which the Shavante are famous and also manufactured the characteristic necklaces from the seeds of a bush, baked hard, pierced one by one and then laboriously strung together.

We went back to visit the Shavante in 1982, twenty-three years after that first meeting, to see how they were faring now that Brazil had caught up with them. I was particularly curious about how the women's lives had changed. This time we could drive, although we left the tarmac and jolted for days over dirt roads which finally degenerated into tracks. When we were thoroughly lost, literally stalking the Shavante in the country-side over which we had once gathered roots and berries and hunted with them, we came at last to the crest of a bluff and saw far below the familiar semicircle of beehive huts.

An hour later we were again among the people who had surrounded us on the airstrip so many years ago. This time there were speeches of welcome to which my husband replied in rusty Shavante. Our hosts appreciated the courtesy but it was no longer strictly necessary. The villagers now spoke Portuguese and had grown worldly wise. Gone were the days when the blond baby might cause a stir among the women, or when the men's council discussed matters relating to hunting and fishing. Now they cross-questioned us about the Malvinas/Falkland Islands war which they had heard about on their transistor radios. During the bitter struggles to retain control of their lands they had become knowledgeable about rational and local politics and Shavante leaders had become famous in Brasilia for their tough and domineering manner of dealing with the authorities.

National elections took place while we were with them and I found myself driving all night to ferry a dozen young Shavante men to the polls. They had been instructed by their chief to vote as soon as the polls opened and then get out of town before the usual election day drinking and fighting started. One of them expertly drove the vehicle back over the difficult trails. When the results came we learned that Mario Juruna, a Shavante running in the cosmopolitan state of Rio de Janeiro, had become the first Indian ever elected to the Federal Chamber of Deputies.

The lives of the Shavante have been transformed in many ways during the last 25 years. Their involvement in a government-sponsored rice cultivation project is very different than their old hunting and gathering subsistence strategies. The men's groups no longer dance around the village every day; the groups of younger men are usually away at the rice fields, where Shavante can be seen driving tractors and bringing in the harvest which have made this part of the country the rice bowl of the Brazilian interior. The men still love hunting and are constantly on the lookout for game, but it has become more of a pastime than a subsistence activity. One elder persuaded me to drive him to visit the Brazilian cowboy who was minding his cattle. On the way he suddenly ordered me to stop the car. He steadied his revolver with a hand on my shoulder and shot a deer from the car window.

Men now wear black jeans or soccer shorts and store-bought red sports shirts. But women still wear shapeless dresses even though they now have sewing machines. Clothes, like body painting—which is still done—appear to be ways for men, not women, to decorate their bodies.

While some Shavante villages do have water piped to communal faucets and a few even have electricity to light half a dozen lamp posts in the village for a couple of hours every evening, the changes over the past twenty years have not lightened the women's labor. The improved water supply has only slightly lessened the additional burden of washing and caring for clothes which has fallen entirely on the women. The women still gather wood and cook the food over open fires as they have since time immemorial. They still rend the subsistence crops, once the men have done the heavy work of clearing the gardens. In addition they are now intensively engaged in animal husbandry. Every woman is expected to raise chickens and "good managers" rear guinea fowl, pigs and even ducks. Yet as the Shavante become increasingly involved in the cash economy, proceeds from women's labor is controlled by men.

Where there are schools for the Shavante, both sexes attend them, but neither the Shavante nor the missionaries or government agencies which run the schools expect women to keep up with men. It is the men who will travel as soon as they are old enough. Some boys have even attended Brazilian schools in faraway towns and a few are at the universities in Sao Paulo, Rio and Brasilia. It is the men who learn how to deal with Brazil and the Brazilians, and who increasingly are acquiring the skills which enable them to enter the Brazilian labor market. Women continue to perform their traditional tasks, but their work has become more onerous. They are now expected to do more with less help from men and little technological assistance.

The most dramatic effect of modernization has, been the downgrading of women's roles in Shavante society. Traditionally, Shavante men and women lived largely separate lives and performed separate tasks, but the collaboration and interdependence between them was clearly understood and was at the heart of Shavante values and their daily lives. Today, Shavante men are sophisticated, and they tend to see the women less as the other pillar of Shavante life and more as a backward category of people relegated to do endless chores.

Africa and Oceania

Africa

Topics Covered in Class

Stereotypes of Africa
Africa's Triple Heritage
Arabs, Europeans, Traditional Africa
Major Sources of Change in Africa
Slave Trade, Missions, Colonialism, Capitalism
Colonial Africa
Africa Today

About the Readings

All of North America and South America have become independent from colonialism by the time that Europe turns its attention to Africa. Because of the Industrial Revolution there is a new drive for riches and resources, and raw materials and markets in Africa. In 1884, the major European powers met in Berlin, Germany and proceeded to put a map of Africa down on a table and divide it up among themselves. The articles in this section describe various methods that the western powers employed to incorporate Africans into their colonial systems.

Ngugi Wa Thiongo's writes an account account of his experience as a student in British schools in Kenya. Kenya was a colony of Great Britain when he was growing up. In "Decolonizing the Mind," the author describes how he was taught English language and culture in school, in a manner designed to undermine the values of traditional African culture. Along with classes in English language, history, and culture, he was taught that anything English is superior to anything African. Today, Thiongo is a highly respected award winning author. His novels and plays have a global audience. This article is a good example of the agency and the Plan B approach long before there was ever a Plan B.

Education is also a central theme in Enid Schildkrout's article, "Schooling and Seclusion." Schildkrout looks at the negative effects of an education program introduced to the Hausa of Nigeria. This is another good example of how changes may affect different parts of a population differently. In this case an attempt to help improve the lives of women actually caused problems for many of them because of the custom of Purdah. The author does not argue against offering education to women, but does assert that these programs should be planned with an understanding of local culture, so that they do not end up hurting the very population that they are attempting to help. Just think of how this program might have been implemented differently if local women were given a voice in the planning.

Cronk and Leech start their article with an account of a missing man, Koisa ole Lengai, but the article is not really about this one man. It is a great example of culture change in Kenya that comes with British colonialism. Koisa was a member of a hunting and gathering group, the Mukogodo. This group did not have direct contact with the British, but their neighbors, the Maasai, did. This article is a good example of what Brian Fagan describes as the "ripple effect". Changes in the Maasai culture led to changes in the culture of their neighbors. Cronl and Leech do a good job of accounting for these changes. Continuing with the theme of change into present time they also point out the the Mukogodo have been subjects of some failed aid projects and explain why.

Finally we have the article by Lila Abu-Lughod about "Change and the Egyptian Bedouin." The Bedouins are an ethnic group living in North Africa. They are also pastoralists who have been experiencing pressure to give up their herds and their nomadic way of life. This is an interesting article, because Abu-Lughod describes how the Egyptian government tried to settle down the Bedouin and assimilate them. Everything that the government did, the Bedouin turned around to work in their favor. It provides an excellent example of agency and how the networks of traditional culture can help people adapt to changes without losing their cultural identity.

Decolonising the Mind

Ngũgĩ wa Thiong'o

I was born into a large peasant family: father, four wives and about twenty-eight children. I also belonged, as we all did in those days, to a wider extended family and to the community as a whole.

We spoke Gĩkũyũ as we worked in the fields. We spoke Gĩkũyũ in and outside the home. I can vividly recall those evenings of storytelling around the fireside. It was mostly the grown-ups telling the children but everybody was interested and involved. We children would re-tell the stories the following day to other children who worked in the fields picking the pyrethrum flowers, tea-leaves or coffee beans of our European and African landlords.

The stories, with mostly animals as the main characters, were all told in Gĩkũyũ. Hare, being small, weak but full of innovative wit and cunning, was our hero. We identified with him as he struggled against the brutes of prey like lion, leopard, hyena. His victories were our victories and we learnt that the apparently weak can outwit the strong. We followed the animals in their struggle against hostile nature—drought, rain, sun, wind—a confrontation often forcing them to search for forms of co-operation. But we were also interested in their struggles amongst themselves, and particularly between the beasts and the victims of prey. These twin struggles, against nature and other animals, reflected real-life struggles in the human world.

Not that we neglected stories with human beings as the main characters. There were two types of characters in such human-centred narratives: the species of truly human beings with qualities of courage, kindness, mercy, hatred of evil, concern of others; and a man-eat-man two-mouthed species with qualities of greed, selfishness, individualism and hatred of what was good for the larger co-operative community. Co-operation as the ultimate good in a community was a constant theme. It could unite human beings with animals against ogres and beasts of prey, as in the story of how dove, after being fed with castor-oil seeds, was sent to fetch a smith working far away from home and whose pregnant wife was being threatened by these man-eating two-mouthed ogres.

There were good and bad story-tellers. A good one could tell the same story over and over again, and it would always be fresh to us, the listeners. He or she could tell a story told by someone else and make it more alive and dramatic. The differences really were in the use of words and images and the inflexion of voices to effect different tones.

We therefore learnt to value words for their meaning and nuances. Language was not a mere string of words. It had a suggestive power well beyond the immediate and lexical meaning. Our appreciation of the suggestive magical power of language was reinforced by the games we played with words through riddles, proverbs, transpositions of syllables, or through nonsensical but musically arranged words.[1] So we learnt the music of our language on top of the content. The language, through images and symbols, gave us a view of the world, but it had a beauty of its own. The home and the field were then our pre-primary school but what is important, for this discussion, is that the language of our evening teaching, and the language of our immediate and wider community, and the language of our work in the fields were one.

And then I went to school, a colonial school, and this harmony was broken. The language of my education was no longer the language of my culture. I first went to Kamaandura, missionary run, and then to another called Maanguuũ run by nationalists grouped around the Gĩkũyũ Independent and Karinga Schools Association. Our language of education was still Gĩkũyũ. The very first time I was ever given an ovation for my writing a composition in Gĩkũyũ. So for my first four years there was still harmony between the language of my formal education and that of the Limuru peasant community.

Reprinted by permission of Ngugi wa' Thiong'o and the Watkins/Loomis Agency.

It was after the declaration of a state of emergency over Kenya in 1952 that all the schools run by patriotic nationalists were taken over by the colonial regime and were placed under District Education Boards chaired by Englishmen. English became the language of my formal education. In Kenya, English became more than a language: it was *the* language, and all the others had to bow before it in deference.

Thus one of the most humiliating experiences was to be caught speaking Gĩkũyũ in the vicinity of the school. The culprit was given corporal punishment—three to five strokes of the cane on bare buttocks—or was made to carry a metal plate around the neck with inscriptions such as I AM STUPID or I AM A DONKEY. Sometimes the culprits were fined money they could hardly afford. And how did the teachers catch the culprits? A button was initially given to one pupil who was supposed to hand it over to whoever was caught speaking his mother tongue. Whoever had the button at the end of the day would sing who had given it to him and the ensuing process would bring out all the culprits of the day. Thus children were turned into witch-hunters and in the process were being taught the lucrative value of being a traitor to one's immediate community.

The attitude to English was the exact opposite: any achievement in spoken or written English was highly rewarded; prizes, prestige, applause; the ticket to higher realms. English became the measure of intelligence and ability in the arts, the sciences, and all the other branches of learning. English became *the* main determinant of a child's progress up the ladder of formal education.

As you may know, the colonial system of education in addition to its apartheid racial demarcation had the structure of a pyramid: a broad primary base, a narrowing secondary middle, and an even narrower university apex. Selections from primary into secondary were through an examination, in my time called Kenya African Preliminary Examination, in which one had to pass six subjects ranging from Maths to Nature Study and Kiswahili. All the papers were written in English. Nobody could pass the exam who failed the English language paper no matter how brilliantly he had done in the other subjects. I remember one boy in my class of 1954 who had distinctions in all subjects except English, which he had failed. He was made to fail the entire exam. He went on to become a turn boy in a bus company. I who had only passes but a credit in English got a place at the Alliance High School, one of the most elitist institutions for Africans in colonial Kenya. The requirements for a place at the University, Makerere University College, were broadly the same: nobody could go on to wear the undergraduate red gown, no matter how brilliantly they had performed in all the other subjects unless they had a credit—not even a simple pass!—in English. Thus the most coveted place in the pyramid and in the system was only available to the holder of an English language credit card. English was the official vehicle and the magic formula to colonial elitedom.

Literary education was now determined by the dominant language while also reinforcing that dominance. Orature (oral literature) in Kenyan languages stopped. In primary school I now read simplified Dickens and Stevenson alongside Rider Haggard. Jim Hawkins, Oliver Twist, Tom Brown—not Hare, Leopard and lion—were now my daily companions in the world of imagination. In secondary school, Scott and G. B. Shaw vied with more Rider Haggard, John Buchan, Alan Paton, Captain W. E. Johns. At Makerere I read English: from Chaucer to T. S. Eliot with a touch of Graham Greene.

Thus language and literature were taking us further and further from ourselves to other selves, from our world to other worlds.

What was the colonial system doing to us Kenyan children? What were the consequences of, on the one hand, this systematic suppression of our languages and the literature they carried, and on the other the elevation of English and the literature it carried? To answer those questions, let me first examine the relationship of language to human experience, human culture, and the human perception of reality.

Language, any language, has a dual character: it is both a means of communication and a carrier of culture. Take English. It is spoken in Britain and in Sweden and Denmark. But for Swedish and Danish people English is only a means of communication with non-Scandinavians. It is not a carrier of their culture. For the British, and particularly the English, it is additionally, and inseparably from its use as a tool of communication, a carrier of their culture and history. Or take Swahili in East and Central Africa. It is widely used as a means of communication across many nationalities. But it is not the carrier of a culture and history of many of those nationalities. However in parts of Kenya and Tanzania, and particularly in Zanzibar, Swahili is inseparably both a means of communication and a carrier of the culture of those people to whom it is a mother-tongue.

Culture transmits or imparts those images of the world and reality through the spoken and the written language, that is through a specific language. In other words, the capacity to speak, the capacity to order sounds in a manner that makes for mutual comprehension between human beings is universal. This is the universality of language, a quality specific to human beings. It corresponds to the universality of the struggle against nature and that between human beings. But the particularity of the sounds, the words, the word order into phrases and sentences, and the specific manner, or laws, of their ordering is what distinguishes one language from another. Thus a specific culture is not transmitted through language in its universality but in its particularity as the language of a specific community with a specific history. Written literature and orature are the main means by which a particular language transmits the images of the world contained in the culture it carries.

Language as communication and as culture are then products of each other. Communication creates culture: culture is a means of communication. Language carries culture, and culture carries, particularly through orature and literature, the entire body of values by which we come to perceive ourselves and our place in the world. How people perceive themselves affects how they look at their culture, at their politics and at the social production of wealth, at their entire relationship to nature and to other beings. Language is thus inseparable from ourselves as a community of human beings with a specific form and character, a specific history, a specific relationship to the world.

So what was the colonialist imposition of a foreign language doing to us children?

The real aim of colonialism was to control the people's wealth: what they produced, how they produced it, and how it was distributed; to control, in other words, the entire realm of the language of real life. Colonialism imposed its control of the social production of wealth through military conquest and subsequent political dictatorship. But its most important area of domination was the mental universe of the colonised, the control, through culture, of how people perceived themselves and their relationship to the world. Economic and political control can never be complete or effective without mental control. To control a people's culture is to control their tools of self-definition in relationship to others.

For colonialism this involved, two aspects of the same process: the destruction or the deliberate undervaluing of a people's culture, their art, dances, religions, history, geography, education, orature and literature, and the conscious elevation of the language of the coloniser. The domination of a people's language by the languages of the colonising nations was crucial to the domination of the mental universe of the colonised.

Take language as communication. Imposing a foreign language, and suppressing the native languages as spoken and written, were already breaking the harmony previously existing between the African child and the three aspects of language. Since the new language as a means of communication was a product of and was reflecting the 'real language of life' elsewhere, it could never as spoken or written properly reflect or imitate the real life of that community. This may in part explain why technology always appears to us as slightly external, *their* product and not *ours*. The word 'missile' used to hold an alien far-away sound until I recently learnt its equivalent in Gĩkũyũ, *ngurukuhi,* and it made me apprehend it differently. Learning, for a colonial child, became a cerebral activity and not an emotionally felt experience.

But since the new, imposed languages could never completely break the native languages as spoken, their most effective area of domination was the third aspect of language as communication, the written. The language of an African child's formal education was foreign. The language of the books he read was foreign. The language of his conceptualisation was foreign. Thought, in him, took the visible form of a foreign language. So the written language of a child's upbringing in the school (even his spoken language within the school compound) became divorced from his spoken language at home. There was often not the slightest relationship between the child's written world, which was also the language of his schooling, and the world of his immediate environment in the family and the community. For a colonial child, the harmony existing between the three aspects of language as communication was irrevocably broken. This resulted in the disassociation of the sensibility of that child from his natural and social environment, what we might call colonial alienation. The alienation became reinforced in the teaching of history, geography, music, where bourgeois Europe was always the centre of the universe.

This disassociation, divorce, or alienation from the immediate environment becomes clearer when you look at colonial language as a carrier of culture.

Since culture is a product of the history of a people which it in turn reflects, the child was now being exposed exclusively to a culture that was a product of a world external to himself. He was being made to stand outside himself to look at himself. *Catching Them Young* is the title of a book on racism, class, sex, and politics in children's literature by Bob Dixon. 'Catching them young' as an aim was even more true of a colonial child. The images of this world and his place in it implanted in a child take years to eradicate, if they ever can be.

Since culture does not just reflect the world in images but actually, through those very images, conditions a child to see that world in a certain way, the colonial child was made to see the world and where he stands in it as seen and defined by or reflected in the culture of the language of imposition.

And since those images are mostly passed on through orature and literature it meant the child would now only see the world as seen in the literature of his language of adoption. From the point of view of alienation, that is of seeing oneself from outside oneself as if one was another self, it does not matter that the imported literature carried the great humanist tradition of the best in Shakespeare, Goethe, Balzac, Tolstoy, Gorky, Brecht, Sholokhov, Dickens. The location of this great mirror of imagination was necessarily Europe and its history and culture and the rest of the universe was seen from that centre.

But obviously it was worse when the colonial child was exposed to images of his world as mirrored in the written languages of his coloniser. When his own native languages were associated in his impressionable mind with low status, humiliation, corporal punishment, slow-footed intelligence and ability or downright stupidity, non-intelligibility and barbarism, this was reinforced by the world he met in the works of such geniuses of racism as a Rider Haggard or a Nicholas Monsarrat; not to mention the pronouncement of some of the giants of western intellectual and political establishment, such as Hume ('. . . the negro is naturally inferior to the whites . . .),[2] Thomas Jefferson ('. . . the blacks . . . are inferior to the whites on the endowments of both body and mind . . .'),[3] or Hegel with his Africa comparable to a land of childhood still enveloped in the dark mantle of the night as far as the development of self-conscious history was concerned. Hegel's statement that there was nothing harmonious with humanity to be found in the African character is representative of the racist images of Africans and Africa such a colonial child was bound to encounter in the literature of the colonial languages.[4] The results could be disastrous.

In her paper read to the conference on the teaching of African literature in schools held in Nairobi in 1973, entitled 'written Literature and Black Images', the Kenyan writer and scholar Professor Micere Mugo related how a reading of the description of Gagool as an old African woman in Rider Haggard's *King Solomon's Mines* had for a long time made her feel mortal terror whenever she encountered old African women. In his autobiography *This Life* Sydney Poitier describes how, as a result of the literature he had read, he had come to associate Africa with snakes. So on arrival in Africa and being put up in a modern hotel in a modern city, he could not sleep because he kept on looking for snakes everywhere, even under the bed. These two have been able to pinpoint the origins of their fears. But for most others the negative image becomes internalised and it affects their cultural and even political choices in ordinary living.

Notes

1. Example from a tongue twister: 'Kaana ka Nikoora koona koora koora: na ko koora koona kaana ka Nikoora koora koora.' I'm indebted to Wangui wa Goro for this example. "Nichola's child saw a baby frog and ran away: and when the baby frog saw Nichola's child it also ran away." A Gĩkũyũ speaking child has to get the correct tone and length of vowel and pauses to get it right. Otherwise it becomes a jumble of *k*'s and *r*'s and *na*'s [Author's note].
2. Quoted in Eric Williams *A History of the People of Trinidad and Tobago,* London 1964, p. 32 [Author's note].
3. Eric Williams, ibid., p. 31 [Author's note].
4. In references to Africa in the introduction to his lectures in *The Philosophy of History,* Hegel gives historical, philosophical, rational expression and legitimacy to every conceivable European racist myth about Africa. Africa is even denied her own geography where it does not correspond to the myth. Thus Egypt is not part of Africa; and North Africa is part of Europe. Africa proper is the especial home of ravenous beasts, snakes of all kinds. The African is not part of humanity. Only slavery to Europe can raise him, possibly, to the lower ranks of humanity. Slavery is good for the African. 'Slavery is in and for itself *injustice* for the essence of humanity is *freedom;* but for this man must be matured. The gradual abolition of slavery is therefore wiser and more equitable than its sudden removal.' (Hegel *The Philosophy of History,* Dover edition, New York: 1956, pp. 91–9.) Hegel clearly reveals himself as the nineteenth-century Hitler of the intellect [Author's note].

Schooling or Seclusion

ENID SCHILDKROUT

Of Nigeria's nineteen states, those in the Muslim north have lagged far behind the others in providing Western education. This situation has been cited as one of the causes of Nigeria's civil war, and as the basis for inequitable access to many occupational opportunities. Successive Nigerian governments have attempted to remedy this situation and in 1976 the military government launched a massive program of Universal Primary Education (UPE). The proceeds of the oil boom were to be poured into educational programs, particularly in the north, with the aim of enrolling all children in primary school by the end of the decade. But Nigeria's oil income has not met the expectations put forth in the development plan under which UPE was conceived, and the program has fallen far short of its original goals. Nevertheless, many children have started going to school and social changes are already apparent.

The dearth of Western education in the north of Nigeria before UPE was largely due to a colonial policy which specifically prohibited Christian missions—the main providers of Western education during the colonial period—from working in the north. Islamic education was, and continues to be, almost universal in the region; Islamic values have often been blamed for the "resistance" to Western education in the area. But the response to UPE clearly demonstrated that "resistance" was more apocryphal than real, at least when the education of males was in question. Families flocked in great numbers to enroll their sons in school. Those who resisted education for boys in the name of Islam were a tiny minority, usually the poorest in society.

The situation for girls is very different, however. A close look shows that it is not Islam, per se, which accounts for the resistance to Western education for girls. In fact a number of local Islamic leaders cited the writings of the 19th century reformer 'Uthman dan Fodio himself to support the notion that women should be educated. Even when Islamic ideology is used as the rationale for resisting Western education for women, the real basis for the resistance is the socioeconomic position of women, the institution of marriage as practiced in the region—and all its associated values—the roles of children which support the sexual division of labor and the restrictions under which women live. There is evidence, however, pointing to change. Not only are women beginning to go to Western school (both girls and boys attended Koranic school in the past and continue to do so), but profound changes in the social system follow this development. In order to understand these changes one must examine in some detail the division of labor in the household and the changes occurring in the traditional marriage system and in the roles of children.

Among the Hausa, the predominant linguistic and ethnic group in northern Nigeria, the Islamic practice of purdah, or seclusion, is virtually universal. In most families married women do not go outside of their homes except to obtain medical care, attend specific ceremonies (with their husband's permission), or occasionally visit relatives. In general women stay at home and depend upon children for virtually all of their communication with the outside world. Children escort women when they do go out; they shop and deliver goods and messages for women. While many women do have income-producing occupations from within the confines of purdah, such as cooking food for sale, trading raw materials, or sewing, they rely on children for procuring goods and selling their products. Street trading is a full-time occupation for many children: almost all these children are trading under the auspices of secluded women.

The enrollment of girls in school poses a severe, if indirect, threat to the institution of purdah. Since Hausa women are so dependent on children, physically removing them from the home threatens to leave women, except those wealthy enough to employ adult servants, without help. In a five-year study of the economic roles of women and children, we found that women who had children helping them with trade had significantly higher incomes than those who did not. In fact, it is in the neighborhoods where women do the most active trading that resistance to Western education for girls is most intense.

The most common reason given for the street trading activities of many Hausa girls is that the proceeds are saved for the girl's dowry. Hausa women's first marriages (many women are divorced and second marriages are less elaborate) are characterized by an extensive series of gift exchanges between the bride's and groom's families and within each family. A girl's relatives provide her with a large quantity of household goods including furniture, which comes from her father, and masses of bowls and pots, which come from female relatives and from her own earnings. These bowls are an important asset for the new bride, and they remain hers to use or sell or pass on to her own daughters. In most cases, the hawking done by young girls is seen as a means of earning this dowry.

The traditional age of marriage for Hausa girls is around eleven or twelve, although child betrothal at a younger age occurs. Most parents deem it imperative that their daughters marry by puberty; there is a great fear that delaying marriage will place the girl's chastity, and hence her marriage prospects, at risk. Since girls enter purdah upon marriage, "childhood" among Hausa girls ends by age eleven or twelve, often earlier. The notion that girls might attend school until the age of seventeen or eighteen is obviously in conflict with the values of this social and cultural system.

There are, then, three interrelated factors which explain the resistance that has been noted among the Hausa to Western education for women: the early age of marriage for girls (men marry when they are able to support their families, in their mid-twenties to early thirties), the dependence of married women on children, and the need for girls to earn money to purchase their dowries. These factors combine to make Western education and marriage appear to be alternatives to many people.

Until the mid-1970s, when attitudes began to change, most Hausa people regarded Western education for women as a very risky prospect, and few families competed for space in the existing girls' boarding schools. After the inception of UPE attitudes began to change, although not in all sectors of the population simultaneously. In those families where men already had some Western education, and where secluded women did not engage in occupations that required the constant assistance of children, girls were enrolled in school. Whereas in 1976 most people claimed that their daughters would not go to post primary school; in 1981 when we conducted a follow-up survey, most of these girls were, surprisingly, still in school.

This first generation of school attenders had not only enrolled in secondary school but had passed the traditional age of marriage. This dramatic development can be explained only with reference to local and national government policies which actively campaigned for women's education and which financed and built many boarding schools for girls. With boarding schools many families were able to accept the risk of delaying marriage. Moreover, the increase of Western education for men meant that many men were interested in women with some education.

The acceptance of Western education for women is by no means universal in northern Nigeria. In those families where education for boys is just starting, education for girls remains at least a generation behind. Moreover, in families where women actively trade with the assistance of children, resistance continues. Five years after our original study of one hundred children, we found that every girl who had not been enrolled in primary school was married and in seclusion by age twelve.

Patterns of sexual inequality are extremely entrenched in northern Nigeria. However, it is already apparent from observations over only five years that girls are being sent to school and kept there beyond the traditional age of marriage. This delays entry into purdah and gives young women a few more years to experience the nondomestic aspects of society. Such experience could lead to resistance to purdah and to a desire for higher education on the part of northern Nigerian women. Inevitably, this has long-range implications for the local and national economy; it will remove many women from occupations that service a rigid sexual division of labor and a rigid division of male and female social space. It could place women in line for jobs in the formal sector and lead to a whole sequence of demands and changes which are still quite remote from the perspective of most Third World women.

"Where's Koisa?"

Lee Cronk and Beth Leech

Although the rate of cultural change has increased tremendously in recent decades, culture change itself is nothing new. One Kenyan people, the Mukogodo, have been changing for decades, first from hunters and gatherers to herders and, more recently, to wage earners, smal-business owners, teachers, and government workers. As Cronk and Leech report, in the process of changing their subsistence they have also changed their language, religious beliefs, and much of the rest of their culture, and gained a better understanding of the world outside their home.

Koisa ole Lengei was born sometime in the 1920s in the Mukogodo hills of north-central Kenya. For the first few years of his life, he lived with his parents and sister in a cave, surviving on honey, wild plants, and wild animals as his ancestors had done for centuries.

The Mukogodo of Koisa's generation spoke a disappearing Cushitic language called Yaaku. In 1969, a German linguist, Bernd Heine, persuaded Koisa to accompany him to the University of Nairobi to teach him the old language. Koisa never came home. After a couple of weeks in Nairobi, he disappeared. Police searches turned up nothing, and Heine later hypothesized in a linguistics journal that Koisa had been killed by criminals.

Our interest in the Mukogodo began with Heine's article. We studied their history, customs, and beliefs, living among them from late 1985 to early 1987 and returning for a short stay in 1992. We went expecting to find a people in transition from the hunting and gathering way of life of Koisa's childhood to one based on raising livestock. Instead, we found a society that had completed the transition to pastoral ways and was beginning a new transition to the ways of Western technological society.

The first transformation occurred about fifty to sixty years ago, when in a period of about ten years in the 1920s and '30s, the Mukogodo changed their economy, language, and way of life from those of the cave dwellers to those of the neighboring Maasai pastoralists. It is interesting and sometimes telling to compare that transition to the one occurring today as Western ideas are brought into Mukogodo by missionaries, the Kenyan government, aid workers, and the Mukogodo themselves.

Bridewealth inflation

Koisa's homeland is a dry forest of cedar and wild olive trees covering a small, rugged range of hills. The area's many riverbeds are dry for all but a few days a year, but small permanent springs of clear water are scattered throughout the forest. On the east and north, the Mukogodo hills drop quickly to a flat, dry plain of thorny, flat-topped acacias and bushy succulents; on the west, they taper off slowly into a series of low, rocky ridges covered with short grass and cactuslike candelabra trees. On the south side, the forest ends at a wide plain of grass and small thorn trees that eventually leads to the foot of Mount Kenya.

In Koisa's childhood, the Mukogodo men, hunters and apiarists, ranged through a territory of more than five hundred square miles. Their many beehives—a man might have had twenty or more—and the hunting of hyraxes, small, woodchuck-like animals, provided most of their food. Other favorite species were buffalo, giraffe, eland, and rhinoceros.

Memories of old Mukogodo religious practices are hazy, but the tribe clearly was monotheistic. The Mukogodo believed that within their territory there were several holy places where they could more easily make

From The World & I, January 1993. Reprinted with permission.

contact with God. The most prominent of these was Ol Doinyo Lossos, at almost seven thousand feet the largest mountain in Mukogodo. On its peak, people made offerings of honey and other foods to request rain, fertility, and good health.

Although many Mukogodo now look back nostalgically on the pre-twentieth-century cave period, those who are old enough to remember it well describe a frightening world of enemies, raids, murder, and fear. The Mukogodo were militarily impotent, scattered among scores of far-flung caves in groups barely larger than nuclear families. Although they had little worth stealing, they often were the victims of larger Kenyan tribes, such as the Maasai, Samburu, and Meru. Around the turn of the century, one of their thirteen lineages was nearly wiped out by a single Meru raid.

The Mukogodo of today are Maasai-speaking herders of sheep, goats, and cattle. They almost never hunt, although they still keep a few beehives, and their territory has shrunk to less than two hundred square miles. About one thousand Mukogodo live there, along with a few hundred people from other tribes. They live in loaf-shaped, Maasai-style houses made of dung, sticks, and mud, and their diet, like that of the Maasai, includes cow blood. There are many other similarities between the two peoples: Mukogodo beads and draped clothing mimic those of the Maasai; their naming, circumcision, and marriage ceremonies follow Maasai models; and although rumors persist among neighboring tribes that the Mukogodo still speak Yaaku secretly, in fact they all speak Maa, the Maasai language.

The driving force behind the changes of the 1920s and '30s was the quest for bridewealth, the gifts a man must pay to his bride's father. Until the 1920s, few Mukogodo kept any domesticated animals. Wives were not expensive: A few beehives built from hollowed logs were enough to release a girl from her father. Around the time when Koisa was born, things began to change, Large tracts of land near Mount Kenya were appropriated for white settlement, forcing several small groups of Maasai-speaking herders into Mukogodo territory. The newcomers soon stopped raiding the Mukogodo and instead began to marry their daughters, paying livestock rather than hives for wives. Few Mukogodo fathers would pass up a chance to get such wealth, and hives were no longer accepted as payment. Soon, it became clear that without herds, no Mukogodo man would marry.

And many Mukogodo men of that period, Koisa included, never did marry. Some, like Koisa, were the last males in their lines of patrilineal descent, and the original thirteen Mukogodo lineages were reduced to eleven. Other Mukogodo men were able to obtain stock, either by trading forest products like elephant tusks and rhino horns or from the marriage of a sister. Out went Mukogodo women, in came stock and, eventually, wives from other groups.

The change was rapid and nearly total. Most of the caves were located deep in the forest, far from good pasture, and by the mid-1930s most Mukogodo had moved to nearby grasslands and built Maasai-style houses. Maasai-speaking women from the neighboring groups married into Mukogodo and raised their children to speak Maasai rather than Yaaku. The few fluent Yaaku speakers still living today—by our count, there were twelve in early 1987—express sadness and bewilderment that few Mukogodo now remember more than the old greeting of "Aichee!"

Western impact

The Mukogodo transition to pastoralism took a heavy toll on cultural traditions, but, in one sense at least, it was successful: The Mukogodo increased their number and reestablished their ability to pay for wives. The changes were necessary for their survival as a people, but it was not as a group that they decided to change. The unplanned transition came as individuals and families, one by one, began living differently. Changes taking place today in Mukogodo are a combination of this same sort of spontaneous adjustment to circumstances and a variety of deliberately planned development projects.

For some Mukogodo, the current changes amount to little more than what one aid worker calls "trouserization": Most men today wear pants, at least in town, instead of the traditional wraparound loincloth, and some women wear Western-style dresses and skirts. Many adults dress in a Western fashion but know nothing of the outside world where their clothes came from. For other Mukogodo, the new era has brought education, health care, an improved standard of living, and new ideologies. Just a few decades after new neighbors and bridewealth inflation changed the face of Mukogodo society, schools, churches, and jobs are changing it again.

Today's children will be the first generation of educated Mukogodo taught in government schools—often built and paid for by Catholic missionaries and foreign aid agencies. Six primary schools and one secondary operate in Mukogodo Division, which includes areas now dominated by non-Mukogodo people. Mukogodo children attend two of the primary institutions, and a few older boys and young men take classes at the secondary school, which opened in 1986. Many families send at least one son to primary school, and those who live close by often send most or all of their children, including daughters.

Motivational and attendance problems plague both students and staff. Parents rarely take an interest in their children's education, and even the best students may be absent as much as half the time. Many teachers consider Mukogodo a miserable assignment, and some are sent there as punishment for misconduct or incompetency in other, less remote parts of Kenya. Yet a growing number of Mukogodo are being trained as teachers and returning home to work. The headmaster of one of the primary schools is a Mukogodo. Two of his relatives teach at other institutions in the division and a third is attending a two-year teachers college.

Most Mukogodo no longer look for God atop Ol Doinyo Lossos. Four churches hold services in the Mukogodo area, though only three are attended by Mukogodo. The Catholics run the largest mission, with a church, a boarding school, and a clinic. The Anglicans also have a complex of buildings, and their services often are conducted by Mukogodo church officials. American Baptist missionaries have been active as well, setting up a church in town and training a Mukogodo lay preacher. So far, Mukogodo church attendance is dominated by a handful of families, but the ideological influence of the churches is felt even in very traditional households. One man enthusiastically recounted the "Mukogodo" myth of origin, complete with the story of Adam's rib and the fall from grace.

For the most part, foreign aid donors in Mukogodo have avoided large, capital-intensive projects, which have long been out of style in development circles, in favor of smaller, simpler projects. Some of the projects have benefitted the Mukogodo. During the drought of 1985, cornmeal from the United States helped feed many who otherwise might have starved. The Catholic mission in Don Dol runs a clinic that provides free health care to the indigent and next-to-free health care for those who can afford to pay a few cents per visit. The Catholics also have provided dormitories so that some children who live too far from a government school to walk home can receive an education.

Plagued projects

Other projects that may seem small and simple to an outsider become hopelessly complicated in a place like Mukogodo, especially when the aid workers and the local people they are helping have conflicting goals, little communication, and almost no knowledge of each other. Take the examples of the gardening classes and the rain tanks.

In 1986, Action Aid (a British non-governmental organization), the Child Welfare Society of Kenya, and the Norwegian aid agency (NORAD) sponsored the introduction of gardening classes to Mukogodo primary schools. In the words of the local NORAD worker in charge of the project, "We must teach these Maasai something about keeping a garden." What they were taught, it seems clear, is that keeping a garden in Mukogodo makes little sense. Despite the construction of heavy brush fences by project employees, the gardens were regularly ravaged by livestock and wild animals, and natural rainfall had to be supplemented by huge quantities of water hauled by donkeys. A small garden of potatoes, spinach, onions, and carrots—about ten yards in diameter—required ten gallons of water a day after the seasonal rains had stopped. That may sound like little water, but a typical Mukogodo woman with five children hauls as little as six or seven gallons (about fifty to sixty pounds) of water a day for up to several miles on her back for all her family's cooking and washing needs. NORAD and Action Aid gave the schools donkeys and plastic jerricans to haul water for the gardens, but owning a donkey is too expensive for most Mukogodo families.

In another local project, Action Aid, the Child Welfare Society, NORAD, and the Peace Corps built concrete rainwater storage tanks at several primary schools in 1985 and 1986. The goal was to provide the schools with water for cooking hot lunches and for the use of the teachers, who usually live at the schools. Although the technology and goals of the project were simple, the water tanks did not function as planned. In some cases, the gutters were mounted incorrectly, so that in a heavy rain, most of the water shot past them and onto the ground. At one school, everyone for up to a mile around came to use the water. In a few weeks, the supply that was meant to last the school several months had been depleted. The heavy use and misuse of the new tank finally wore out the faucet, rendering the entire tank useless. A replacement faucet had not been purchased when we left Mukogodo in February 1987, and the situation remained unchanged upon a return visit last year.

The construction of the new tanks also encouraged the schools to be lazy about maintenance of older, smaller tanks they already had, and at least one school ended up with no working water tanks. To make up for the water loss, the school had to obtain further funds from donors to buy another donkey, a cart, a yoke, and several more plastic jerricans to haul even more water two miles from a well.

Simple, small, and apparently promising projects can fail for reasons other than complexity or inappropriateness. In 1985, World Vision, a Christian donating agency, gave a honey refinery to the Anglican Church in Mukogodo. Given the traditional Mukogodo expertise in beekeeping, nothing could seem better suited to the area, yet the refinery never has been used. When Mukogodo have tried to sell honey to the church, they have been turned away. The reason seems to involve tribalism and religious prejudice rather than simple ineptitude. Most of the people involved with the church are Kikuyu, members of Kenya's largest tribe. The Kikuyu privately refer to the Mukogodo and other Maasai-speakers by the biblical pejorative "dogs and evildoers" because these peoples circumcise their sons and daughters. They have refused to accept the honey because they want to have as little to do with the Mukogodo beekeepers as possible.

Modern Mukogodo

Development aid projects sometimes have helped the Mukogodo in times of need, but they seldom have sparked indigenous efforts to raise the standard of living. In that regard, the Mukogodo themselves are the best development workers of all. Kelasinga LeSakui, the lay minister of the local Baptist Church, has almost singlehandedly started two cooperative businesses. The first, a small cafe that offers tea, doughnut-like *mandazis*, and, on good days, maize and beans, is doing a good business. The other, newer venture is a cooperative chicken coop. Each member contributes a few chickens, and the profits from the sale of eggs and chickens are shared. Most Mukogodo follow Maasai food taboos and find the mere idea of eating a chicken disgusting, so their sales are all to people of other tribes in the nearby town of Don Dol. But a few Mukogodo have begun to feed eggs to their children, and tastes may change within the next few decades.

Both of Kelasinga's businesses were begun without outside funds. Start-up money was supplied by the participants, a disproportionate share from Kelasinga's own pocket (he has a job with the forestry service, which administers parts of Mukogodo territory). The local Baptist missionary, Jerry Daniels, donated a couple hundred dollars for a new chicken coop several months after the cooperative was started, but he insists the original idea was Kelasinga's.

Fifty years after the transition to pastoralism and almost twenty years after Koisa's disappearance, the quest for bridewealth continues to contribute to cultural change and economic development among the Mukogodo. Young men now routinely venture beyond Don Dol to Nairobi and other Kenyan cities and towns for temporary jobs to earn money to pay for wives. Wages are low—most are employed as night watchmen at sixty to seventy-five dollars a month—and wives are expensive. A girl might cost as much as ten cows and other gifts totaling as much as two thousand dollars.

The work trips are taken in order to continue the Maasai marriage customs and social patterns, but what the men see outside Mukogodo and bring home is one of the greatest sources of new ideas and knowledge. A city offers the first glimpse of tall buildings, masses of people, electricity, unfamiliar tribes and races, telephones, movies, businesses more complex than a general store, global politics, and different social customs. Men who have seen the outside world are more likely to allow their children to attend school, and some have gotten ideas from the city that helped them start their own small businesses.

The people of Koisa ole Lengei's generation have seen the Mukogodo way of life change twice. The second of the changes is still occurring, and most of Koisa's contemporaries do not yet understand the new world of which they are now part. Those who still remember the old language rattled on in it hopefully to us in the belief that Koisa went with the linguist to the land of the white people and taught them all to speak Yaaku.

Slightly younger people made demands based on that belief. "Write your father," instructed one man in his fifties. "Write your father in America and tell him to find Koisa. Tell him to come home."

Younger Mukogodo, many of whom have worked in Nairobi and are well aware of its dangers, know better. One young father in his mid-twenties, Menye Sapukian LeLeitiko, took charge when an older woman accosted us with questions and accusations about Koisa's disappearance. LeLeitiko did not try to explain that Koisa was dead but merely that Europe, where the linguist was from, is very far from our home in America, and that Koisa clearly is not in America. The geographical knowledge was new to the woman, and it seemed to satisfy her.

LeLeitiko has high hopes for his children, two girls ages one and three. He hopes they get more education than their mother, who did not attend school, and more than the five years of school he attended. Perhaps they will get jobs as teachers and, unlike the women of today, go beyond their homes in the hills. They already know more about the world beyond Mukogodo than their forefathers ever thought possible. They know that Koisa ole Lengei is not coming home.

Change and Egyptian Bedouins

LILA ABU-LUGHOD

Although they may appear as coastal communities on a map, Bedouin groups along the northern edge of the Egyptian Western Desert orient themselves south toward the desert where, until sedentarization, their migrations had taken them. Permanent water sources attract them to the coastal region during the summer season when the desert is parched. So does the need to sow barley in the fall and harvest in early summer. Coastal towns and markets, roads and a water pipeline also exert a pull. But their nostalgia for the inland desert, "up country" is strong. Although they had last migrated seven years previous to my arrival, the members of the community in which I lived all spoke with fond recollection of the "good old days" when they spent months at a time in the desert. They described the flora and fauna, the grasses so delectable to the gazelle, the umbellifer that opens the appetite, the herb that boiled with tea cures sundry maladies, the wild hares that must be hunted at night, and the game birds that suddenly take flight from the midst of a shrub. They praised the good "dry" foods of desert life and disparaged as unhealthy the fresh vegetable stews now an important part of their diet. They remembered with pleasure the milk products so plentiful in springtime when rains have created desert pastures. They savored memories of the taste of milk given by ewes who have fed on aromatic wormwood.

Before I went to do research among the Egyptian Bedouin tribes known as Awlad 'Ali I had envisioned Bedouins as noble desert roamers living in tents and herding animals. Instead I found that these same people who touted the joys of the desert lived in houses (at least many of them did), wore wristwatches and plastic shoes, listened to radios and cassette players, and traveled in Toyota pickup trucks. They had no camel herds. Like Bedouins in other parts of the Arab world, the Bedouins in northern Egypt are settling, in part on their own and in part as a result of government development projects to encourage the trend. They are all involved in a cash economy.

To understand the meaning of plastic shoes and Toyota trucks, and the less obvious changes Awlad 'Ali have undergone in the last few decades, we need to remember that the Bedouins' fortunes have always been tied to more than the state of rainfall and pasture, despite the fact that their traditional economy was based primarily on herds of camels, sheep, and goats, supplemented by rainfed cereal cultivation along the Mediterranean coast, and a bit of trade. Their movements and livelihood were determined by internal competition with other tribal groups who shared their way of life, but also by external political and economic events including World War II, battles of which were fought on their soil. They have been affected by shifts in the relations between Libya and Egypt, not to mention the internal affairs of each state. The nomads were in contact with numerous indigenous and foreign groups who lived in the region, for whatever length of tine. Being within the borders of the Egyptian state has had more than a negligible influence on them, particularly during periods when the central government sought to extend its control. Yet, despite significant contact and changes in the Bedouin economy and lifestyle, the Bedourins have maintained a distinct identity.

In the Modern State: Development and Adaptation

The greatest challenge to the Awlad 'Ali's traditional way of life and their distinctive cultural identity has come in the last thirty years. In the 1950s Nasser's administration attempted efforts to sedentarize and exert political control over those Bedouins still living in the Western Desert. Ideological and material motives underlay the government's interest in integrating the Bedouins into the Egyptian state, economy, and national "culture."

Although military rule ended in the 1950s, special privileges regarding taxation and military conscription were revoked, a local system of government established, and the jurisdiction of the legal system extended to the area, government efforts to incorporate this province have met with only partial success. The persistence of Bedouin autonomy and values can be seen in a number of arenas. Unofficially, elections on the national parliament are still decided on the basis of tribal affiliations. Young men still try to avoid conscription into the Egyptian army by escaping to Libya or into the desert with the herds. Most disputes are settled by customary law. While serious crimes such as homicides cannot be kept from the authorities, the judgments of the state courts are still not considered valid by Bedouins. Since they want a culprit released as quickly as possible so they can settle matters according to customary law, Awlad 'Ali are often uncooperative in the courts.

In general, the Awlad 'Ali resent the government for imposing restrictions and curtailing their freedom to live their own lives and run their own affairs. Arrests and jailings carry no stigma for the Bedouins; rather they evoke self-righteous curses of the government agents responsible. Most people live outside the law, wittingly or unwittingly, smuggling, crossing closed borders, carrying unlicensed firearms, avoiding conscription, not registering births, foregoing identity papers, evading taxes and taking justice into their own hands.

More fundamental changes in the lives of the semi-nomadic desert Awald 'Ali were ushered in by government-sponsored development projects rather than political reforms. These projects have not always achieved their aims, and their effects have not always been intentional; yet, in concert with Bedouin initiatives, they have radically altered the Bedouins' basic economy and work patterns. The priorities of the government have been to settle the nomads and expand agriculture though land reclamation.

The government used several techniques to encourage the Bedouins to settle. Government cooperative societies provided subsidized food and fodder. Planners hoped that the ready availability of fodder would eliminate the need for seasonal migrations. It did, but not for the reasons they imagined. The herds increased to sizes which the desert pastures could not sustain. This limited the number of groups that could migrate and the length of time that could be spent in the desert. In the traditional economy, barley was planted in the fall. After the sowing, most family members moved to the desert pastures for a number of months, leaving behind a few people to watch the crop. In summer, the desert contingents returned to harvest the crop and to summer near the permanent water sources near the coast. Some members of each family engaged in cultivation, some in herding. With fodder provided to the animals, however, labor power was diverted from herding to agriculture. Once tractors were introduced, cultivation required less labor. As Bujra points out, this freed many "to participate in other activities outside the cultivation herding cycle"; some turned to lucrative smuggling rather than legitimate alternatives [Bujra 1973: 149].

The government also subsidized orchards of almond, olive, and fig trees. This discouraged nomadism, since orchards require more attention and protection than barley crops. With the introduction of a water pipeline along the coast, of social and medical services (however inadequate), and of employment opportunities, the attractions of the coastal settlements became harder to resist. Many Bedouins moved to the towns and cities.

The land reclamation projects in the Western Desert, mostly in Mariut, were less successful in inducing Awlad 'Ali to settle. Undertaken to increase agricultural production and to relieve population pressure in the Delta, the projects have been beset by technical and social problems. They displaced large numbers of Bedouins, overrunning their traditional grazing and watering spots, but convinced only a few to turn to farming. Even those Bedouins wealthy enough to purchase the newly-irrigated lands preferred not to remain on them. The introduction of irrigation altered the face of the desert in adjacent areas. Along with the greenery and availability of vegetables have come the less salutary mosquitoes and rats which plague those living in the Mariut area. The fevers of which many Bedouins complain are often attributed to "the coming of the water." Nor are the many strangers in the area particularly welcome.

Commercial ventures have contributed more to the sedentarization of the Bedouins and to the transformation of their traditional way of life than have government-sponsored projects. These ventures were at best indirectly encouraged by government efforts; mostly they came into collision with government plans. Trade was not new to the Awlad 'Ali. Dates, quail, and barley had been early sources of income, if only through exchange. Smuggling was not unknown. But now Bedouins participate in a cash economy. They market their animals, barley, wool, olives and olive oil, figs, and almonds. They buy much of their food and other necessities in the towns, or at daily or weekly markets. Smuggling became big business in the 1950s and many Bedouins became wealthy through it. In the 1970s, the opening of the Egyptian economy allowed the Bedouins to profit from new commercial opportunities. With the boom in the private sector, development of the northwest coast for tourism has begun. The Bedouins are now scrambling for title to coastal land so they can sell it to developers from the cities. With the proceeds from these legitimate and illegal ventures, they invest in new businesses, urban properties, agricultural land, and their herds. Sheep are still the basis of their lifestyle, if not their economy. The wealthiest men, hopping between Alexandria, Cairo and Mirsa Matruh in their Mercedes, are still judged by the size of their herds.

The new economic opportunities radically altered not just the volume but the distribution of wealth. An economy based on herds and cereal cultivation is dependent on rainfall. In a region that averages 24 inches per year and has periods of drought every seven years or so, assets are precarious. Herds can be wiped out in a season. Rain might or might not fall on a plot one had sown. Although there were always rich and poor among the Bedouins, fortunes could reverse unpredictably. Wealth could not be securely concentrated in the hands of any one person or family. Now the social stratification has become more marked and fixed. The wealthy have the capital to invest in lucrative ventures while the poor do not. Economic, political, and social status are increasingly coterminous. Formerly they were not tied: status and leadership were based more on genealogy and reputation. Wealthy merchants cannot afford a few months absence in the desert. They build houses near the roads and settle. Poorer families still try to subsist on their herds and barley and are less likely to settle. They pasture their sheep in the desert and have inland as semi-nomads. They cannot afford to buy land or build houses. But cash is essential and they usually send at least one family member to Libya to earn money. Some young men find unskilled work in the towns. The poor also depend on help from wealthier kinsmen or patrons for whom they work and from whom they receive loans and "gifts."

Yet the transformation of the social order is not as radical as it first appears. For one thing, the disintegration of the tribal system is hardly imminent. Kinship ties still cross-cut wealth differentials, and the vertical links of tribal organization overshadow horizontal links of incipient class formations. The introduction of individual ownership and control over resources is beginning to undermine the economic bases of the tribal system, but ideologically the tribe remains a powerful system. Government attempts to undermine tribalism have failed. Cooperative societies introduced by the government to break down the lineage system in fact strengthened lineage loyalties by providing new resources to be distributed [Bujra 1973:156]. Leadership was assumed by traditional lineage heads and the distribution of favors tended to follow lineage lines.

Secondly, the new wealth is often used to realize old ideals. In the past, wealth was secondary to reputation and generosity was the keystone of reputation. It was the responsibility of the wealthy to redistribute their wealth through hospitality, feasting and providing in numerous ways for the less fortunate. Although there are exceptions, people tend to use their new wealth to the same ends. A wealthy man entertains, assists kinsmen and non-kin in brideprice debts. He is expected to assist poor relations by setting them up in small businesses, like starting them off with a small herd, or including them in his own endeavors. In return he gains clients and reputation. Large families were always an ideal and now wealth is used to support larger families. People disapprove of men who use their wealth selfishly. The enhancement of physical comfort beyond a certain minimum level is the lowest priority in the use of wealth.

Just as new opportunities are used to realize old ideals, new commodities are incorporated as functional equivalents of traditional items. Probably three-quarters of the population live in houses now. Houses are prestigious, since they cost more than tents and symbolize the more urban lifestyle of the wealthy. However, Bedouins live in these houses as if they were tents. They position themselves in the open doorways where they can have a good view. Along one wall in each room is a pile of woven rugs a woman has made or inherited. These are folded and stacked neatly as they traditionally are in the tents. There is virtually no furniture and what there is is rarely used. Woven straw mats are placed wherever people plan to sit, as in the tents. Even in the most modern houses equipped with kitchens, the sinks go unused, since the water rarely runs, and the counters, cluttered with pots being stored out of reach of the children, are never used for food preparation. Modern brides require beds, yet most beds are judged so uncomfortable that they are immediately abandoned for a small mattress or a couple of blankets on the floor. By contrast, the wardrobe is a staple of Egyptian Bedouins who readily appreciate its utility as a storage facility for anything from clothing to guns to sacks of sheepfat.

Many Bedouin, in fact, pitch tents next to their houses. This is where people prefer to sit and where most daytime activities take place. People say they feel constricted in houses, even though they appreciate their utility for storage and the protection of material belongings.

The automobile and pickup truck are now popular throughout the Western Desert. Since only the wealthier men own motor vehicles, these are cherished as status objects in much the same way horses were in the past. Accordingly, the purchase of a new car occasions a sheep-sacrifice and a trip to the holyman to get a protective amulet to hang on the rearview mirror. Men are identified by and with their cars. They want to be photographed with them. In young girls' playful rhyming ditties, young men are referred to not by name but by the color or make of the cars they drive, as in the following two examples:

Welcome you who drives a Jeep
I'd make you tea with milk if it weren't shameful

Toyotas when they first appeared
brought life's light then disappeared

Like their animate antecedents, cars are used not just for transport but for ritual. Brides used to be carried from their natal homes to the grooms' in a litter mounted on a camel. Accompanying them were men and women riding on horses, donkeys, or whatever could be mustered, singing, dancing, and firing rifles. Now, although the size of the bridal procession is equally important, its composition has changed; Toyotas, Datsuns, and Peugeots race. The bride rides in a car with a red blanket on the roof, perhaps in imitation of the litter.

Conclusion

The Bedouins' sense of cultural identity remains strong. It is true that most Bedouin men are at least aware of events in the world political arena, and some hold opinions on the relative merits of the superpowers. They have some knowledge of Egypt's positions and international involvements. But their passions are only truly aroused by tribal affairs—intra-Bedouin disputes, reconciliations, alliances and hostilities. The Bedouins may listen to the radio and hear Egyptian programs, but their excitement is reserved for one radio program called *Iskandanyya-Matruuh* (Alexandria-Matruh). Once a week they crowd around small radios and listen with rapt attention and visible enjoyment to this program which features traditional Bedouin songs, poems, and greetings for various parties, all identified by name and tribal affiliation.

Dr. Abou-Zeid's sanguine prediction made in 1959 about the impact government development projects would have on the Awlad 'Ali rings hollow nearly twenty-five years later. He wrote:

But the crowning achievement of these projects will be the reduction of the cultural and social contrast which exists at present between the Western Desert, with its nomadic and semi-nomadic inhabitants, and the rest of the country. This contrast is manifested in the different patterns of social relationships, the different values and modes of thought, and the different structure prevailing in the desert and the Nile Valley [Abou-Zeid 1959:558].

Bedouin identity is tied to tribal ideology and a standard of morality based on honor and modesty. By means of these values Awlad 'Ali still distinguish themselves from and feel superior to foreigners and other Egyptians, peasant and urban. Thus the most visible changes in their mode of life, from plastic shoes, to houses, to Toyotas, do not signal the disintegration of their culture and society, although they may be part of a more fundamental transformation which will eventually erode the social bases of this ideology.

References

Abou-Zeid, A. H. 1959 *The Sedentarization of Nomads in the Western Desert of Egypt.* UNESCO International Social Science Journal 11:550–558.
Buira, A. S. 1973 "The Social Implications of Developmental Policies: A Case Study from Egypt" in *The Desert and the Soren.* C. Nelson, ed. Institute of International Studies, University of California, Berkeley.

Africa and Oceania

Oceania

Topics Covered in Class

Types of Islands
Three Culture Areas
Polynesia, Micronesia, Melanesia
Historical Experience
Recent Themes
Contemporary Issues

About the Readings

The Pacific Islands were the last big area on Earth to be settled. Today the large cultural area of Oceania is divided in three different culture areas, Polynesia, Micronesia, and Melanesia. Many of people living on these islands have experienced very rapid change in just three generations. The outside world did not even know that the interior of the island of New Guinea was actually inhabited until the 1940's. Many anthropologists went to New Guinea to do fieldwork in the 1960s and 70s, hoping to find groups that had had little or no contact with the outside world. Richard Sorenson was one of those anthropologists. He began his study of the Fore in the early 1960s, and at that time the Fore had already begun to change. In 1977, Sorenson wrote the now classic article about the Fore, "Growing Up Fore Is to Be 'In Touch' and Free." The Fore were a horticultural group living in the highlands of New Guinea. After a road was built and they were exposed to Western culture the Fore began to change very rapidly. According to the author this change was a result of the Fore childrearing customs that produced children predisposed to taking on new adventures and exploring new opportunities. That's exactly what the Fore did after contact. The article provides a good illustration of the concepts introduced in Unit I: cultural integration, culture clash, and the ripple effect.

Growing Up as a Fore Is to Be 'In Touch' and Free

E. RICHARD SORENSON

Untouched by the outside world, they had lived for thousands of years in isolated mountains and valleys deep in the interior of Papua New Guinea. They had no cloth, no metal, no money, no idea that their homeland was an island or that what surrounded it was salt water. Yet the Fore (for'ay) people had developed remarkable and sophisticated approaches to human relations, and their child-rearing practices gave their young unusual freedom to explore. Successful as hunter-gatherers and as subsistence gardeners, they also had great adaptability, which brought rapid accommodation with the outside world after their lands were opened up.

It was alone that I first visited the Fore in 1963—a day's walk from a recently built airstrip. I stayed six months. Perplexed and fascinated, I returned six times in the next ten years, eventually spending a year and a half living with them in their hamlets.

Theirs was a way of life different from anything I had seen or heard about before. There were no chiefs, patriarchs, priests, medicine men or the like. A striking personal freedom was enjoyed even by the very young, who could move about at will and be where or with whom they liked. Infants rarely cried, and they played confidently with knives, axes, and fire. Conflict between old and young did not arise; there was "no generation gap."

Older children enjoyed deferring to the interests and desires of the younger, and sibling rivalry was virtually undetectable. A responsive sixth sense seemed to attune the Fore hamlet mates to each other's interests and needs. They did not have to directly ask, inveigle, bargain or speak out for what they needed or wanted. Subtle, even fleeting expressions of interest, desire, and discomfort were quickly read and helpfully acted on by one's associates. This spontaneous urge to share food, affection, work, trust, tools, and pleasure was the social cement that held the Fore hamlets together. It was a pleasant way of life, for one could always be with those with whom one got along well.

Ranging and planting, sharing, and living, the Fore diverged and expanded through high virgin lands in a pioneer region. They hunted out their gardens, tilled them while they lasted, then hunted again. Moving ever away from lands peopled and used they had a self-contained life with its own special ways.

The underlying ecological conditions were like those that must have encompassed the world before agriculture set its imprint so broadly. Abutting the Fore was virtually unlimited virgin land, and they had food plants they could introduce into it. Like hunter-gatherers they sought their sources of sustenance first in one locale and then another, across an extended range, following opportunities provided by a providential nature. But like agriculturalists they concentrated their effort and attention more narrowly on selected sites of production, on their gardens. They were both seekers and producers. A pioneer people in a pioneer land, they ranged freely into a vast territory, but they planted to live.

Cooperative groups formed hamlets and gardened together. When the fertility of a garden declined, they abandoned it. Grass sprung up to cover these abandoned sites of earlier cultivation, and, as the Fore moved on to other parts of the forest, they left uninhabited grasslands to mark their passage.

The traditional hamlets were small, with a rather fluid system of social relations. A single large men's house provided shelter for 10 to 20 men and boys and their visiting friends. The several smaller women's houses each normally sheltered two married women, their unmarried daughters and their sons up to about six years of age. Formal kinship bonds were less important than friendship was. Fraternal "gangs" of youths formed the hamlets; their "clubhouses" were the men's houses.

During the day the gardens became the center of life. Hamlets were virtually deserted as friends, relatives and children went to one or more garden plots to mingle their social, economic and erotic pursuits in a pleasant and emotionally filled Gestalt of garden life. The boys and unmarried youths preferred to explore and hunt in the outlying lands, but they also passed through and tarried in the gardens.

Daily activities were not scheduled. No one made demands, and the land was bountiful. Not surprisingly the line between work and play was never clear. The transmission of the Fore behavioral pattern to the young began in early infancy during a period of unceasing human physical contact. The effect of being constantly "in touch" with hamlet mates and their daily life seemed to start a process which proceeded by degrees: close rapport, involvement in regular activity, ability to handle seemingly dangerous implements safely, and responsible freedom to pursue individual interests at will without danger.

While very young, infants remained in almost continuous bodily contact with their mother, her house mates or her gardening associates. At first, mothers' laps were the center of activity, and infants occupied themselves there by nursing, sleeping, and playing with their own bodies or those of their caretakers. They were not put aside for the sake of other activities, as when food was being prepared or heavy loads were being carried. Remaining in close, uninterrupted physical contact with those around them, their basic needs such as rest, nourishment, stimulation, and security were continuously satisfied without obstacle.

By being physically in touch from their earliest days, Fore youngsters learned to communicate needs, desires and feelings through a body language of touch and response that developed before speech. This opened the door to a much closer rapport with those around them than otherwise would have been possible, and led ultimately to the Fore brand of social cement and the sixth sense that bound groups together through spontaneous, responsive sharing.

As the infant's awareness increased, his interests broadened to the things his mother and other caretakers did and to the objects and materials they used. Then these youngsters began crawling out to explore things that attracted their attention. By the time they were toddling, their interests continually took them on short sorties to nearby objects and persons. As soon as they could walk well, the excursions extended to the entire hamlet and its gardens, and then beyond with other children. Developing without interference or supervision, this personal exploratory learning quest freely touched on whatever was around, even axes, knives, machetes, fire, and the like. When I first went to the Fore, I was aghast.

Eventually I discovered that this capability emerged naturally from Fore infant-handling practices in their milieu of close human physical proximity and tactile interaction. Because touch and bodily contact lend themselves naturally to satisfying the basic needs of young children, an early kind of communicative experience fostered cooperative interaction between infants and their caretakers, also kinesthetic contact with the activities at hand. This made it easy for them to learn the appropriate handling of the tools of life.

The early pattern of exploratory activity included frequent return to one of the "mothers." Serving as home base, the bastion of security, a woman might occasionally give the youngster a nod of encouragement, if he glanced in her direction with uncertainty. Yet rarely did the women attempt to control or direct, nor did they participate in the child's quests or jaunts.

As a result Fore children did not have to adjust to rule and schedule in order to find their place in life. They could pursue their interests and whims wherever they might lead and still be part of a richly responsive world of human touch which constantly provided sustenance, comfort, diversion, and security.

Learning proceeded during the course of pursing interests and exploring. Constantly in touch with people who were busy with daily activities, the Fore young quickly learned the skills of the life from example. Muscle tone, movement, and mood were components of this learning process; formal lessons and commands were not. Kinesthetic skills developed so quickly that infants were able to causally handle knives and similar objects before they could walk.

Even after several visits I continued to be surprised that the unsupervised Fore toddlers did not recklessly thrust themselves into unappreciated dangers, the way our own children tend to do. But then, why should they? From their earliest days, they enjoyed a benevolent sanctuary from which the world could be confidently viewed, tested and appreciated. This sanctuary remained ever available, but did not demand, restrain or impose. One could go and come at will.

In close harmony with their source of life, the Fore young were able confidently, not furtively, to extend their inquiry. They could widen their understanding as they chose. There was no need to play tricks or deceive in order to pursue life.

Emerging from this early childhood was a freely ranging young child rather in tune with his older and younger hamlet mates, disinclined to act out impulsively, and with a capable appreciation of the properties of potentially dangerous objects. Such children could be permitted to move out on their own, unsupervised and unrestricted. They were safe.

Such a pattern could persist indefinitely, re-creating itself in each new generation. However, hidden within the receptive character it produced was an Achilles heel; it also permitted adoption of new practices, including child-handling practices, which did not act to perpetuate the pattern. In only one generation after Western contact, the cycle of Fore life was broken.

Attuned as they were to individual pursuit of economic and social good, it did not take the Fore long to recognize the value of the new materials, practices and ideas that began to flow in. Indeed, change began almost immediately with efforts to obtain steel axes, salt, medicine, and cloth. The Fore were quick to shed indigenous practices in favor of Western example. They rapidly altered their ways to adapt to Western law, government, religion, materials and trade.

Sometimes change was so rapid that many people seemed to be afflicted by a kind of cultural shock. An anomie, even cultural amnesia, seemed to pervade some hamlets for a time. There were individuals who appeared temporarily to have lost memory of recent past events. Some Fore even forgot what type and style of traditional garments they had worn only a few years earlier, or that they had used stone axes and had eaten their dead close relatives.

Remarkably open-minded, the Fore so readily accepted reformulation of identity and practice that suggestion or example by the new government officers, missionaries and scientists could alter tribal affiliation, place names, conduct and hamlet style. When the first Australian patrol officer began to map the region in 1957, an error in communication led him to refer to these people as the "Fore." Actually they had had no name for themselves and the word, Fore, was their name for a quite different group, the Awa, who spoke another language and lived in another valley. They did not correct the patrol officer but adopted his usage. They all now refer to themselves as the Fore. Regional and even personal names changed just as readily.

More than anything else, it was the completion of a steep, rough, always muddy Jeep road into the Fore lands that undermined the traditional life. Almost overnight their isolated region was opened. Hamlets began to move down from their ridgetop sites in order to be nearer the road, consolidating with others.

The power of the road is hard to overestimate. It was a great artery where only restricted capillaries had existed before. And down this artery came a flood of new goods, new ideas and new people. This new road, often impassable even with four-wheel-drive vehicles, was perhaps the single most dramatic stroke wrought by the government. It was to the Fore an opening to a new world. As they began to use the road, they started to shed traditions evolved in the protective insularity of their mountain fastness, to adopt in their stead an emerging market culture.

The Coming of the Coffee Economy

"Walkabout," nonexistent as an institution before contact, quickly became an accepted way of life. Fore boys began to roam hundreds of miles from their homeland in the quest for new experience, trade goods, jobs, and money. Like the classic practice of the Australian aborigine, this "walkabout" took one away from his home for periods of varying length. But unlike the Australian practice, it usually took the boys to jobs and schools rather than a solitary life in traditional lands. Obviously it sprang from the earlier pattern of individual freedom to pursue personal interests and opportunity wherever it might lead. It was a new expression of the old Fore exploratory pattern.

Some boys did not roam far, whereas others found ways to go to distant cities. The roaming boys often sought places where they might be welcomed as visitors, workers or students for a while. Mission stations and schools, plantation work camps, and the servants' quarters of the European population became way-stations in the lives of the modernizing Fore boys.

Some took jobs on coffee plantations. Impressed by the care and attention lavished on coffee by European planters and by the money they saw paid to coffee growers, these young Fore workers returned home with coffee beans to plant.

Coffee grew well on the Fore hillsides, and in the mid-1960s, when the first sizable crop matured, Fore who previously had felt lucky to earn a few dollars found themselves able to earn a few hundred dollars. A rush to coffee ensued, and when the new gardens became productive a few years later, the Fore income from coffee jumped to a quarter of a million dollars a year. The coffee revolution was established.

At first the coffee was carried on the backs of its growers (sometimes for several days) over steep, rough mountain trails to a place where it could be sold to a buyer with a jeep. However, as more and more coffee was produced, the villagers began to turn with efforts to planning and constructing roads in association with neighboring villages. The newly built roads, in turn, stimulated further economic development and the opening of new trade stores throughout the region.

Following European example, the segregated collective men's and women's houses were abandoned. Family houses were adopted. This changed the social and territorial arena for all the young children, who hitherto had been accustomed to living equally with many members of their hamlet. It gave them a narrower place to belong, and it made them more distinctly someone's children. Uncomfortable in the family houses, boys who had grown up in a freer territory began to gather in "boys' houses," away from the adult men who were now beginning to live in family houses with their wives. Mothers began to wear blouses, altering the early freer access to the breast. Episodes of infant and child frustration, not seen in traditional Fore hamlets, began to take place along with repeated incidents of anger, withdrawal, aggressiveness and stinginess.

So Western technology worked its magic on the Fore, its powerful materials and practices quickly shattering their isolated autonomy and life-style. It took only a few years from the time Western intruders built their first grass-thatched patrol station before the Fore way of life they found was gone.

Fortunately, enough of the Fore traditional ways were systematically documented on film to reveal how unique a flower of human creation they were. Like nothing else, film made it possible to see the behavioral patterns of this way of life. The visual record, once made, captured data which was unnoticed and unanticipated at the time of filming and which was simply impossible to study without such records. Difficult-to-spot subtle patterns and fleeting nuances of manner, mood and human relations emerged by use of repeated reexamination of related incidents, sometimes by slow motion and stopped frame. Eventually the characteristic behavioral patterns of Fore life became clear, and an important aspect of human adaptive creation was revealed.

The Fore way of life was only one of the many natural experiments in living that have come into being through thousands of years of independent development in the world. The Fore way is now gone; those which remain are threatened. Under the impact of modern technology and commerce, the entire world is now rapidly becoming one system. By the year 2000 all the independent natural experiments that have come into being during the world's history will be merging into a single world system.

One of the great tragedies of our modern time may be that most of these independent experiments in living are disappearing before we can discover the implication of their special expressions of human possibility. Ironically, the same technology responsible for the worldwide cultural convergence has also provided the means by which we may capture detailed visual records of the yet remaining independent cultures. The question is whether we will be able to seize this never-to-be repeated opportunity. Soon it will be too late. Yet, obviously, increasing our understanding of the behavioral repertoire of humankind would strengthen our ability to improve life in the world.

Tasmania, Australia, Japan and Conclusions

Topics Covered in Class

Tasmania
> The Tasmanian Extinction
> Genocide

Australia
> Terra Nullius
> The Lost Generations
> Forced Assimilation

Japan
> Early History
> The Shogunate
> Isolationism
> Meiji Restoration
> WW II/ The Occupation
> Article 9
> Japan Today

About the Readings

The worst thing that can happen when two cultures come into contact with each other is genocide, the killing off of one group by another. The past century is probably the genocidal in known world history. Most recent cases of genocide have involved groups of people who have lived as neighbors for generations and then turn on each other. The most complete and rapid case of genocide is associated with a contact event. It occurred on the island of Tasmania. From 1800 to 1876 an entire aboriginal population was wiped out by a combination on British colonial policies.

Many British settlers in Australia envied the settlers in Tasmania for "getting rid of their aborigine problem." Australia was much larger than Tasmania and so was its native population. The Australians instituted many policies that resembled those that we have seen in the United States and elsewhere.

One of these policies was forced assimilation in the form of boarding schools and adoptions. Aboriginal children were taken away from their families and adopted by white families or placed in boarding schools.

These children are called the "Lost Generation". As many as 100,000 children were taken from their homes. In the article, Stolen Girlhoods, Christine Cheater tells the story of girls that were placed in boarding schools. She documents both their experiences and their resistance.

I have saved Japan for the end of the semester, because it has a very different history of contact with the West. European powers never colonized Japan. The Japanese saw themselves as the civilized peoples and the Europeans as the barbarians. For two centuries after contact, Japan managed to effectively isolate itself from European and American influence. In the 1850s the United States forced Japan into a trade relationship and changes began to accumulate. The Japanese had a strong military at this time. They were also ardent nationalists who realized that they had to modernize and industrialize. Even though Japan has heavily borrowed from the West, they have distinctively stayed Japanese. Today, Japan is the only Non-Western nation classified as First World.

We are all aware of the global leadership role that Japan plays today both economically and politically. We often think of how much Japan has "Westernized" since after WWII. However, we often overlook the impact to the spread of Japanese culture to other parts of the world. In Unit I, we read the article on the globalization of Japanese cuisine, sushi. Despite the fact that sushi is now popular all over the world, it remains associated with its Japanese origins. Japanese popular cultural exports are almost too numerous to mention. Those that students are most familiar with are probably anime (i.e., Speed Racer), karaoke, and transformers. Hip-Hop in Japan is a great example of the globalization and localization of popular culture. Ian Condry is an anthropologist who did field research on Hip-Hop culture in Japan. Part of his research was as a participant observer attending Hip-Hop clubs in Tokyo's Little Harlem. It is a good example of diffusion including the two important aspects of the concept—borrowing and incorporation. The article explores how this distinctively American import both affirms and challenges modern Japanese culture.

Throughout the text you have read about many incidents of culture contact. There are many commonalities and many differences. You have seen the themes of modernization, commercialization, religious revitalization, globalization, and localization repeated over and over again in different context. You have seen a change in Western attitudes to Non-Western cultures and a change in their attitudes toward us. The final section reflects on some of these changes.

Stolen Girlhood
Australia's Assimilation Policies and Aboriginal Girls

CHRISTINE CHEATER

In Darlene Johnson's short film *Two Bob Mermaid*,[1] an Australian Aboriginal mother peers through a wire fence watching her daughter, the two-bob mermaid, as she swims in the whites-only pool in Moree in northern New South Wales. The two-bob mermaid is pale skinned: she can pass as a white girl. As she leaves the pool with her white friends, a group of Aboriginal girls call out "Tidda" (or sister), a reminder of her hidden identity.[2] Like most of the creative works produced by Australia's Aboriginal people, *Two Bob Mermaid* is semiautobiographical. The Aboriginal mother is Darlene Johnson's grandmother, and the girl who passes for white is her mother. The film is a statement about the impact of racism on the lives of the women in her family. Swimming in the whites-only pool was an act of defiance, a brief chance to experience the privileges of a white girl that ended when the New South Wales Aboriginal Protection Board removed Johnson's mother from her family and sent her to live in a girls' home. Johnson suffered a similar fate, as did many Aboriginal girls. Some families suffered through three or four generations of child removal by the various Australian states.

This treatment resulted from the girls' standing as young members of a colonized people. From the first years of British colonization, Aboriginal Australians were viewed as an impediment to the successful settlement of the country and, after 1901, as a stain on Australia's projected image as a white nation.[3] According to historian Russell McGregor, solutions to what was termed the "Aboriginal problem" ranged from violence, to protection, to assimilation.[4] Aboriginal children became the focus of Australia's assimilation policies, because British officials thought that the way to break Australian Aboriginal culture was to break the link between parent and child. As other authors in this volume, especially Nancy Stockdale and Corrie Decker, have shown, this attitude influenced the treatment of indigenous children in many British dominions and became the guiding principal of assimilation policies in all the Australian states until the 1960s.[5] State governments defined Aboriginality according to physical appearance and lifestyle. Any person who looked Aboriginal, who lived in an Aboriginal community, or who socialized with other Aboriginal people required assimilation into mainstream society. Authorities thought that the fastest way to achieve this end was to remove children, especially female children of mixed descent, from their families.

Across Australia, authorities singled out children like Darlene Johnson and her mother because they could pass for white but continued to identify and socialize with other members of Moree's Aboriginal community. By removing these children from their families, authorities hoped to break their links with Aboriginal communities and thereby facilitate their absorption into white society. Similar practices occurred in other settler states, such as the Native boarding systems in North America, but in Australian states they were taken to extremes. In one of the first studies of the impact of assimilation policies on Aboriginal families, historian Peter Read called children who were removed from their families and placed in institutional or foster care "the stolen generations."[6] He found that even children who were not taken lived with the constant threat of permanent separation from their parents or of losing a sibling.

Since Read's study, the impact of child removal has become a dominant theme both in Australian Aboriginal studies and in the history of Australian childhood. In 1994, a nationwide judicial inquiry on "the stolen generations" estimated that around 20 percent of Australia's Aboriginal children were removed from their families and recommended the gathering of oral histories from the people involved.[7] The result was an oral history collection of 340 interviews conducted with removed children, their families, welfare workers; and

Cheater, Christine, "Stolen Girlhood: Australia's Assimilation Policies and Aboriginal Girls" in *Girlhood: A Global History*, edited by Jennifer Helgren and Colleen A. Vasconcellos (New Brunswick: Rutgers University Press, 2010), 250-266.

policy makers.[8] These interviews reveal that although each Australian state developed separate assimilation policies, these policies and their impact on the lives of Aboriginal children followed similar trajectories.[9]

In this chapter I draw on these oral histories, along with the memoirs of four Aboriginal women, to reveal the experiences of girls trapped by the assimilation process. According to historian Heather Goodall, the majority of Aboriginal children removed from their families before the 1950s were girls.[10] Although Goodall based her observations on data from New South Wales, similar trends occurred in the other Australia states. To explain why girls bore the brunt of the assimilation polices, I first analyze the historical context in which these policies were developed between 1890 and 1950, and argue that anxiety about the girls' sexual behavior and demands for cheap domestic servants caused authorities to remove girls in higher numbers than boys. Second, I examine policy implementation and its impact on the lives of Aboriginal girls. Although removal disrupted girls' childhoods and their emotional well-being, they found ways to resist, forming bonds with one another and taking advantage of opportunities to be themselves.

Australian Protection and Assimilation Policies

The Australian states developed separate Aboriginal welfare policies, but they copied each other's legislation and were imbued with similar ideologies. The philosophical underpinning of their policies was inherited from their British founders, who thought that civilizing or Christianizing Australia's Aboriginal people would lift them from their savage state, teach them the virtue and advantages of good work habits, and eventually turn them into useful members of colonial society. The training of children featured strongly in their thinking in that both Christian and enlightenment philosophies viewed children as more malleable than adults and therefore more easily civilized. Settlers countered these views by observing that Aboriginal children who had been taken in by white families threw off their clothes and reverted to savagery when they rejoined their communities. High mortality rates among Aboriginal communities in contact with white society further fueled the settlers' belief that that the Aborigines were members of a primitive race heading toward extinction and that attempts to assimilate them were futile.[11]

Australian state governments aligned Aboriginal communities with other groups of people who required constant supervision, such as criminals, the diseased, the disabled, and the insane. They appointed Aboriginal Protection Officers who acted in loco parentis for Aboriginal people and had the power to remove any Aboriginal child deemed in physical or "moral" danger, the blanket excuse used when taking children from their families.[12] Under the guise of protecting Aboriginal people from the vices of white society and their own inadequacies, protection officers confined Aboriginal people to camps on the edges of country towns or placed them on church- or state-run reserves. Most of these areas were controlled by a superintendent, who drew up arbitrary rules of behavior, enforced standards of cleanliness, issued rations, decided when medical help was needed, and regulated movement in and out of the missions.[13]

In the 1890s, anthropologists noted that although the numbers of so-called full-blood Aborigines were declining, the numbers of "half-castes" were increasing.[14] At the same time, state governments became concerned that the birth rate was declining among white middle-class women, leading to white fears that Australia was in danger of becoming a nation of the "feebleminded." Included among the feebleminded were the rising numbers of "half-caste," "quadroon," "octoroon," or "yellow" children in rural areas. Supposedly the small number of white women in remote rural towns, the large number of lonely men, and sexually promiscuous Aboriginal women caused this problem.[15] In response, authorities designed policies to curtail miscegenation by controlling the movement of Aboriginal women. Women who found work in white communities needed papers to leave the mission and had to ask permission if they wanted to return to visit their families. Aboriginal women who remained on the mission lived under the constant threat of family dislocation, a threat that was used to control dissent.[16] The ultimate threat was the removal of children, who were then either placed in the mission's dormitory or sent to children's institutions or foster homes.

Initially authorities modeled the institutionalization of Aboriginal children on North American and Canadian Native American assimilation schools, but over time the permanent separation of children from their families became common practice. To make escape difficult, children were sent to homes on the other side of the state. Their names were changed, they were told their parents did not want them, and they were punished if they talked about their homes or spoke their native tongue. Siblings were separated according to age and gender, or according to the discretion of protection officers. Parents' attempts to trace their children were thwarted, and those who persisted were branded as troublemakers and subject to separation from their spouses, imprisonment, or exile to another mission.

Authorities justified these actions on the grounds that Aboriginal parents were unable to provide a moral upbringing for the children or to care for them financially, but in truth they were concerned about solving the "half-caste" problem. In addition to controlling miscegenation, authorities wanted to ensure that "half-castes" did not become a drain on state finances. Therefore, "half-caste" children had to be trained to be productive members of society, and the easiest way to achieve this goal was to place children in institutions where they could learn a trade. Most commentators agreed that it would be easy to assimilate children of mixed descent into the lower levels of white society. Because history had shown that Aboriginal children reverted to traditional behaviors if returned to their parents, removal would be permanent.

A two-tiered welfare system emerged—one level promoted the protection of "full-bloods," and the other level controlled the assimilation of "half-castes." Such distinctions, however, were arbitrary, based on perceived levels of acculturation as defined by white authorities. Aboriginal people who lived in remote northern communities and had little contact with white people were "full-bloods" in need of protection, whereas Aboriginal people who lived in southern regions, near towns, or who had regular contact with white people were "half-castes" in need of assimilation.

Protecting Aboriginal Girls

Child removal policies targeted girls in higher numbers than boys for various interrelated reasons, namely, the girls' sexual vulnerability, the authorities' desire to whiten the Aboriginal population through appropriate marriages, and an ongoing demand for cheap domestic servants. Generally girls were perceived to be in greater moral danger than boys. Until the early twentieth century, white men outnumbered white women in Australia's frontier settlements by as many as ten to one, and white men in these settlements often kidnapped or formed liaisons with Aboriginal girls.[17] Because many white men were of the opinion that Aboriginal women peaked, in looks and sexual maturity, around the age of eighteen, girls seized for this purpose were often between twelve and eighteen years of age, with some as young as nine. Attempts to ban cross-racial liaisons proved ineffectual. Often stockmen disguised the girls in men's clothing and passed them off as "drover's boys," making it easy for authorities to ignore the situation. In remote areas, police officers were usually single men who frequently used their position to coerce sexual favors. If a situation did gain public attention, district magistrates only reluctantly prosecuted offenders. In response, official inquiries into the problem urged the removal of young Aboriginal women and girls from the communities.[18]

Taking on the role of the girls' protectors, the states removed girls to remote mission stations or institutions where they could be protected while learning a useful trade. In his 1899 annual report, Walter Roth, protector of Aborigines in north Queensland, noted that girls were "tampered with by unscrupulous whites" and thus needed to be "protected by the missionaries, and, through them, by the State. [Otherwise] they are sent back to their camps as bad girls and left there to ultimate disease and ruin."[19] In 1902, Roth reinforced his views, stating that half-caste girls living in native camps on cattle stations should be removed to mission stations or reformatories, and on no account should girls be sent to male-only residences because such placements offered no protection from white bosses.[20]

Although government officials promoted the notion that girls needed to be protected from the corrupting influence of unscrupulous white men, the settlers claimed that girls welcomed their attention. One cattleman complained that the girls' presence made it impossible to hire young white men, as the girls soon "dragged them down to their level."[21] White women echoed these concerns. According to historian Ann McGrath, "White women were shocked by the black woman's more open approach to sex and felt threatened by white men's interests."[22] They perceived adolescent girls as acting in a flirtatious and overtly sexual manner and blamed the girls' parents for encouraging them. Such feelings were particularly evident among the white women who moved onto remote pastoral stations and faced the possibility that their husbands had formed relationships with adolescent girls and that some of the children on the station might be his.

As a result, settlers demanded that Aboriginal girls be removed to institutions where they could be socialized and taught virtuous behavior. Meanwhile authorities, worried that sexual promiscuity would increase the
number of half-castes in rural regions, supported policies that explicitly aimed to control the sexual activity of
fertile Aboriginal women by removing the girls from their families before they reached puberty. Goodall estimates that between 1912 and 1921, 81 percent of child removals in New South Wales were girls removed for
this reason.[23] These girls were placed in single-sex institutions where they were cut off from all contact with
parents and communities while being trained to work as domestic servants. Through these means, authorities
hoped to socialize the girls into becoming chaste, pliable women who conformed to Christian ideals of womanhood and who would pass these values on to the next generation.

The less-populated northern states expressed similar concerns. From the 1930s, assimilation policies in
Queensland, the Northern Territory, and Western Australia revolved around the removal of half-caste children (mainly girls) from their families. Through an ironic twist of reasoning and one that reveals their eugenic
ambitions, authorities here encouraged institutionalized girls to marry either light-skinned half-caste men or
lower-class white men. Marriage to lower-class white men alleviated the shortage of single white women in
rural areas and provided a morally sanctioned outlet for the men's natural urges. Marriage to light-skinned
half-castes, if continued across a number of generations, would gradually whiten the Aboriginal population
and "breed out the colour."[24]

Historian Russell McGregor has labeled these tactics "Civilisation by Blood."[25] They were designed to
transform Australia into a white nation through the gradual bleaching of the Aboriginal population.[26] The
control of Aboriginal women and girls was central to this process. Beginning in the 1930s, no Aboriginal
women could marry without the permission of Aboriginal protectors or mission superintendents who vetted
their choice of husband. Although whites had blamed Aboriginal women for the rise in the number of half-
castes, they also believed that young girls could be trained to control their sexuality and develop the habits of
respectable women if they were isolated from the corrupting influences of their families.

In a debate on the issue in 1936, a Western Australia member of Parliament summed up popular opinion
on the treatment of half-caste children and the reasons why it was necessary to remove girls from their families:

> We contaminated their blood and there is an obligation on us to see that the half-castes, at least, have
> an opportunity to earn a living, I refer particularly to the girls. . . . I understand that up to the age of
> eight, nine or ten, half-caste-children are capable of learning well at school. From then on to the age
> of puberty—and that is the dangerous time—they need to be taught other things, most important mat-
> ters being . . . sex questions and cleanliness. They should be given a reasonable education and trained
> to take their place as domestics in the homes of white people.

Their removal to foster homes or institutions was necessary because "the native girl is a child of nature, and
her character is not sufficiently strong to withstand the urge of nature."[27]

The idea that half-caste girls should be trained as domestic servants was another underlying reason why
girls were removed in larger numbers than boys. As Australia industrialized, white working-class women
moved out of low paid domestic service and into the factories, leaving white middle-class women struggling
to find suitable domestic servants. Women living on pastoral stations in rural areas felt the shortages most.
They not only were responsible for running the household but also were expected to help manage the property. Moreover, medical experts warned that in the heat of the tropics, too much heavy work would undermine
a white woman's health and fertility. In these regions, middle-class white women took in Aboriginal girls to
help with domestic or farm chores, accepting that it was their duty to train the girls to be good housekeepers
and to control their sexual behavior. Their motivations were also self-serving. They needed domestic servants
and feared that, if left unsupervised, the Aboriginal girls, with their supposed loose morals, would attract the
men of the household.

In southern regions, Aboriginal Protection Boards used the shortage of domestic servants to secure employment for Aboriginal girls in controlled, low-paid positions. The boards viewed domestic service as good
training in housekeeping and as an efficient means of injecting white values into Aboriginal communities. For
instance, the New South Wales Protection Board expressed the hope that "having been removed from the en-

vironment of camp life at a fairly early age, trained and placed in first class private homes, the result must be that the standards of life of this younger generation will be superior to those of their parents, thus paving the way for the general absorption of these people into the general population."[28] Consequently the boards placed institutionalized girls in domestic service during their adolescent years.

Girls bound into this form of indentured labor were usually between fourteen and twenty-one years old. Authorities viewed adolescent Aboriginal girls as semi-mature adults. They were sexually mature and capable of adult work, but because of their perceived childlike attributes they had to be guided into suitable work. Domestic service, under the supervision of good housewives, seemed an ideal solution. It trained the girls in skills suited to their level of intelligence while alleviating the ongoing shortage of white women willing to work as domestic servants.[29] The Protection Boards relied on the housewives to protect the girls, but in many instances the boards were returning the girls to the same "moral dangers" used to justify their removal from their communities.

The boards did little to protect the girls from the unwanted attentions of male members of the household. Instead, board members asserted that respectable middle-class white men would not be attracted to Aboriginal girls without provocation. If the girls complained, they were called liars and moved to another position. The boards attributed any pregnancy to the low moral character of the girl. Thus pregnant girls, some as young as fourteen, were returned to an institution or placed in a reformatory. When their babies reached the age of two or three, the girls were sent to another position while the babies remained in the institution, thereby perpetuating the next generation of child removal.

Assimilating Aboriginal Girls

Once caught in the assimilation system, a girl suffered psychological distress and disruption of her childhood. Particularly onerous were the numerous separations that the assimilation system inflicted. The first separation occurred when a girl was taken from her parents and placed in an institutional home or in the mission dormitory. She next faced a series of separations as she matured and progressed through age-segregated dormitories until she was old enough to be placed in domestic service. Once in service she could be moved from position to position until she reached the age of twenty-one. At twenty-one, training ended and authorities expected the woman to remain in domestic service until she married. After marriage, a woman could either move onto a mission to raise her children or apply for an exemption on the grounds that she and her husband were capable of earning a living in white society.

Within institutions and missions, girls suffered the continual turn over of staff. Sue Gordon, who in the 1940s, at the age of four, was placed in Sister Kate's Home for Nearly White Children in Perth, remembers how caregivers "flowed in and out of our lives . . . the kids . . . watched house mothers leave on a regular basis, and we were the permanent fixtures."[30] According to Margaret Tucker, who in the 1910s was removed to Cootamundra Aboriginal Girls Home in central New South Wales at the age of thirteen, the girls' ability to cope with the lack of permanent ties and affection depended on their character, but mostly, she recalled, "we got used to accepting our fate."[31] The fatalism of this comment underscores the emotional and psychological distress the system inflicted on these girls.

Under usual conditions, Aboriginal girls learned from their mothers, grandmothers, and aunts. They played with sisters and cousins, and throughout their lives networks of women and girls of all ages supported them. The constant separations, however, limited the girls' abilities to form emotional attachments and denied them the normal friendships and learning activities of girlhood. When asked to recall their lives in the institutions, many women talked about loss of family and girlhood. Many commented that they had no mothers or normal girlhood memories. They felt they had been taught how to work but not how to live. They could clean a house but not raise a child. Most knew nothing about boys or sex until they left the mission. They had not been given the chance to make personal choices about what to wear, what to eat, or how to spend their time. They missed the endless social interactions that informed these mundane decisions and lacked skills that girls naturally developed through socialization with their mothers, other women, older girls, and their peers.

Because she was in her teens when she was taken from her family, Margaret Tucker remembered her Aboriginal name (Lilardia), her people (Wirrardjerie), her country, and her life before she was taken.[32]

Her father was an itinerant sheep shearer who was away for long periods of time. Her mother worked as a domestic servant. Because work was scarce, the family moved regularly between Aboriginal settlements, and occasionally Margaret and her three sisters were left in the care of members of their extended family while their mother worked in a nearby town or on a farm. They lived in tin shacks with dirt floors in camps comprising four or five families who supplemented their meager wages by hunting and gathering. In these camps, women taught their children how to live off the land, how to fish, which roots and leaves to gather, where to find duck eggs and honey, how to cook directly on an open fire, and which berries could be used as medicine.

Margaret's grandparents told her stories about aunts, uncles, and cousins as well as stories from the Dreamtime, a term referring to the myths and traditional stories of Australia's Aboriginal people. She felt that "in spite of our walkabout existences, and often hard times, those days were the happiest of my life."[33] Her semi-traditional upbringing was typical of that of Aboriginal girls, who learned by watching and doing and whose maturation into womanhood was gradual and based on physical development. Other girls who were removed after the age of five also remembered living in tin shacks; having lots of aunts, uncles, and cousins; gathering bush tucker; hearing stories told by their grandparents; singing around the campfire; and enjoying a wonderful sense of freedom.

Even as girls enjoyed traditional childhoods, the threat of removal clouded their existence. Margaret's family was wary of the police, and the girls were taught to make themselves scare if any were seen near the camp. As arbitrary child removals became more common, Aboriginal communities organized signaling systems that warned of the approach of police or welfare officers. Children were taught to hide if they saw a black car, their usual means of transport, and in the north, where light-skinned children were routinely removed, mothers darkened the children's skin with charcoal. Some parents tried to turn these stratagems into games, but the children soon realized the consequences of being caught. Older girls matured quickly and took on the responsibility of organizing lookouts and hiding younger children from police or welfare officers. These girls spent their childhood in a state of constant vigilance, their play tempered by a wariness of strangers, responsibility for the safety of younger playmates, and constant fear that they or their siblings would be taken.

When Margaret and her sisters turned five, their parents sent them to the closest mission school. They were soon taken. The girls were given no warning and only got to say good-bye because of the delaying tactics of their teacher, who sent a message to their mother that the police had arrived to take her girls to Cootamundra Aboriginal Girls Home. Margaret recalled that her mother followed them to the police station "thinking she could beg once more for us. . . . My last memory of her for many years was her waving pathetically, as we waved back and called out good-bye to her."[34] Margaret considered herself lucky. Usually children had no opportunity to say good-bye to their parents.

Welfare officers preferred to take the children from schools or during their walk home, and their parents only later learned their fate. Some officers acted out of callous indifference to the feelings of Aboriginal families, but some found the act of removing children distressing. They wanted to avoid scenes of wailing women and children or confrontations like the one witnessed by Isobel Edwards when a welfare inspector came to take her from her home: "Donaldson came to our home and he asked mum if she had the children ready, and she said 'No, and you're not taking them.' Then dad stepped out from the bedroom door with a double-barrelled shotgun he had and he said 'You lay your hands on my kids Donaldson and you'll get this.' . . . when old dad stepped towards him old Donaldson went for his life."[35] Isobel was allowed to stay with her family, but usually parents accepted the inevitable, and the girls were told that they were going on a holiday. Oral histories taken as a result of the 1994 national inquiry revealed that parents acquiesced for a number of reasons. Some parents wanted to spare their children the trauma of their grief and humiliation. Some hoped to control where the children were sent and to maintain contact with them. Some bargained with welfare officers, offering older or light-skinned children in the hope of keeping one or two children at home.

After they were in the system, children were separated from their siblings according to gender and age.[36] This practice was carried out to suit the needs of the institutions, which received inadequate funding from the government. Most institutions grew their own food, and all relied on the children to clean the buildings. The children were grouped and housed according to the tasks they could perform. An increased workload accompanied each graduated move through the dormitories. The little girls were expected to strip and make their beds, clean the dormitory, scrub floors, feed the chickens, and help with the cooking and washing. Older girls carried wood and water for washing, bathed the younger girls, served the food, mended clothes, and worked in the laundry, dairy, or gardens after school. Most girls did not mind these tasks because they relieved the boredom of the strict routine: rise, wash, strip and make beds, eat breakfast, wash up, walk to school, sit for lessons, walk back, work, bathe, eat dinner, do homework, say prayers, and go to bed.

Weekends broke the monotony. Because the missions and institutions were chronically understaffed, caregivers used the weekends to visit friends and relatives or to pursue personal interests. After supervising Sunday services and assigning a few chores, the staff let the girls pursue their own interests. The weekends became prized times when the girls recaptured their girlhood and played in the bush as they had at home. They spent these precious days walking, climbing trees, or swimming. Girls who remembered traditional food-gathering skills taught the others how to eat bush tucker.

Weekends became the time when the girls forged friendships. During the week, daily routines and barracks-like accommodations limited their ability to form or maintain personal attachments. Ruth Hegarty was placed in a dormitory after her parents were forced to move to Queensland's Cherbourg mission during the Great Depression. Because Ruth was under five, she and her mother were separated from her father and brothers and placed in the nursery. She stayed with her mother until she started school and then moved into the little girls' dormitory, which was separated from the nursery by a lattice. Ruth was only allowed to talk to her mother with permission, and opportunities to see her mother were limited. Ruth had her own routines, and her mother was expected to work, first in the sewing room and later as a domestic outside the mission. Her mother's wages paid for Ruth's upkeep. Ruth found that as she grew up, she grew away from her mother and became "more dependent upon those girls I shared my life with in the dormitory."[37]

Even though girls were subject to continuous separations as they aged, many found themselves moving through the system with a core group of friends who became surrogate sisters. On cold nights they piled into the same bed to keep each other warm, they told each other stories, looked after new girls in the dormitory, played together, formed gangs, squabbled, and teased one another. As Ruth stated, "Our lives were governed by the same polices and what happened to one, happened to all of us. No one was treated as special or given privileges. We were treated identically, dressed identically, our hair cut identically. Our clothes and bald head were a give away. We were dormitory girls."[38] Dormitory friendships were particularly important for girls who were placed in institutions as babies or at an early age. They became sisters in a system in which family relationships were ignored. Even after they had left the institution, the girls attempted to maintain these friendships. Dormitory sisters often formed support networks that operated like extended families. These networks were particularly important for the girls who could not reestablish traditional family ties.

For Glenyse Ward, who as an infant was placed in a Catholic mission in Western Australia in the 1950s, her dormitory friends were her only family. At the age of five she moved from an infants' home in the city to a rural mission. On arrival she was given over to the care of a big girl who "soaked my dress with tears and squeezed me nearly to death. Then the big girl knelt down with me so that the smaller girl who had been pushing and shoving . . . could give me a big slopping kiss on the cheek. Little did I know that the big girl who was crying and the little girl who kissed me were my natural sisters. They were Nita and Sally." Two years later Nita, then fourteen, became a working girl and was sent to work for a white family. Sally, who was closer to Glenyse's age, remained in the same dormitory for a number of years, becoming a close friend, but no closer than five other girls who moved through the system with them. By the time she was ten, Glenyse thought of the mission as home and the caregivers as her parents. When a group of girls ran away, she decided to stay because "I felt that I was in my home already." When told by one of the other girls that the mission was not her home and asked where her mother was, Glenyse replied that the care-giver, who "wakes me up every morning," was her mother.[39]

Friendships developed away from the watchful eyes of the caregivers. On the weekends and after lights out, the girls were free to be children. They could joke, tell stories, and speak their own language. All institutions had a ghost that older girls invented to frighten younger girls and became the topic of many stories. In addition, each group of friends had a secret garden, a special place where they acted out their fantasies. For Ruth and her friends it was the duck pond, where the girls played at being movie stars and smoked cigarettes of rolled leaves or butts filched from the garbage bins.[40] For girls at Cootamundra Aboriginal Girls Home it was a grass field where the girls played at being hairdressers. They pretended that the little hillocks of grass were heads of hair and plaited the tufts into ponytails and decorated them with twigs.[41]

Because staff did not let the girls keep personal possessions, including toys, the girls collected buttons, pins, and bits of broken china and buried them in secret locations around the missions.[42] Girls showed these little collections, known as "secrets," to friends and told stories about how each piece was found. Collections could be built up through gambling with cards made from pages torn out of exercise books. Ruth's friend Pearl had a collection of safety and bobby pins that had been won from the other girls in card games and hopscotch. The extent to which the girls were able to develop friendships or play in this fashion depended on the culture of the institution. At Sister Kate's, for instance, girls were not allowed to sit next to friends or relatives at meal times, and they were punished if they talked or laughed during the meal.

Not being allowed to talk during meals was a common form of discipline and was enforced by most institutions as a means of controlling the girls' behavior. Another method of control was regimentation. Girls who did not finish their tasks satisfactorily or who missed the bell for the start of the next activity were punished. Punishments were varied, arbitrary, and ranged from the withdrawal of privileges to life-threatening beatings. The intensity and type of punishment depended on the personality of the care-giver. A priest at Glenyse's mission struck girls on the head if they failed to complete tasks to his satisfaction. The matron at Ruth's mission withheld privileges and had the girls perform extra duties to win them back. The cook at Margaret's mission flogged the girls with a wooden spoon if they failed to remember her instructions.

Over time, forms of punishment became institutionalized. Oral histories taken for the 1994 national inquiry spoke of ongoing incidents of physical, psychological, and sexual abuse. Interviewees accused some institutions of perpetrating all forms of child abuse. Sandra Hill, who was placed in Sister Kate's Home for Nearly White Children in the 1950s, described the discipline in that institution as "never-ending" abuse. A routine punishment for bed wetters was to stand the offender on a milk crate with the wet sheet draped over her head while the rest of the children filed past on their way to church. Children who refused to eat were force fed, and beatings were common. Sandra recalled, "One day Barbara [my older sister] happened to touch [my little sister] and she screamed and she lifted up her top and she had welts all the way across her back where she had been beaten."[43] Aboriginal Protection Boards made no attempt to control these abuses, but the girls organized small rebellions against the regimentation and abuses suffered.

Mostly these rebellions revolved around stealing food, for the girls were always hungry. They stole eggs from the hen house, fruit from the orchard, and anything they could lay their hands on from the kitchen. More adventurous girls raided nearby farms. The food was either eaten on the spot or hidden in the bush and eaten on the weekends. Sneaking baths after lights out and playing tricks on staff were other forms of rebellion. Staff whose actions were seen to be unjust might find their washing in the dirt or all the fruit in their garden stolen. If the girls were homesick or felt they had been unjustly punished too often, they ran away. Most girls made at least one attempt to escape.

When girls decided to run away it was usually in small groups from the same dormitory, and their destination was often one of the girls' homes. Even if they managed to escape for two or three days, the runaways rarely reached their destination because hunger eventually forced them to beg for food. Farmers who lived near institutions watched for runaways and reported their location to the police. Luckier girls were given a good feed while waiting to be sent back. One successful escape involved an epic 1,600-kilometer journey on foot by three girls—Molly (14), Grade (11), and Daisy (8)—who absconded from Moore River Mission in 1931. Because they were light-skinned, they had been sent south from their home in the Pilbara region in far north Western Australia. From the start Molly resented being locked in the dormitory at night and was determined to go home.[44]

Unlike other runaways, Molly knew where she was going. Her father had worked on the rabbit-proof fence that ran the length of the state, and Molly planned to head northeast until she found the fence to follow home. She also knew how to live off the land, hide their tracks, and misdirect any white people they met who might report them to the police. Molly and Daisy made it back to their home at Jigalong after nine weeks, but Gracie, who was told her mother was working on a station farther south, was caught and shipped to an institution in Perth. The press reported on the girls' trek, embarrassing the Aboriginal Protection Board. When a local police officer spied Molly living with her relatives, he offered to pick her up, but the chief protector of Aborigines declared that he "did not desire any further action re: half-caste Molly because she has been a costly woman to the Department. Very heavy expenditure was incurred in securing her and when she decamped a lot of undesirable publicity took place."[45]

Although Molly's bid for freedom succeeded, most girls' attempts failed because they simply did not know enough about life outside the institution. The schools that were attached to each institution taught only elementary subjects, namely, reading, writing, and simple arithmetic. Teachers did not teach the girls anything about their own culture, nor did they impart any practical information on how to survive in white society. None of the girls were given the opportunity to extend their education past the age of fourteen. According to Ruth, "We were trained simply to be a source of cheap labour."[46] This training ensured that the girls knew nothing of the world outside the mission.

By the age of fourteen, the age when they were expected to start earning their keep, some girls living in institutions had never visited the nearest town, handled money, or interacted with adults other than their teachers and caregivers. Little wonder they experienced difficulties on being placed in domestic service. There the girls had to overcome not only ignorance but also loneliness and the sheer hard labor of domestic service. They were expected to clean, cook, wash, iron, garden, and chop and carry firewood. If the family had young children, the girls were expected to look after them, and in rural areas many took on extra duties as farm laborers. The amount of work and treatment varied. Although some families treated the girls fairly, others garnished their wages, and all viewed them as cheap labor. Their bedrooms were in out buildings, garden sheds, or above garages, and they were not allowed to eat with the family or use indoor bathrooms. When visitors called, the girls were expected to keep out of sight, or mistresses paraded them as incompetent maids in training.[47]

This kind of treatment shocked many girls, for the institutions had sheltered them from blatant racism.[48] Nor had the institutions taught them how to stand up for themselves. Shy girls harangued for not completing their tasks or for performing unsatisfactorily did not know how to react. They were isolated from the support networks they had developed in the institutions and were forced to cope as best they could. Margaret Tucker's first employer hid her mother's letters and rationed her food to the point where she was starving. She became depressed and attempted suicide by eating rat poison, after which the board moved her to another position. Ruth Hegarty learned to manipulate the system by accumulating numerous complaints about her "bad" attitude and thus spent her teen years being moved from position to position. Glenyse Ward began "playing a dummies life" and took revenge on her employer's uncompromising demands by raiding the refrigerator, using her employer's shower and perfume, and playing the piano when they were out.[49] After two years with the same employer Glenyse ran away and found employment in a country hospital.

Still, most girls stayed with their employers because they had nowhere to go and did not realize that their skills enabled them to earn a living. Margaret also ran away but went back because she felt vulnerable living on her own. Furthermore, her only way of finding her family was through the New South Wales Aboriginal Protection Board. This dependence on the Protection Boards and the girls' ignorance kept them tied to the institutions and helped perpetuate multigenerational child removals. Ruth claimed that although girls had been trained as good domestics, when it came to more serious matters, such as sex education, they had to learn by trial and error. She became a single mother at the age of eighteen: "I was painfully aware that our lives were beginning to mirror those of our mothers. We were still dormitory girls and so were our babies, and it looked as if it was continuing on through our children. The enormous irony for me was that, instead of ever reaching a point in life where I could escape from this system, the cycle had begun again."[50] Determined not to let this happen, Ruth turned to a married friend for help in raising her baby. Although girls like Ruth suffered separation from their families, more resilient girls were able to establish new support networks and, through their friendships, reestablish contact with Aboriginal communities.

Conclusion

The desire of white Australians to build a new Britannia in the Southern Hemisphere inspired Australia's assimilation polices before the 1950s. To achieve the desired end, authorities aimed to replace Aboriginal culture with white Australian working-class culture by breaking the links between generations. In a pattern that was repeated in places such as Palestine and Mombasa, girls became a focus of these policies because of their gender. Authorities believed that the girls, destined to become mothers, could become the conduits through which white values would enter indigenous communities. Girls, moreover, were supposedly easier to train, and half-caste girls in particular offered a medium for "breeding out the colour." Aboriginal girls removed from their families routinely faced control over their sexual knowledge and activities, experiences similar to girls in other modernizing cultures, or countries intent on building a modern nation-state. Welfare officers removed girls from corrupting influences, namely, Aboriginal communities, and placed them in institutions where they were trained as domestic servants, skills that would also make them good home-makers and by extension good citizens.

Consequently, Aboriginal girls lost their childhood and adolescent years in a haze of hard work. Their education was abridged, their contact with friends and family was limited, and the girls were isolated in a hostile environment where few cared about their emotional needs. The girls survived this system through small acts of resistance and the creation of spaces where they could be themselves. Most important, they survived by banding together and remaking families and their culture. Older girls looked after younger girls and taught them remembered traditions. Girls living in the same dormitory became a substitute family. They were sisters. Although many bore the scars of years spent in an uncaring environment, many became community leaders intent on rebuilding the family ties that Australia's assimilation polices were designed to break.

NOTES

1. *Two Bob Mermaid*, video recording, written and directed by Darlene Johnson (Sydney: Australian Film Institute, 1996).

2. I recognize that "aborigine" is a generic description, but capitalized it is a term that is "owned" by Australia's Aboriginal people, and in this chapter I use it to refer to them. I also employ the term "white," which is commonly used to designate Australians of European descent.

3. Upon the federation of Australian states in 1901, Australia's Aboriginal people were excluded from census counts and denied the right to vote.

4. Views on the status and fate of the Australian Aboriginal race varied throughout the eighteenth and nineteenth centuries, but a dominant theme was the need either to protect Aboriginal people from the vices of white society or to assimilate them. See Russell McGregor, *Imagined Destinies: Aboriginal Australians and the Doomed Race Theory, 1880–1936* (Melbourne: Melbourne University Press, 1997).

5. Australian states began abandoning their assimilation policies in the 1960s but continued to remove children in fewer numbers until the 1980s.

6. Peter Read, *The Stolen Generations: The Removal of Aboriginal Children in New South Wales, 1883–1969* (Sydney: Ministry of Aboriginal Affairs, 1983).

7. The report was published as *Bringing Them Home: Report of the National Inquiry into the Separation of Aboriginal and Torres Straight Islander Children from Their Families* (Sydney: Human Rights and Equal Opportunity Commission, 1997).

8. The collection is housed in the National Library of Australia. Excerpts were published in Doreen Mellor and Anna Haebich, eds., *Many Voices: Reflections on Experiences of Indigenous child Separation* (Canberra: National Library of Australia, 2002).

9. For a comprehensive overview of the various state policies, see Anna Haebich, *Broken Circles: Fragmenting Indigenous Families, 1800–2000* (Fremantle: Fremantle Arts Centre Press, 2000).

10. Heather Goodall, "Saving the Children: Gender and Colonization of Aboriginal Children in New South Wales, 1788–1990," *Aboriginal Law Bulletin* 44 (June 1990): 6–9.

11. It has been estimated that within two to three years of contact with settlers, nearby Aboriginal populations declined by up to 80 percent.

12. Although some removals were triggered by child abuse or starvation, most removals were arbitrary and depended on the whim of missionaries, protection officers, or the police.

13. In New South Wales, the Aboriginal Protection Board appointed the superintendents. In the other states, church mission boards appointed the superintendents, who ran them under the auspices of Aboriginal Protection Boards.

14. Between 1880 and 1900, the percentage of the Aboriginal population known to be of mixed descent rose from 27 percent to 55 percent.

15. The ratio of white men to white women varied over time and from place to place. Generally a ratio of around five to one applied to most regions before the 1890s. In frontier settlements, however, especially mining towns and in tropical regions, this ratio could rise to over ten men for every woman.

16. The methods used to control the movement of Aboriginal people, their living conditions, and their ability to resist white authorities varied over time and from state to state and in some cases from mission to mission.

17. Liaisons ranged from prostitution to long-term de facto relationships.

18. For example; the 1905 Western Australian Royal on the Condition of the Natives and the 1913 South Australian Royal Commission on the Aborigines commented on the vulnerability of Aboriginal girls, the problems of protecting them from sexual exploitation, and their consequent need for institutionalized care.

19. Walter E. Roth, *Northern Protector of Aborigines Annual Report, 1899,* Queensland State Archives, ID 7328, 10.

20. Walter E. Roth, *Northern Protector of Aborigines Annual Report, 1902,* Queensland State Archives, ID 7328.

21. T.G.H. Strelow, Central Australian Field Diary (unpublished), October 26, 1935, South Australian Museum, AA316.

22. Ann McGrath, *Born in the Cattle* (Sydney: Allen and Unwin, 1987), 73.

23. Heather Goodall, "Assimilation Begins in the Home: The State and Aboriginal Women's Work as Mothers in New South Wales, 1900s to 1960s," in "Aboriginal Workers," special issue, *Labour History 69* (November 1995): 81.

24. Breeding out the color was a policy proposed by Western Australia's chief protector of Aborigines, A. O. Neville, in *Australia's Coloured Minority: Its Place in the Community* (Sydney: Currawong Publishing, 1947).

25. McGregor, *Imagined Destinies,* 142.

26. From the nation's inception, politicians and settlers clung to the notion that only whites should populate Australia. Politicians passed laws, commonly called the White Australia Policy, to prevent Asian immigration, and Aboriginal people did not receive full citizenship until 1967.

27. *Western Australia Parliamentary Debates* (1936), 822, as quoted in Haebich, *Broken Circles,* 278.

28. As quoted in Goodall, "Assimilation Begins in the Home," 83.

29. Studies of domestic labor in Australia have noted that an ongoing concern of middle-class women before the widespread use of domestic appliances was the shortage of suitable maids. Cf. Beverley Kingston, *My Wife, My Daughter, and Poor Maryann* (Melbourne: Nelson, 1975), 29–55.

30. Mellor and Haebich, *Many Voices,* 201.

31. Margaret Tucker, *If Everyone Cared: Autobiography of Margaret Tucker* (Melbourne: Grosvenor Books, 1986), 101.

32. Australian Aboriginal people call tribal areas "country." Margaret's family moved around campsites in Wirrardjerie country, namely, land along the Murray, Murrumbidgee, and Lachlan rivers. This region was one of the few where superintendents did not control the campsites.

33. Tucker, *If Everyone Cared,* 61.

34. Ibid., 93–94.

35. As quoted in Peter Read, *A Rape of the Soul so Profound: The Return of the Stolen Generations* (Sydney: Allen and Unwin, 1999), 32.

36. It was standard practice on mission stations and in institutions to segregate children according to gender and age. See Haebich, *Broken Circles,* 342–348; and Mellor and Haebich, *Many Voices,* 166–207.

37. Ruth Hegarty, *Is That You Ruthie?* (St. Lucia: Queensland University Press, 1999), 51.

38. Ibid., 4.

39. Glenyse Ward, *Unna You Fullas* (Broome: Magabala Books, 1991), 2, 72, 70.

40. Hegarty, *Is That You Ruthie?* 63.

41. Mellor and Haebich, *Many Voices,* 81.

42. Only a few homes provided balls, books, and board games, which were kept under lock and key. Many of the oral histories related how children made their toys from bits of rubbish or natural materials and hid them from the staff. Cf. Mellor and Haebich, *Many Voices,* 172, 187.

43. Ibid., 201, 202.

44. This escape was popularized in *Rabbit Proof Fence,* video recording, directed by Phillip Noyce (Canberra: Ronin Films, 2002).

45. Commissioner of Aboriginal Affairs, as quoted in Doris Pilkington, *Follow the Rabbit Proof Fence* (St. Lucia: Queensland University Press, 2002), 125.

46. Hegarty, *Is That You Ruthie?* 75.

47. Many of the girls' oral histories and memoirs mention feeling isolated and lonely while working as domestic servants, being overwhelmed by the number of duties they were expected to perform, and being ostracized or mistreated by their mistresses. An overview of the problems they faced can be found in Jennifer Sabironi, "I Hate Working for White People," *Hecate* 19, no. 2 (1993): 7–29.

48. Some interviewees claimed that they were so isolated from the realities of life in the outside world that they did not think of themselves as black and were unprepared for the racism they encountered when sent into service. Cf. Mellor and Haebich, *Many Voices,* 181–185.

49. Glenyse Ward, *Wandering Girl* (Broome: Magabala Books, 1987), 131.

50. Hegarty, *Is That You Ruthie?* 126.

Japanese Hip-Hop and the Globalization of Popular Culture

IAN CONDRY

Introduction

Japanese hip-hop, which began in the 1980s and continues to develop today, is an intriguing case study for exploring the globalization of popular culture. Hip-hop is but one example among many of the transnational cultural styles pushed by entertainment and fashion industries, pulled by youth eager for the latest happening thing, and circulated by a wide range of media outlets eager to draw readers and to sell advertising. In Tokyo, a particular combination of local performance sites, artists, and fans points to ways that urban areas are crucibles of new, hybrid cultural forms. Hip-hop was born in the late 1970s in New York City as a form of street art: rapping on sidewalk stoops, outdoor block parties with enormous sound systems, graffiti on public trains, and breakdancing in public parks. In its voyage to Japan, the street ethic of hip-hop remains, but it is performed most intensely in all-night clubs peppered around Tokyo. This paper examines these nightclubs as an urban setting that helps us grasp the cultural dynamics of Japanese hip-hop. In particular, the interaction between artist-entrepreneurs and fans in live shows demonstrates how "global" popular culture is still subject to important processes of localization.

Anthropologists have a special role in analyzing such transnational forms because of their commitment to extended fieldwork in local settings. Ethnography aims to capture the cultural practices and social organization of a people. This offers a useful way of seeing how popular culture is interwoven with everyday life. Yet there is a tension between ethnography and globalization, because in many ways they seem antithetical to each other. While ethnography attempts to evoke the distinctive texture of local experience, globalization is often seen as erasing local differences. An important analytical challenge for today's media-saturated world is finding a way to understand how local culture interacts with such global media flows.

On one hand, it seems as if locales far removed from each other are becoming increasingly the same. It is more than a little eerie to fly from New York to Tokyo and see teenagers in both places wearing the same kinds of fashion characteristic of rap fans: baggy pants with boxers on display, floppy hats or baseball caps, and immaculate space-age Nike sneakers. In Tokyo stores for youth, rap music is the background sound of choice. Graffiti styled after the New York City aerosol artists dons numerous walls, and breakdancers can be found in public parks practicing in the afternoon or late at night. In all-night dance clubs throughout Tokyo, Japanese rappers and DJs take to the stage and declare that they have some "extremely bad shit" *(geki yaba shitto)*—meaning "good music"—to share with the audience. For many urban youth, hip-hop is the defining style of their era. In 1970s Japan, the paradigm of high school cool was long hair and a blistering solo on lead guitar. Today, trendsetters are more likely to sport "dread" hair and show off their scratch techniques with two turntables and a mixer. In the last few years, rap music has become one of the best-selling genres of music in the United States and around the world as diverse youth are adapting the style to their own messages and contexts.

But at the same time, there are reasons to think that such surface appearances of sameness disguise differences at some deeper level. Clearly, cultural setting and social organization have an impact on how movies and television shows are viewed. Yet if we are to understand the shape of cultural forms in a world that is increasingly connected by global media and commodity flows, we must situate Japanese rappers in the context of contemporary Japan. When thinking about how hip-hop is appropriated, we must consider, for example, that most Japanese rappers and fans speak only Japanese. Many of them live at home with their parents, and they all went through the Japanese education system. Moreover, even if the origin of their beloved music genre is overseas, they are caught up in social relations that are ultimately quite local, animated primarily by face-to-face interactions and telephone calls. So while these youth see themselves as "hip-hoppers" and "B-Boys" and "B-Girls," and associate themselves with what they call a "global hip-hop culture," they also live in a day-to-day world that is distinctly Japanese.

For those interested in studying the power of popular culture, there is also a more practical question of research methods. How does a lone researcher go about studying something as broad and unwieldy as the globalization of mass culture? One of the tenets of anthropological fieldwork is that you cannot understand a people without being there, but in the case of a music genre, where is "there"? In the fall of 1995, I began a year and a half of fieldwork in Tokyo, and the number of potential sites was daunting. There were places where the music was produced: record companies, recording studios, home studios, and even on commuter trains with handheld synthesizers. There were places where the music was promoted: music magazines, fashion magazines, TV and radio shows, night-clubs, and record stores. There was the interaction between musicians and fans at live shows, or in mediated form on cassettes, CDs, and 12-inch LPs. To make matters worse, rap music is part of the larger category of "hip-hop." Hip-hop encompasses not only rap, but also breakdance, DJ, graffiti, and fashion. The challenge was to understand the current fascination among Japanese youth with hip-hop music and style, while also considering the role of money-making organizations. How does one situate the experiential pleasures within the broader structures of profit that produce mass culture?

As I began interviewing rappers, magazine writers, and record company people, I found a recurring theme that provided a partial answer. Everyone agreed that you cannot understand Japanese rap music without going regularly to the clubs. Clubs were called the "actual site" *(genba)* of the Japanese rap scene.[1] It was there that rappers performed, DJs learned which songs elicit excitement in the crowd, and breakdancers practiced and competed for attention. In what follows, I would like to suggest that an effective tool for understanding the globalization of popular culture is to consider places like Japanese hip-hop nightclubs in terms of what might be called "genba globalism." by using participant–observation methods to explore key sites that are a kind of media crossroads, we can observe how globalized images and sounds are performed, consued, and then transformed in an ongoing process. I use the Japanese term "genba" to emphasize that the processing of such global forms happens through the local language and in places where local hip-hop culture is produced. In Japanese hip-hop, these clubs are important not only as places where fans can see live shows and hear the latest releases from American and Japanese groups, but also as places for networking among artists, writers, and record company people. In this essay, I would like to point out some of the advantages of considering key sites as places to understand the cross-cutting effects of globalization. To get a sense of what clubs are about, let's visit one.

Going to Harlem on the Yamanote Line

A visit to Tokyo's Harlem is the best place to begin a discussion of Japanese hip-hop. Opened in the summer of 1997, Harlem is one of many all night dance clubs, but as the largest club solely devoted to hip-hop and R&B, it has become the flagship for the Japanese scene (at least, at the time of this writing in February 2001). Nestled in the love hotel area of the Shibuya section of Tokyo, Harlem is representative of the otherworldliness of clubs as well as their location within the rhythms and spaces of mainstream Japan.

If we were visiting the club, we would most likely meet at Shibuya train station around midnight because the main action seldom gets started before 1 A.M. Most all-night revelers commute by train, a practice that links Tokyo residents in a highly punctual dance. The night is divided between the last train (all lines stop by 1 A.M. at the latest) and the first train of the morning (between 4:30 and 5 A.M.). The intervening period is when clubs *(kurabu)* are most active.[2] shortly after midnight. Shibuya station is the scene for the changing of the guard: those heading home, running to make their connections for the last train, and those like us heading out, dressed up, and walking leisurely because we will be spending all night on the town. The magazine stands are closing. Homeless men are spread out on cardboard boxes on the steps leading down to the subways. The police observe the masses moving past each other in the station square towards their respective worlds. Three billboard-size TVs looming overhead, normally spouting pop music videos and snowboard ads during the day, are now dark and silent. The throngs of teenagers, many in their school uniforms, that mob Shibuya during afternoons and all weekend have been replaced by a more balanced mix of college students, "salarymen" and "career women," and of course more than a few B-Boys and B-Girls—the hip-hop enthusiasts in baggy pants and headphones. The sidewalks are splashed with light from vending machines—cigarettes, soda, CDs, beer (off for the night), and "valentine call" phone cards. A few drunken men are being carried by friends or lie in their suits unconscious on the sidewalk.

To get to Harlem, we walk uphill along Dôgenzaka Avenue toward a corner with a large neon sign advertising a capsule hotel, where businessmen who have missed their last train can sleep in coffin-like rooms. We pass disposable lamppost signs and phone booth stickers advertising various sex services. An elderly man in the back of a parked van is cooking and selling *takoyaki* (octopus dumplings) to those with the late-night munchies. The karaoke box establishments advertise cheaper rates at this hour. Turning right at a Chinese restaurant, we move along a narrow street packed with love hotels, which advertise different prices for "rest" or "stay." In contrast to the garish yellow sign advertising the live music hall, On-Air East, about fifty meters ahead, a nondescript door with a spiffy, long-haired bouncer out front is all that signals us that Harlem is inside. It seems there are always a couple of clubbers out front talking on their tiny cell phones. Up the stairs, past a table filled with flyers advertising upcoming hip-hop events, we pay our ¥3000 each (around $25, which may seem expensive, but is only about half again as much as a movie ticket). We move into the circulating and sweaty mass inside.

Traveling to a club instills a sense of moving against the mainstream in time and space. Others are going home to bed as the clubber heads out. When the clubber returns home in the morning, reeking of smoke and alcohol, the train cars hold early-bird workers as well. So the movement to and from the club, often from the distant suburbs, gives clubbers a sense of themselves as separate, flaunting their leisure, their costumes, and their consumer habits. During the course of my year-and-a-half of fieldwork, between the fall of 1995 and the spring of 1997, I went to over a hundred club events around Tokyo and I began to see that clubs help one understand not only the pleasures of rap in Japan, but also the social organization of the scene and the different styles that have emerged. This becomes clear as you spend time inside the clubs.

Inside the Club

Inside the club, the air is warm and thick, humid with the breath and sweat of dancing bodies. Bone-thudding bass lines thump out of enormous speakers. There is the scratch-scratch of a DJ doing his turntable tricks, and the hum of friends talking, yelling really, over the sound of the music. The lighting is subdued, much of it coming from a mirrored ball slowly rotating on the ceiling. The fraternity house smell of stale beer is mostly covered up by the choking cigarette haze, but it is best not to look too closely at what is making the floor alternately slippery and sticky. The darkness, low ceiling, black walls, and smoky murk create a space both intimate and claustrophobic. Almost everyone heads for the bar as soon as they come in. An important aspect of clubbing is the physical experience of the music and crowded setting.

Harlem is a larger space than most of the Tokyo clubs, and can hold upwards of one thousand people on a crowded weekend night. On the wall behind the DJ stage, abstract videos, *anime* clips, or edited Kung Fu movies present a background of violence and mayhem, albeit with an Asian flavor. Strobe lights, steam, and moving spotlights give a strong sense of the space, and compound the crowded, frenetic feeling imposed by the loud music. The drunken revelry gives clubs an atmosphere of excitement that culminates with the live show and the following freestyle session. But an important part of clubbing is also the lull before and after the show, when one circulates among the crowd, flirting, networking, gossiping, or simply checking out the scene. Clubs are a space where the diffuse network of hip-hop fans comes together in an elusive effort to have fun. To the extent that a "community" emerges in the hip-hop scene, it revolves around specific club events and the rap groups that draw the crowd.

Much of the time is spent milling around, talking, drinking, and dancing. The live show often produces a welcome rise in the excitement level of the clubbers. Some events feature several live acts, often followed by a freestyle session. The rap show will usually begin between 1:00 and 1:30 A.M. Formats vary depending on the club and the event. "B-Boy Night" at R-Hall (organized by Crazy-A) was held one Sunday a month and would start with a long breakdancing show, with many groups each doing a five-minute routine. Then a series of rap groups would come on, each doing two or three songs. At other shows, like FG Night, sometimes a series of groups would perform, while on other nights only one group would do a show followed by a more open-ended freestyle. Nevertheless, there were many similarities, and a characteristic live show would proceed as follows. Two rappers take the stage (or step up into the DJ booth), as the DJ prepares the music. For people enamored of live bands, the live show of a rap concert may strike one as a bit lifeless. The music is either pre-recorded on a digital audio tape (DAT) or taken from the breakbeats section of an album.[3] The flourish of a lead guitar, bass, or drum solo is replaced in the hip-hop show by the manic scratching of a record by a DJ who deftly slides a record back and forth across the slip mat laid on the turntable and works the mixer to produce the rhythmic flurries of sampled sound.

The rappers begin with a song introducing themselves as a group. Every group seems to have its own introductory song of self-promotion:

rainutsutaa ga rainut shi ni yatte kita doko ni kita? Shibuya!	Rhymester has come to rhyme where are we? Shibuya!
hai faa za dopesuto da oretachi kyo cho gesuto da	we are By Phar the Dopest we are tonight's super guests
makka na me o shita fuktuô ore tojo	The red-eyed owl [You the Rock] I've arrived on stage

These songs tend to be brief, only a couple of minutes long. Between the first and second song, the rappers ask the audience how they feel. A common catchphrase was "How do you feel/My crazy brothers."[4] The group will introduce by name the rappers and DJ, and also make sure everyone remembers the name of the group. The rappers will comment about how noisy the crowd is. Crowds are more often criticized for not being worked up enough rather than praised for their excitement.

The second song tends to be the one the group is most famous for. On stage, each rapper holds a cordless microphone right up to his mouth, and a rapper might steady the mic by holding his index finger under his nose. The other arm is gesticulating, palm out in a waving motion at the audience. A bobbing motion in the head and shoulders can be more or less pronounced.

Between the second and third song, the group will usually demand some call-and-response from the audience, almost always as follows:

Call	Response	Call	Response
ie yo ho	*ho*	Say, ho	ho
ie yo ho ho	*ho ho*	Say, ho ho	ho ho
ie yo ho ho ho	*ho ho ho*	Say ho ho ho	ho ho ho
sawage!	[screams]	Make noise!	[screams]

The third and usually final song tends to be a new song, often introduced in English as "brand new shit," a revolting image for English-speakers perhaps, but apparently heard by the audience as a cooler way of saying "new song" than the Japanese *shinkyoku*. if the song is about to be released as a record or CD, this information is also announced before the song's performance. If there are other rap groups in the audience, this is also the time for "shout outs" (praise for fellow hip-hoppers) as in "Shakkazombie in da house" or "Props to king Giddra" and once even, "Ian Condry in da house." After the third song, there is seldom talk besides a brief goodbye in English: "Peace" or "We out." Encores are rare, but freestyle sessions, discussed below, are ubiquitous. After the show, rappers retreat backstage or to the bar area, but never linger around the stage after performing. The year 1996 was also a time of a "freestyle boom," when most shows were closed with an open-ended passing of the microphone. Anyone could step on stage and try his or her hand at rapping for a few minutes. This has been an important way for younger performers to get the attention of more established acts. There is a back-and-forth aspect of performance in the clubs that shows how styles are developed, honed, and reworked in a context where the audience is knowledgeable, discriminating, and at times participates in the show itself.

It is important to understand that over the years, this kind of feedback loop has helped determine the shape of current Japanese rap styles. One of my main sites was a weekly Thursday night event that featured another collection of rap groups called Kitchens. Hip-hop collectives such as Kitchens, Little Bird Nation, Funky Grammar Unit, and Rock Steady Crew Japan are called "families" (*famirii,* in Japanese). The different groups often met at clubs or parties, at times getting acquainted after particularly noteworthy freestyle sessions. Over time some would become friends, as well as artistic collaborators, who performed together live or in the studio for each others' albums. Such families define the social organization of the "scene." What is interesting is how they also characterize different aesthetic takes on what Japanese hip-hop should be. Kitchens, for example, aim to combine a pop music sensibility with their love for rap music, and, like many such "party rap" groups, they appeal to a largely female audience. The Funky Grammar Unit aims for a more underground sound that is nonetheless accessible, and they tend to have a more even mix of men and women in the audience. Other families like Urbarian Gym (UBG) are less concerned with being accessible to audiences than with conveying a confrontational, hard-core stance. The lion's share of their audiences are young males, though as UBG's leader, Zeebra, breaks into the pop spotlight, their audiences are becoming more diverse.

The lull that precedes and follows the onstage performance is a key time for networking to build these families. In all, the live show is at most an hour long, at times closer to twenty minutes, and yet there is nowhere for the clubbers to go until the trains start running again around 5 A.M. It is not unusual for music magazine writers to do interviews during club events, and record company representatives often come to shows as well, not only as talent scouts but also to discuss upcoming projects. I found that 3:00 to 4 A.M. was the most productive time for fieldwork because by then the clubbers had mostly exhausted their supply of stories and gossip to tell friends, and were then open to finding out what this strange foreigner jotting things in his notebook was doing in their midst.

Japanese cultural practices do not disappear just because everyone is wearing their hip-hop outfits and listening to the latest rap tunes. To give one example, at the first kitchens event after the New Year, I was surprised to see all the clubbers who knew each other going around and saying the traditional New Year's greeting in very formal Japanese: "Congratulations on the dawn of the New Year. I humbly request your benevolence this year as well." There was no irony, no joking atmosphere in these statements. This is a good example of the way that globalization may appear to overshadow Japanese culture, but one needs to spend time in clubs with the people to see how surface appearances can be deceiving.

In many ways, then, it is not surprising that rappers, DJs, breakdancers, record company people, and magazine editors all agree you cannot understand the music unless you go to the clubs. There is an intensity of experience in hearing the music at loud volume, surrounded by a crush of dancing people, while drinking alcohol and staying out all night, that gives the music an immediacy and power it lacks when heard, say, on headphones in the quiet of one's room. Indeed, it is difficult to convey in words the feeling of communal excitement during a particularly good show, when one gets wrapped up in a surge of energy that is palpable yet intangible. It is this emotional experience that in many ways counteracts any fears that it is all "merely imitation," which is the most common criticism of the music.

At the same time, going to a club involves a strange mix of the extraordinary and the routine. On one hand, you visit a place with bizarre interior design, listen to music at exceedingly high volume, stay out all night and, often, get drunk. It is a sharp contrast to an ordinary day of school or work. We must also recognize, however, that while a club may strive to be a fantastic microcosm, it is still embedded in Japan's political-economic structures, characteristic social relations, and the contemporary range of cultural forms. It is not by chance that clubs tend to attract people of specific class, age, sexuality, and to some extent locale. Moreover, if you go regularly to clubs, after a while it becomes just another routine. It is largely predictable what kind of pleasures can be expected, and also the generally unpleasant consequences for work or school after a nigh without sleep.[5] Clubbing offers freedom and constraints. This tension is the key to understanding how clubs socialize the club-goers by structuring pleasure in characteristic ways.

I have only suggested some of the ways that clubs offer insight into the ways that global hip-hop becomes transformed into a local form of Japanese hip-hop, but we can see how an idea of "genba globalism" can help us understand the process of localization. Globalism is refracted and transformed in important ways through the actual site of urban hip-hop clubs. Japanese rappers perform for local audiences in the Japanese language and use Japanese subjects to build their base of fans. In contrast to club events with techno or house music, hip-hop events emphasize lyrics in the shows and the freestyle sessions. There is a wide range of topics addressed in Japanese hip-hop, but they all speak in some way to the local audience. Dassen 3 uses joking lyrics ridiculing school and television. Scha Dara parr is also playful, emphasizing things like their love of video games and the kind of verbal repartee characteristic of close buddies. When Zeebra acts out his hard-core stance, he tells of drug use in California, expensive dates with girlfriends, and abstract lyrics about hip-hop as a revolutionary war. Rhymester's lyrics are often set in a club or just after a show, for example, describing an imagined, fleeting love affair with a girl on a passing train. Some songs refer to cultural motifs going back centuries, such as a song performed by Rima and Umedy about a double-suicide pact between lovers, remade as a contemporary R&B and hip-hop jam.

Understanding Globalization in Local Terms

Rap music in Japan offers an interesting case study of the way popular culture is becoming increasingly global in scope, while at the same time becoming domesticated to fit with local ideas and desires. At the dawn of the twenty-first century, entertainment industries are reaching wider markets and larger audiences. The film *Titanic*, for example, grossed over $1.5 billion, the largest amount ever for a film, and two-thirds of this income came from overseas. In music, there are global pop stars too, like Britney Spears and Celine Dion. In rap music, the Fugees could be considered global stars. Their 1996 album "The Score" sold over 17 million copies worldwide. More recently, Lauryn Hill's 1998 solo album revealed that the transnational market for hip-hop is still growing, and most major rap stars do promotional tours in Japan. An important feature of pop culture commodities is that they tend to be expensive to produce initially, but then relatively cheap to reproduce and distribute. Compact disks are one of the most striking examples. Although studio time is expensive (between $25,000 for a practically homemade album to upwards of $250,000 for state-of-the-art productions), the CDs themselves cost about eighty cents to produce, including the packaging. Obviously, the more one can sell, the higher the return, and this helps explain the eagerness of entertainment businesses to develop new markets around the world.

Less clear are the kinds of effects such globalized pop culture forms might have. The fluidity of culture in the contemporary world raises new questions about how we are linked together, what we share and what divides us. The spread of popular culture seems in some ways linked with a spread in values, but we must be cautious in our assessment of how and to what extent this transfer takes place. It is safe to say that the conventional understanding of globalization is that it is producing a homogenization of cultural forms. From this perspective, we are witnessing the McDonaldization and the Coca-Cola colonization of the periphery by powerful economic centers of the world system. The term "cultural imperialism" captures this idea, that political and economic power is being used "to exalt and spread the values and habits of a foreign culture at the expense of the native culture."[6] In some ways, anthropology as a discipline emerged at a time when there was a similar concern that the forces of modernity (especially missionaries and colonial officials) were wiping out "traditional cultures," and thus one role for ethnographers was to salvage, at least in the form of written documents, the cultures of so-called "primitive peoples." Many people view globalization, and particularly the spread of American pop culture, as a similar kind of invasion, but the idea that watching a Disney movie automatically instills certain values must be examined and not simply assumed. In some ways the goals of anthropology—combating simplistic and potentially dangerous forms of ethnocentrism—remain as important today as when the discipline was born.

The example of Japanese hip-hop gives us a chance to examine some recent theorizing on globalization. The sociologist Malcolm Waters offers a useful overview of globalization, which he defines as follows:

> A social process in which the constraints of geography on social and cultural arrangements recede, and in which people become increasingly aware that they are receding.[7]

A key aspect of this definition is not only that the world is increasingly becoming one place, but that people are becoming increasingly aware of that. This awareness may lead to a heightened sense of risk, such as global warming or the "love bug" virus, or to a rosy view of increased opportunities, for example, to get the most recent hip-hop news in real time or to download the latest music instantly via the Internet.

It is important to recognize, however, that globalization involves much more than Hollywood movies and pop music. Waters does a good job of analyzing three aspects of globalization, namely, economic, political, and cultural. He contends that globalization processes go back five hundred years, and that the relative importance of economic, political, and cultural exchanges has varied over that time.[8] From the sixteenth to nineteenth centuries, economics was key. In particular, the growth of the capitalist world system was the driving force in linking diverse regions. During the nineteenth and twentieth centuries, politics moved to the fore. Nation-states produced a system of international relations that characterized global linkages with multinational corporations and integrated national traditions. Now, at the dawn of the twenty-first century, cultural forms are leading global changes in both politics and economics. Waters argues that a "global idealization" is producing politics based on worldwide values (e.g., human rights, the environment, anti-sweatshop movement) and economic exchanges centered on lifestyle consumerism. The key point is that while economics and then politics were the driving forces in globalization of previous centuries, it is cultural flows that are increasingly important today. If he is right, and I would argue he is, this points to the importance of studying the kinds of ideals that are spread around the globe.

What ideals are spread by hip-hop in Japan? Clubbing certainly promotes an attitude that stresses leisure, fashion, and consumer knowledge of music over other kinds of status in work and school. Although it is important to recognize that the effects of lyrics are somewhat complicated, it is worth considering, to some extent, the messages carried by the music. Although rappers deal with a wide variety of subjects, one theme appears again and again, namely, that youth need to speak out for themselves. As rapper MC Shiro of Rhymester puts it, "If I were to say what *hip-hop* is, it would be a 'culture of the first person singular.' In hip-hop, . . . rappers are always yelling, 'I'm this.'" Such a message may seem rather innocuous compared to some of the hard-edged lyrics one is likely to hear in the United States, but it is also a reflection of the kind of lives these Japanese youth are leading. In Japan, the education system tends to emphasize rote memorization and to track students according to exams. Sharply age-graded hierarchies are the norm, and may be especially irksome in a situation where the youth are likely to live with their parents until they get married. Moreover, the dominant ideology that harmony of the group should come before individual expression ("the nail that sticks up gets hammered down") makes for a social context in which the hip-hop idea that one should be speaking for oneself is, in some limited sense, revolutionary. At the very least, it shows how global pop culture forms are leading not to some simple homogenization, but rather adding to a complex mix that in many ways can only be studied ethnographically through extended research in local sites.

Another important theorist of globalization is Arjun Appadurai, who proposes that we consider contemporary cultural flows in terms of movement in five categories: people or ethnicity, ideology, finance, technology, and media. He adds the suffix "-scape" to each to highlight that the deterritorialization of cultural forms is accompanied by new landscapes of cultural exchange, thus we have "ethnoscapes, ideoscapes, financescapes, technoscapes, and mediascapes" (others have added "sacriscapes" to describe the spread of religion, and one might add "leisurescapes" for the spread of popular culture). The key point about these landscapes is that they are "non-isomorphic," that is, they don't map evenly onto each other. Appadurai notes, for example, that the "Japanese are notoriously hospitable to ideas and are stereotyped as inclined to export (all) and import (some) goods, but they are notoriously closed to immigration"[9] (1996:37). Migration and electronic mass media are the main driving forces to Appadurai's theorization. One of the problems with Appadurai's theory, however, is that the notion of "-scapes" draws us away from considering how flows of technology, media, finance, and people are connected. An alternative is to consider key sites, *genba* if you will, of various sorts depending on one's interests as a way to see how new, hybrid forms of culture are produced. "Genba globalism" aims to show how artists, fans, producers, and media people are actively consuming and creating these new forms.

One thing that anthropologists offer to the advancement of human knowledge is a clear sense of the ways people interact in specific places. At one time, anthropologists would choose a village or island to map in elaborate detail. Now in a media-filled world, we face different analytical challenges, but the techniques of fieldwork—learning the language, participating in daily life, observing rituals, and so on—can still be used. One of Appadurai's conclusions is that exchanges along these different "-scapes" are leading not only to a deterritorialization of cultural forms, but also to an increased importance of the "work of the imagination".[10] In other words, as identities can be picked up from a variety of media sources, the construction of "who we are" arises increasingly from how we imagine ourselves, rather than from where we live. Life in urban areas seems to make this aspect of identity—as imagination and as performance—all the more salient. What I hope I have drawn attention to is the way the hip-hop nightclubs give us a chance to bring some of this work of the imagination down to the level of daily life.

Conclusion: Global Pop and Cultural Change

In the end, the globalization of popular culture needs to be understood as two related yet opposing trends of greater massification and deeper compartmentalization. On one hand, the recording industry is reaching larger and larger markets, both within Japan and around the world, as mega-hits continue to set sales records. On the other hand, there is an equally profound if less visible process by which niche scenes are becoming deeper and more widely connected than before, and in the process, new forms of heterogeneity are born. Although I have only been able to touch on a few of its aspects here, Japanese rap music is a revealing case study of the social location, cultural role, and capitalist logic of such micro-mass cultures. It is important to recognize, however, that these micro-mass cultures also have the potential to move into the mainstream.

The distinction between "scene" and "market" highlights what is at stake when we try to analyze the cultural and capitalist transformations associated with globalization. Information-based and service industries are growing rapidly, promising to reorganize the bounds of culture and commodities, yet we need close readings of how such emerging economies influence everyday lives. Although B-Boys and B-Girls go to great lengths to distinguish the "cultural" from the "commercial" in their favored genre, it is rather the linkage of the two in the circuits of popular culture that offers the deepest insight. In the end, the winds of global capitalism that carried the seeds of rap music to Japan can only be grasped historically with a close attention to social spaces, media forms, and the rhythms of everyday life.

Walking to a hip-hop club in Tokyo, one is confronted with a tremendous range of consumer options, and it is this heightened sense of "you are what you buy" that has in many ways become the defining feature of identity in advanced capitalist nations, at least among those people with the money to consume their preferred lifestyle. At the same time, it is important to be sensitive to the ways that, outward appearances notwithstanding, the consumers of things like hip-hop are embedded in a quite different range of social relations and cultural meanings. It makes a difference that B-Boys and B-Girls, listening to American hip-hop records, still feel it is important to go around to their friends and associates with the traditional New Year's greeting of deference and obligation. This is an example of the ways social relations within the Japanese rap scene continue to carry the weight of uniquely Japanese practices and understandings.

It is likely, too, that "global pop" will become more heterogeneous as the entertainment industries in other countries develop. There are reasons to think that, in music at least, the domination of American popular music as the leading "global" style seems likely to be a temporary situation. In the immediate postwar period in Japan, Western music initially dominated sales. Today, three-fourths of Japan's music market is Japanese music to one-fourth Western. Moreover, although American music currently constitutes about half of global sales, this is down from 80 percent a decade ago. It is quite possible that as local record companies mature in other countries, they will, as in Japan, come to dominate local sales. Certainly, multinational record companies are moving in this direction of developing local talent and relying less on Western pop stars. Moreover, although Japan is a ravenous importer of American popular culture, it has some notable exports as well. Some are more familiar than others, but they include the Mighty Morphin' Power Rangers, karaoke, "Japanimation," *manga* (Japanese comic books), mechanical pets, Nintendo or the Sony Play-Station video games, and of course, Pokémon.

Just as it would seem strange to Americans if someone claimed Pokémon is making U.S. kids "more Japanese," it is dangerous to assume that mass culture goods by themselves threaten to overwhelm other cultures. The anthropologist Daniel Miller has been a proponent for taking a closer look at the ways such goods are woven into everyday lives. He argues that mass commodities are better analyzed in terms of an "unprecedented diversity created by the differential consumption of what had once been thought to be global and homogenizing institutions."[11] Miller's emphasis on the active and creative aspects of consumption is characteristic of a broad trend within the social sciences to view global commodities in terms of their local appropriations, and to represent local consumers with a greater degree of agency than found in other works that emphasize "cultural imperialism." it is this perspective that seems to me the best characterization of what is going on in Japan.

It is easy to see how the "sameness" aspect of globalization is promoted. Music magazines, TV video shows, and record stores promote similar artists whether in Japan or the United States. A new album by Nas is met with a flurry of publicity in the Japanese and English-language hip-hop magazines available in Tokyo. This relates in part to the structure of record companies and their marketing practices. In this sense, the widening and increasingly globalized market for popular culture does appear to be leading to greater homogenization. But it is primarily a process of homogenizing what is available, regardless of where you are. I would argue that the global marketing blitz of megahit productions like the film *Titanic* and the music of Celine Dion and Lauryn Hill reflect a homogenization of *what* is available, but not *how* it is interpreted. Although it is more difficult to see, in part because it is hidden beneath similar clothes, hairstyles, and consumption habits, different interpretations are generated in different social contexts. By attending to "actual sites" of cultural production and consumption, we can more clearly gauge the ways local contexts alter the meanings of globalization. "Keeping it real" for hip-hoppers in Japan means paying attention to local realities.

Notes

1. The word *"genba"* is made up of the characters "to appear" and "place," and it is used to describe a place where something actually happens, like the scene of an accident or of a crime, or a construction site. In the hip-hop world the term is used to contrast the intense energy of the club scene with the more sterile and suspect marketplace.
2. Hip-hop is not the only style for club music. Techno, House, Reggae, Jungle/Drum 'n' Bass, and so on, are some of the other popular club music styles. Live music tends to be performed earlier in the evening, usually starting about 7 P.M., and finishing in time for the audience to catch an evening train home. In contrast to "clubs," "discos" must by law close by 1 A.M.
3. The term "breakbeats" refers to the section of a song where only the drums, or drums and bass, play. It is the break between the singing and the melodies of the other instruments, hence "breakbeats." This section can be looped by a DJ using two turntables and a mixer with cross-fader, and produces a backing track suitable for rapping.
4. In Japanese, *chôoshi wa dô dai/ikarera kyôdai.* The masculinity of Japanese rap is here indexed by the calling out to "brothers" and also by the use of the masculine slang *dai* instead of *da*.
5. Youthful Japanese clubbers use the mixed English-Japanese construction "all *suru*" (do all) to mean "stay out all night in a club." For example, the following exchange occurred between two members of the female group Now. Here, the sense of routine outweighs the excitement. A: *konban mo ooru suru ka na?* (Are we staying out all night again?) B: *Tabun.* (Probably) A: *Yabai.* (That sucks.)
6. John Tomlinson, *Cultural Imperialism: A Critical Introduction* (London: Printer Publishers, 1991), p. 3.
7. Malcolm Waters, *Globalization* (London: Routledge, 1995, p. 3).
8. Waters, pp. 157–164.
9. Argun Appadurai, *Modernity at large: Cultural dimensions of globalization* (Minneapolis: University of Minnesota Press, 1996), p. 37.
10. Appadurai, p. 3.
11. Daniel Miller, "Introduction: Anthropology, modernity and consumption," in Daniel Miller (ed.), *Worlds Apart: Modernity through the Prism of the Local* (London: Routledge, 1995), p. 3.

Conclusion

Conclusion

▼

Topics Covered in Class

Expansion of European States
Neo-Europes
What Happens at Contact
Resistance
Assimilation
Pluralism
Development Issues
Foreign Aid
Applied Anthropology

About the Readings

In this section I will review the material that we have covered from the beginning to the end of the semester in class.

John Bodley's article, The Price of Progress, fits well into this section. It is an article that is often assigned at the end of a variety of anthropology courses.

In the chapter, "Price of Progress," the author raises some interesting questions and makes some astute observations. He examines the meaning of the word, "progress," demonstrating an ethnocentric bias in how we Westerners use this term to refer specifically to economic change and development. He also points out the cultural bias inherent in the concept of standard of living. We tend to see progress (Westernization) as a positive event leading to improvements in people's lives. Bodley shows us that tribal peoples often pay a high price for progress, including poor health, loss of land, loss of independence, loss of the right to follow their own lifestyle, and even death.

Bodley's objective in writing this article is not to offer solutions to all these problems, but to make us aware of them. Many Americans think that as soon as we get involved with the politics and economics in another country, life will be better for the people. We have learned in this course that is not necessarily the case. We will end the course with an explanation of the role that applied anthropology has the potential to play in present and future programs designed to improve peoples' lives. We should also recognize and support the efforts of Native Peoples to improve their lives by helping them make their voices heard and giving them more power or agency in influencing their future.

Bodley: The Price of Progress

This is a great article for the end of the course. By now you should realize programs directed toward modernization and development do not always benefit Fourth World Peoples. Bodely does a good job of documenting this in the final chapter of his book, Victims of Progress.

- Explain what Bodley means when he writes about Diseases of Development and Ecocide?
- Why is urbanization a mixed blessing for small-scale cultures?
- What is the long range impact of malnutrition?
- What is meant by the term, standard of living? Is this concept ethnocentric?
- Does Bodley offer solutions to the problems that he writes about?

> *In aiming at progress . . . you must let no one suffer by too drastic a measure, nor pay too high a price in upheaval and devastation, for your innovation.*
>
> —René Maunier[1]

Until recently, government planners always considered economic development and material progress beneficial goals that all societies should want to strive toward. The social advantages of progress—as defined in terms of increased incomes, higher standards of living, greater security, and better health—are thought to be positive, universal goods to be obtained at any price. Although one might argue that indigenous peoples should not be forced to sacrifice their own cultures and autonomy to obtain these benefits, government planners have historically felt that the loss of cultural autonomy would be a small price to pay for such obvious advantages.

In earlier chapters, evidence was presented to demonstrate that autonomous indigenous peoples have not chosen progress to enjoy its advantages and that the real reason governments have pushed progress upon them was to obtain resources, not primarily to share the benefits of progress with indigenous peoples. It was also shown that the price of forcing progress on unwilling recipients included the deaths of millions of indigenous people, as well as their loss of land, political sovereignty, and the right to follow their own lifestyle. This chapter does not attempt to further summarize that aspect of the cost of progress, but instead analyzes the specific effects of the participation of indigenous peoples in the global economy. In direct opposition to the usual interpretation, it is argued here that the benefits of progress are often both illusory and detrimental to indigenous peoples when they have not been allowed to control their own resources and define their relationship to the market economy.

Progress and The Quality of Life

One of the primary difficulties in assessing the benefits of progress and economic development for any culture is that of establishing a meaningful measure of both benefit and detriment. It is widely recognized that standard of living, which is the most frequently used measure of progress, is an intrinsically ethnocentric concept that relies heavily upon indicators that lack universal cultural relevance. As a less ethnocentric alternative, the

Happy Planet Index, which uses self-reported life satisfaction levels, life expectancy, and ecological footprint to rank nations, shows that some of the smallest, least developed nations rank as the happiest.[2] Vanuatu, the "happiest" country in the world, had just over two hundred thousand people in 2007 and a per capita GDP of under $3,000. More than half (65 percent) of the population derived its living from the subsistence sector.[3] A top ranking on Happy Planet Index requires high satisfaction, good life expectancy, and a very small ecological footprint. Such factors as GDP and per capita income may be especially irrelevant measures of actual quality of life for autonomous indigenous peoples. For example, in its 1954 report, the Trust Territory government indicated that since the Micronesian population was still largely satisfying its own needs within a cashless subsistence economy: "Money income is not a significant measure of living standards, production, or well-being in this area."[4] Unfortunately, within a short time the government began to rely on an enumeration of specific imported consumer goods as indicators of a higher standard of living in the islands, even though many tradition-oriented islanders felt that these new goods symbolized a reduction of their quality of life.

A more useful measure of the benefits of progress might be based on a formula for evaluating cultures devised by anthropologist Walter R. Goldschmidt in 1952.[5] According to these less ethnocentric criteria, the important question to ask is: *Does progress or economic development increase or decrease a given society's stability or its ability to satisfy the physical and psychological needs of its population?* This question is a far more direct measure of quality of life than are the standard economic correlates of development, and it is universally relevant. Specific indication of this standard of living could be found for any society in the nutritional status and general physical and mental health of its population, incidence of crime and delinquency, demographic structure, family stability, and the society's relationship to its natural resource base. We might describe a society that has high rates of malnutrition and crime and one that degrades its natural environment to the extent of threatening its continued existence as having a lower standard of living than another society in which these problems do not exist.

For decades development experts used increases in Gross National Product as a measure of "progress," but a new measure of "Genuine Progress" that discounted for the negative aspects of growth suggested that as much of 60 percent of America's GDP between 1950 and 2002 was lost to social and environmental costs.[6] Since then the deficiencies of GDP as a measure of human well-being have been widely recognized,[7] but so far only one country, the Kingdom of Bhutan, has specifically replaced GDP as a development goal with a real alternative, Gross National Happiness.[8]

Careful examination of the data, which compare the former condition of self-sufficient indigenous peoples with their condition following their incorporation into the world-market economy, leads to the conclusion that their standard of living is often lowered, not raised, by economic progress—and often to a dramatic degree. This is perhaps the most outstanding and inescapable fact to emerge from the years of research anthropologists have devoted to the study of culture change and modernization. Despite the best intentions of those who have promoted change and improvement, all too often the results have been poverty, longer working hours, much greater physical exertion, poor health, social disorder, discontent, discrimination, overpopulation, and environmental deterioration—combined with the destruction of the small-scale culture.

Diseases of Development

Perhaps it would be useful for public health specialists to start talking about a new category of diseases. . . . Such diseases could be called the "diseases of development" and would consist of those pathological conditions which are based on the usually unanticipated consequences of the implementation of developmental schemes.[9]

Economic development increases the disease rate of affected peoples in at least three ways. First, to the extent that development is successful, developed populations suddenly become vulnerable to all of the chronic "lifestyle" diseases suffered almost exclusively by "advanced" peoples,[10] including diabetes, obesity, hypertension, and a variety of circulatory problems. Second, development disturbs existing environmental balances and may dramatically increase some bacterial and parasite diseases. Finally, when development goals prove unattainable, an assortment of poverty diseases may appear in association with the crowded conditions of urban slums and the general breakdown in small-scale socioeconomic systems.

Outstanding examples of the first situation can be seen in the Pacific, where some of the most successfully transformed small-scale societies are found. In Micronesia, where development progressed more rapidly than perhaps anywhere else, the population doubled between 1958 and 1972. However, the number of patients treated for heart disease in the local hospitals nearly tripled, the incidence of mental disorders increased eight-fold, and by 1972 hypertension and nutritional deficiencies began to make significant appearances for the first time.[11]

Although some critics argue that the Micronesian figures simply represent better health monitoring due to economic progress, rigorously controlled data from Polynesia show a similar trend. The progressive acquisition of modern degenerative diseases was documented by an eight-member team of New Zealand medical specialists, anthropologists, and nutritionists, whose research was funded by the Medical Research Council of New Zealand and the World Health Organization. These researchers investigated the health status of a genetically related population at various points along a continuum of increasing cash income, modernizing diet, and urbanization. The extremes on this acculturation continuum were represented by the relatively traditional Pukapukans of the Cook Islands and the essentially Europeanized New Zealand Maori; the busily developing Rarotongans, also of the Cook Islands, occupied the intermediate position. In 1971, after eight years of work, the team's preliminary findings were summarized by Dr. Ian Prior, cardiologist and leader of the research team, as follows: "We are beginning to observe that the more an islander takes on the ways of the West, the more prone he is to succumb to our degenerative diseases. In fact, it does not seem too much to say our evidence now shows that the farther the Pacific natives move from the quiet, carefree life of their ancestors, the closer they come to gout, diabetes, atherosclerosis, obesity, and hypertension."[12]

In Pukapuka, where progress was limited by the island's small size and its isolated location—some 480 kilometers from the nearest port—the annual per capita income was only about $36 and the economy remained essentially at a subsistence level. Resources were limited and the area was visited by trading ships only three or four times a year; thus, there was little opportunity for intensive economic development. Predictably, the population of Pukapuka was characterized by relatively low levels of imported sugar and salt intake and a presumably related low level of heart disease, high blood pressure, and diabetes. In Rarotonga, where economic success was introducing town life, imported food, and motorcycles, sugar and salt intakes nearly tripled, high blood pressure increased approximately ninefold, diabetes increased two- to threefold, and heart disease doubled for men and more than quadrupled for women. Meanwhile, the number of grossly obese women increased more than tenfold. Among the New Zealand Maori, sugar intake was nearly eight times that of the Pukapukans, gout in men was nearly double its rate on Pukapuka, diabetes in men was more than fivefold higher, and the incidence of heart disease in women was more than sixfold greater than that of women on Pukapuka. The Maori were, in fact, dying of "European" diseases at a greater rate than the average New Zealand European.

Government development policies designed to bring about changes in local hydrology, vegetation, and settlement patterns and to increase population mobility, and even programs aimed at reducing some diseases, have frequently led to dramatic increases in disease rates because of the unforeseen effects of disturbing the preexisting order. Charles C. Hughes and John M. Hunter[13] published an excellent survey of cases in which development led directly to increased disease rates in Africa. They concluded that hasty development intervention in relatively balanced local cultures and environments resulted in "a drastic deterioration in the social and economic conditions of life."

Self-sufficient populations in general have presumably learned to live with the endemic pathogens of their environments, and in some cases they have evolved genetic adaptations to specific diseases, such as the sickle-cell trait, which provided immunity to malaria. Unfortunately, however, outside intervention has entirely changed this picture. In the late 1960s, the rate of incidence of sleeping sickness suddenly increased in many areas of Africa and even spread to areas where the disease had not formerly occurred, due to the building of new roads and migratory labor, both of which caused increased population movement. Forest-dwelling peoples such as the Aka in central Africa explicitly attribute new diseases such as AIDS and Ebola to the materialism associated with roads and new settlements.[14]

Large-scale relocation schemes, such as the Zande Scheme, had disastrous results when natives were moved from their traditional disease-free refuges into infected areas. Dams and irrigation developments inadvertently created ideal conditions for the rapid proliferation of snails carrying schistosomiasis (a liver fluke disease), and major epidemics suddenly occurred in areas where this disease had never before been a problem. DDT-spraying programs have been temporarily successful in controlling malaria, but there is often a rebound effect that increases the problem when spraying is discontinued, and resistant strains of the malarial mosquitoes are continually evolving.

Urbanization is one of the prime measures of development, but it is a mixed blessing for most small-scale cultures. Urban health standards are abysmally poor and generally worse than in rural areas for the former villagers who have crowded into the towns and cities throughout Africa, Asia, and Latin America seeking wage employment out of new economic necessity. Infectious diseases related to crowding and poor sanitation are rampant in urban centers, and greatly increased stress and poor nutrition aggravate a variety of other health problems. Malnutrition and other diet-related conditions are, in fact, one of the characteristic hazards of progress faced by indigenous peoples and are discussed in the following sections.

The Hazards of Dietary Change

The diets of indigenous peoples are admirably adapted to their nutritional needs and available food resources. Even though these diets may seem bizarre, absurd, and unpalatable to outsiders, they are unlikely to be improved by drastic modifications. Given the delicate balances and complexities involved in any subsistence system, change always involves risks, but for indigenous people the effects of dietary change have been catastrophic. The benefits of traditional subsistence-based diets are dramatically demonstrated by the negative health effects explicitly connected with the "nutrition transition," the shift to diets based on highly processed commercial foods.[15] This negative process was first identified as a complex of conditions called the Saccharine Disease, caused by a reduction in dietary fiber associated with the shift to refined commercial foods.[16]

Under normal conditions, food habits are remarkably resistant to change, and indeed people are unlikely to abandon their traditional diets voluntarily in favor of dependence on difficult-to-obtain exotic imports. In some cases it is true that imported foods may be identified with powerful outsiders and are therefore sought as symbols of greater prestige. This may lead to such absurdities as Amazonian Indians choosing to consume imported canned tuna fish when abundant high-quality fish are available in their own rivers. Another example of this situation occurs in tribes where mothers prefer to feed their infants expensive and nutritionally inadequate canned milk or formula from unsanitary, but high-status, baby bottles. The high status of these items is often promoted by traders and clever advertising campaigns.

Aside from these apparently voluntary changes, it appears that more often dietary changes are forced upon unwilling indigenous peoples by circumstances beyond their control. In some areas, new food crops have been introduced by government decree or as a consequence of forced relocation or other government policies designed to end hunting, pastoralism, or shifting cultivation. Food habits have also been modified by massive disruption of the natural environment by outsiders—as when sheepherders transformed the Australian Aborigines' foraging territory or when European invaders destroyed the bison herds that were the primary element in the Plains Indians' subsistence patterns. Perhaps the most frequent cause of diet change occurs when formerly self-sufficient peoples find that wage labor, cash cropping, and other economic development activities that feed resources into the world-market economy must inevitably divert time and energy away from the production of subsistence foods. Many indigenous peoples in transforming cultures suddenly discover that, like it or not, they are unable to secure traditional foods and must spend their newly acquired cash on costly and often nutritionally inferior manufactured foods.

Overall, the available data seem to indicate that the dietary changes that are linked to involvement in the world-market economy have tended to reduce rather than raise the nutritional levels of the affected peoples. Specifically, the vitamin, mineral, and protein components of their diets are often drastically reduced and replaced by enormous increases in starch and carbohydrates, often in the form of white flour and refined sugar.

Any deterioration in the quality of a given population's diet is almost certain to be reflected in an increase in deficiency diseases and a general decline in health status. Indeed, as indigenous peoples have shifted to a diet based on imported manufactured or processed foods, there has been a dramatic rise in malnutrition, a massive increase in dental problems, and a variety of other nutrition-related disorders. Nutritional physiology is so complex that even well-meaning dietary changes have had tragic consequences, In many areas of Southeast Asia, government-sponsored protein supplementation programs, which supplied milk to protein-deficient populations, caused unexpected health problems and increased mortality. Officials failed to anticipate that in cultures where adults do not normally drink milk, they no longer produce the enzymes needed to digest it, resulting in milk intolerance.[17] In Brazil, a similar milk distribution program caused an epidemic of permanent blindness by aggravating a preexisting vitamin A deficiency.[18]

Teeth and Progress

There is nothing new in the observation that savages, or peoples living under primitive conditions, have, in general, excellent teeth. . . . Nor is it news that most civilized populations possess wretched teeth which begin to decay almost before they have erupted completely, and that dental caries is likely to be accompanied by periodontal disease with further reaching complications.19

Anthropologists have long recognized that undisturbed indigenous peoples are often in excellent physical condition. And it has often been noted specifically that dental caries and the other dental abnormalities that plague globalscale societies are absent or rare among indigenous peoples who have retained their diets. The fact that indigenous food habits may contribute to the development of sound teeth, whereas modernized diets may do just the opposite, was illustrated as long ago as 1894 in an article in the *Journal of the Royal Anthropological Institute* that described the results of a comparison between the teeth of ten Sioux Indians and a comparable group of Londoners.[20] The Indians, who were examined when they came to London as members of "Buffalo Bill's Wild West Show," were found to be completely free of caries and in possession of all their teeth, even though half of the group was over thirty-nine years of age. The Londoners' teeth were conspicuous for both their caries and their steady reduction in number with advancing age. The difference was attributed primarily to the wear and polishing caused by the Indian diet of coarse food and the fact that they chewed their food longer, encouraged by the absence of tableware.

One of the most remarkable studies of the dental conditions of indigenous peoples and the impact of dietary change was conducted in the 1930s by Weston Price,[21] an American dentist who was interested in determining what contributed to normal, healthy teeth. Between 1931 and 1936, Price systematically explored indigenous areas throughout the world to locate and examine the most isolated peoples who were still living relatively self-sufficiently. His fieldwork covered Alaska, the Canadian Yukon, Hudson Bay, Vancouver Island, Florida, the Andes, the Amazon, Samoa, Tahiti, New Zealand, Australia, New Caledonia, Fiji, the Torres Strait, East Africa, and the Nile. The study demonstrated both the superior quality of aboriginal dentition and the devastation that occurs as modern diets are adopted. In nearly every area where traditional foods were still being eaten, Price found perfect teeth with normal dental arches and virtually no decay, whereas caries and abnormalities increased steadily as new diets were adopted. In many cases the change was sudden and striking. Among Inuit (Eskimo) groups subsisting entirely on traditional food he found caries totally absent, whereas in groups eating a considerable quantity of store-bought food, approximately 20 percent of their teeth were decayed. This figure rose to more than 30 percent with Inuit groups subsisting almost exclusively on purchased or government-supplied food and reached an incredible 48 percent among the native peoples of Vancouver Island. Unfortunately for many of these people, modern dental treatment did not accompany the new food, and their suffering was appalling. The loss of teeth was, of course, bad enough in itself, and it certainly undermined the population's resistance to many new diseases, including tuberculosis. But new foods were also accompanied by crowded, misplaced teeth, gum diseases, distortion of the face, and pinching of the nasal cavity. Abnormalities in the dental arch appeared in the new generation following the change in diet, while caries appeared almost immediately even in adults.

Price reported that in many areas the affected peoples were conscious of their own physical deterioration. At a mission school in Africa, the principal asked him to explain to the native schoolchildren why they were not physically as strong as children who had had no contact with schools. On an island in the Torres Strait the Aborigines knew exactly what was causing their problems and resisted—almost to the point of bloodshed—

government efforts to establish a store that would make imported food available. The government prevailed, however, and Price was able to establish a relationship between the length of time the government store had been established and the increasing incidence of caries among a population that had shown an almost 100 percent immunity to them before the store had been opened.

In New Zealand, the Maori, who in their aboriginal state are often considered to have been among the healthiest, most perfectly developed of peoples, were found to have "advanced" the furthest. According to Price: "Their modernization was demonstrated not only by the high incidence of dental caries but also by the fact that 90 percent of the adults and 100 percent of the children had abnormalities of the dental arches."[22]

Malnutrition

Malnutrition, particularly in the form of protein deficiency, has become a critical problem for indigenous peoples who must adopt new economic patterns. Population pressures, cash cropping, and government programs have all tended to encourage the replacement of previous crops and other food sources that were rich in protein with substitutes high in calories but low in protein. In Africa, for example, protein-rich staples such as millet and sorghum are being systematically replaced by high-yielding manioc and plantains, which have insignificant amounts of protein. The problem is increased for cash croppers and wage laborers whose earnings are too low and unpredictable to allow purchase of adequate amounts of protein. In some rural areas, agricultural laborers have been forced systematically to deprive non-productive members (principally children) of their households of minimal nutritional requirements to satisfy the need of the productive members of the household. This process has been documented in northeastern Brazil following the introduction of large-scale sisal plantations.[23] In urban centers, the difficulties of obtaining nutritionally adequate diets are even more serious for tribal immigrants because costs are higher and poor-quality foods often are more tempting.

One of the most tragic, and largely overlooked, aspects of chronic malnutrition is that it can lead to abnormal brain development and apparently irreversible brain damage; chronic malnutrition has been associated with various forms of mental impairment or retardation. Malnutrition has been linked clinically with mental retardation in both Africa and Latin America,[24] and this appears to be a worldwide phenomenon with serious implications.[25]

Optimistic supporters of progress will surely say that all of these new health problems are being overstressed and that the introduction of hospitals, clinics, and other modern health institutions will overcome or at least compensate for all of these difficulties. However, it appears that uncontrolled population growth and economic impoverishment will likely keep most of these benefits out of reach for many indigenous peoples, and the intervention of modern medicine has at least partly contributed to the problem in the first place.

The generalization that global-scale culture frequently has a negative impact on the health of indigenous peoples has found broad empirical support worldwide,[26] but these conclusions have not gone unchallenged. Some critics argue that the health of indigenous peoples was often poor before modernization, and they point specifically to low life expectancy and high infant mortality rates.[27] Demographic statistics on self-sufficient indigenous peoples are often problematic because precise data are scarce, but they do show a less favorable profile than that enjoyed by many global-scale societies. However, it should be remembered that our present life expectancy is a recent phenomenon that has been very costly in terms of medical research and technological advances. Furthermore, the benefits of our health system are not equally enjoyed by all members of our society. We could view the formerly high infant mortality rates as a relatively inexpensive and egalitarian small-scale public health program that offered the reasonable expectation of a healthy and productive life for those surviving to age fifteen.

Some critics also suggest that certain indigenous peoples, such as the New Guinea highlanders, were "stunted" by nutritional deficiencies created by their natural diet, which was "improved" through "acculturation" and cash cropping.[28] Although this argument suggests that the health question requires careful evaluation, it does not invalidate the empirical generalizations already established. Nutritional deficiencies undoubtedly occurred in densely populated zones in the central New Guinea highlands. However, the specific case cited above may not be widely representative of other indigenous groups even in New Guinea, and it does not address the facts of outside intrusion or the inequities inherent in the contemporary development process.

Ecocide

"How is it," asked a herdsman . . . "how is it that these hills can no longer give pasture to my cattle? In my father's day they were green and cattle thrived there; today there is no grass and my cattle starve." As one looked one saw that what had once been a green hill had become a raw red rock.[29]

Progress not only brings new threats to the health of indigenous peoples, it also imposes new strains on the ecosystems upon which they must depend for their ultimate survival. The introduction of new technology, increased consumption, reduced mortality rates, and the eradication of all previous controls have combined to replace what for many indigenous peoples was a relatively stable balance between population and natural resources with a new system that is unbalanced. Economic development is forcing ecocide on peoples who were once careful stewards of their resources. There is already a trend toward widespread environmental deterioration in indigenous areas, involving resource depletion, erosion, plant and animal extinction, and a disturbing series of other previously unforeseen changes.

After the initial depopulation suffered by many indigenous peoples during their engulfment by frontiers of national expansion, their populations began to experience rapid growth. Authorities generally attribute this growth to the introduction of commercial medicine and new health measures and the termination of chronic intergroup violence, which reduced mortality rates, as well as to new technology, which increased food production. Certainly all of these factors played a part, but merely reducing mortality rates would not have produced the rapid population growth that most indigenous areas have experienced if traditional birth-spacing mechanisms had not been eliminated at the same time. Regardless of which factors were most important, it is clear that all of the natural and cultural checks on population growth have suddenly been pushed aside by culture change, while indigenous lands have been steadily reduced and consumption levels have risen. In many areas, environmental deterioration due to overuse of resources has set in, and in other areas such deterioration is imminent as resources continue to dwindle relative to the expanding population and increased use. Of course, population expansion by indigenous peoples may have positive political consequences, because where they can retain or regain their status as local majorities, they may be in a more favorable position to defend their resources against intruders.

Swidden systems and pastoralism, both highly successful economic systems under former conditions, have proven particularly vulnerable to increased population pressures and outside efforts to raise productivity beyond its natural limits. Research in Amazonia demonstrates that population pressures and related resource depletion can be created indirectly by official policies that restrict swidden people to smaller territories. Resource depletion itself can then become a powerful means of forcing indigenous people into participating in the world-market economy—thus leading to further resource depletion. For example, Foley C. Benson and I[30] showed how the Shipibo Indians in Peru were forced to further deplete their forest resources by cash cropping in the forest area to replace the resources that had been destroyed earlier by the intensive cash cropping necessitated by the narrow confines of their reserve. In this case, some species of palm trees that had provided critical housing materials were destroyed by forest clearing and had to be replaced by costly purchased materials. Research by Daniel R. Gross and others[31] showed similar processes at work among four indigenous groups in central Brazil and demonstrated that the degree of market involvement increases directly with increases in resource depletion.

The settling of nomadic herders and the removal of prior controls on herd size have often led to serious overgrazing and erosion problems where these had not previously occurred. There are indications that the desertification problem in the Sahel region of Africa was aggravated by programs designed to settle nomads. The first sign of imbalance in a swidden system appears when the planting cycles are shortened to the point that garden plots are reused before sufficient forest regrowth can occur. If reclearing and planting continue in the same area, the natural patterns of forest succession may be disturbed irreversibly and the soil can be impaired permanently. An extensive tract of tropical rain forest in the lower Amazon of Brazil was reduced to a semiarid desert in just fifty years through such a process.[32] The soils in the Azande area are also now seriously threatened with laterization and other problems as a result of the government-promoted cotton development scheme.[33]

The dangers of overdevelopment and the vulnerability of local resource systems have long been recognized by both anthropologists and indigenous peoples themselves, but the pressures for change have been overwhelming. In 1948 the Maya villagers of Chan Kom complained to Robert Redfield[34] about the shortening of their swidden cycles, which they correctly attributed to increasing population pressures. Redfield told them, however, that they had no choice but to go "forward with technology."[35] In Assam, swidden cycles were shortened from an average of twelve years to only two or three within just twenty years, and anthropologists warned that the limits of swiddening would soon be reached.[36] In the Pacific anthropologists warned of population pressures on limited resources as early as the 1930s.[37] These warnings seemed fully justified, considering the fact that the crowded Tikopians were prompted by population pressures on their tiny island to suggest that infanticide be legalized. The warnings have been dramatically reinforced since then by the doubling of Micronesia's population in the fourteen years between 1958 and 1972, from 70,600 to 114,645, while consumption levels have soared. By 1985 Micronesia's population had reached 162,321.

The environmental hazards of economic development and rapid population growth have become generally recognized only since worldwide concerns over environmental issues began in the early 1970s. Unfortunately, there is as yet little indication that the leaders of nations in transformation are sufficiently concerned with environmental limitations. On the contrary, governments are forcing indigenous peoples into a self-reinforcing spiral of population growth and intensified resource exploitation, which may be stopped only by environmental disaster or the total impoverishment of the indigenous peoples.

The reality of ecocide certainly focuses attention on the fundamental contrasts between small- and global-scale systems in their use of natural resources. In many respects the entire "victims of progress" issue hinges on natural resources, who controls them, and how they are managed. Indigenous peoples are victimized because they control resources that outsiders demand. The resources exist because indigenous people managed them conservatively. However, as with the issue of the health consequences of economic globalization, some anthropologists minimized the adaptive achievements of indigenous groups and seemed unwilling to concede that ecocide might be a consequence of cultural change. Critics attacked an exaggerated "noble savage" image of indigenous people living in perfect harmony with nature and having no visible impact on their surroundings.[38] They then showed that indigenous groups do in fact modify the environment, and they concluded that there is no significant difference between how indigenous peoples and global-scale societies treat their environments. For example, Charles Wagley declared that Brazilian Indians such as the Tapirapé "are not 'natural men.' They have human vices just as we do. . . . They do not live 'in tune' with nature any more than I do; in fact, they can often be as destructive of their environment, within their limitations, as some civilized men. The Tapirape are not innocent or childlike in any way."[39]

Anthropologist Terry Rambo demonstrated that the Semang of the Malaysian rain forests have a measurable impact on their environment. In his monograph *Primitive Polluters*,[40] Rambo reported that the Semang live in smoke-filled houses. They sneeze and spread germs; breathe and thus emit carbon dioxide. They clear small gardens, contributing "particulate matter" to the air and disturbing the local climate because cleared areas proved measurably warmer and drier than the shady forest. Rambo concluded that his research "demonstrates the essential functional similarity of the environmental interactions of primitive and civilized societies"[41] in contrast to a "noble savage" view, which, according to Rambo, mistakenly "claims that traditional peoples almost always live in essential harmony with their environment,"[42]

This is surely a false issue. To stress, as I do, that small-scale indigenous societies tend to manage their resources for sustained yield within relatively self-sufficient and resilient subsistence economies is not to portray them as either childlike or "natural." Nor is it to deny that tribal societies "disrupt" their environment and may never be in absolute "balance" with nature.[43] The crucial point is that the total consumption of natural resources, or ecological footprint, of self-sufficient tribal peoples in their territory is minuscule in comparison to the ecological footprint of commercial societies. For example, the Asháninka use only 0.24 percent of the biological potential of their territory, whereas Americans in 2001 were using the equivalent of nearly 200 percent. The elevated American consumption rate was only possible because of their use of fossil fuels and reliance on global trade.[44]

The ecocide issue is perhaps most dramatically illustrated by two sets of satellite photos taken over the Brazilian rain forests of Rondônia.[45] Photos taken in 1973, when Rondônia was still a tribal domain, show virtually unbroken rain forest. The 1987 satellite photos, taken after just fifteen years of highway construc-